SCHOLA LATINA

I

KEY

GH

GLOSSAHOUSE

WILMORE, KY

www.glossahouse.com

Schola Latina I Key

GlossaHouse, LLC
110 Callis Circle
Wilmore, KY 40390

Publisher's Cataloging-in-Publication Data

Stephenson, Ken (revised by Thomas Caucutt and Ruth Baldwin)
    Schola Latina I KEY/ Wilmore, KY: GlossaHouse, 2023

xiv, 202 pages ; 22 cm.– (LAETA— Latin Ancient Educational Tools & Aids)

ISBN: 978-1-63663-064-9 (paperback)

Library of Congress Control Number:

Corrected Version, June 2024

Cover Design by T. Michael W. Halcomb

Book Layout and volume editing by Thomas Caucutt and Ruth Baldwin

Original content by Ken Stephenson who grants GlossaHouse the rights to publish *Schola Latina I & II*

Select maps used with permission from Ancient World Mapping Center at https://awmc.unc.edu/.

SCHOLA LATINA

I

KEY

BY

KEN STEPHENSON

REVISED BY

THOMAS CAUCUTT   RUTH BALDWIN

GH

GLOSSAHOUSE

WILMORE, KY

www.glossahouse.com

LAETA
Latin Ancient Educational Tools & Aids

SERIES EDITOR

T. Michael W. Halcomb

LAETA

The Latin term LAETA is an adjective that means "fertile" or "welcoming," especially when describing land. It is also a term that captures the link between this series and its Hebrew (HA'ARETS) and Greek (AGROS) counterparts also bearing land-related names and published by GlossaHouse. In keeping with those series, LAETA functions as an acronym: Latin Ancient Educational Tools & Aids. This series exists because, while there are many great resources on Latin, more can and always will need to be created. Thus, LAETA welcomes new and innovative works, those that make a contribution, however big or small, to the journey of learning Latin. The long-term aim is to create a tiered curriculum suite featuring innovative readers, grammars, specialized studies, and similar resources that will both encourage and foster the use of Latin. Additionally, the LAETA series endeavors to facilitate the creation and publication of innovative and inexpensive print and digital resources within the context of the global community.

Table of Contents

Preface

Welcome to Latin, one of the most durable and influential languages in the western world for over two thousand years! Although Latin is considered to be a dead language because there are fewer than 100 native speakers who have learned it from childhood, it is far from being either useless or forgotten. In fact, Latin has been in use continuously ever since the Romans dominated Europe and the Mediterranean, even if it is no longer a living language.

For a brief time, the Romans forged an empire spanning several continents, hundreds of peoples, religions, cultures, and languages. But this alone cannot explain why those conquered peoples readily embraced Roman culture, laws, or the Latin language. Nor can it explain why the Latin language was still in use centuries after the Roman Empire had fallen. Perhaps Latin has survived so long because under Roman rule – for the first time in history – more people than ever before were given rights of citizenship, freedom, property, literacy, education, and legal protection. The advantages were obvious even to the enemies of Rome.

But what is the importance of studying Latin now? We now enjoy prosperity and opportunity unequaled since Romans times, but we still have much to gain from the Romans. Our American republic, our laws, our modern sciences, our medicine, our currency, and our language are built in part upon the foundation of ancient Rome. To study Rome and its language is really to study our own history: Latin is the key to our past.

Latin may also provide a key to our future. After all, even in modern times we share many of the same difficulties and concerns which faced the Romans:

- What is the best way to care for refugees?
- How can immigrants become citizens?
- Who should have protection under the laws of our land?
- Can we avoid destructive political rivalry, riots, and injustice at home?
- How can we guard against or prevent terrorism?
- Should we get involved in a war abroad on behalf of other nations?
- Can we keep the value of our money constant?
- What is the best solution for poverty?

Even in these modern times Latin is a valuable tool because it can unlock many resources of past ages for our instruction. Latin offers us an opportunity to learn from the mistakes and successes of the Romans, the one civilization in all of world history most like our own. Surely Latin is far from being dead or even useless to us!

This course cannot give you a complete knowledge of Latin, but it will open a little doorway into a vast world. You will learn only the most basic aspects of the Latin language, but by building on these little by little, you can gain all the skills you need to explore that whole world on your own.

Eāmus!
(Let's go!)

Pronunciation

Several different methods of pronouncing Latin exist. The following notes correspond to what is known as "classical" pronunciation.

Vowels

If you were to say the word "no" very slowly, you would discover that your pronunciation of the vowel "o" probably started something like "uh" and ended something like "oo." Such glides do not occur in single vowels in Latin. There are six vowels in Latin, and these six vowels may be pronounced either long or short. A macron (a small horizontal mark above the vowel) indicates a long vowel. A short vowel has no macron. Below are each of the six Latin vowels, both short and long, with an English word to help guide your pronunciation:

Short vowels		Long vowels	
a	as in *a*lter	**ā**	as in f*a*ther (twice as long as short *a*)
e	as in p*e*t	**ē**	as in th*ey*
i	as in p*i*n	**ī**	as in sk*i*
o	as in *o*ff	**ō**	as in t*o*tal
u	as in p*u*t	**ū**	as in r*u*le
y	as in p*u*t	**ȳ**	as in r*u*le

Macrons

Macrons are small horizontal bars written above long vowels in Latin. Macrons indicate the proper pronunciation and length of vowels and give important clues to a word's use and meaning within a sentence.

Diphthongs

Diphthongs are vowel combinations. Below are some common to Latin:

ae	like *i* in k*i*te
au	like *ou* in lo*u*d
ei	like *e* in h*e*y
eu	like *eu* in f*eu*d
ui	like *uey* in gl*uey*

Consonants

The consonants are pronounced as in English with the following exceptions:

b	as in English (except before *s* and *t,* where it is pronounced *p)*
c	always like *c* in *c*ar
ch	always like *k* in *k*ite
g	always like *g* in *g*ap
i	like *y* in *y*et (only when it begins a word or precedes a vowel)
ph	like *ph* in *ph*one
r	trilled or rolled
s	always like *s* in *s*ing
th	like *t* in *t*ell
v	like *w* in *w*ine

Accents and Syllables

The Latin accent is a musical one: accented syllables are spoken with a higher pitch than other syllables and not necessarily with any more force.

In two-syllable words, the first syllable is always accented. In longer words, the accent comes either on the next-to-last syllable (if that one is long) or on the third-to-last syllable (if the next-to-last isn't long). Latin words are never stressed or accented on the last syllable.

audēmus	au·dē´mus
iūra	iū´·ra
nostra	nos´·tra
dēfendere	dē·fen´de·re

A syllable is long if it contains a long vowel (with a macron) or if it contains a vowel and is followed by two consonants.

At the Beginning of Class

Magister: Salvēte, discipulī. Hello, students.

Discipulī: Salvē, magister. Hello, teacher.

Magister: Surgite. Ōrēmus. Stand up. Let's pray.

Omnēs: Domine Deus, adiūvā nōs Lord God, help us

linguam Latīnam discere. Amen. to learn the Latin language. Amen.

Omnēs: Pater noster, quī in caelī es, Our Father, You who are in heaven,

sanctificētur nōmen tuum; may Your name be made holy;

veniat rēgnum tuum; may Your kingdom come;

fīat voluntās tua may Your will be done

sicut in caelō et in terrā. on earth just as in heaven.

Pānem nostrum cōtīdiānum dā nōbīs hodiē, Our daily bread

dā nōbīs hodiē, give us today,

et dimitte nōbīs debita nostra and forgive us our debts

sicut et nōs dimissimus debitōribus nostrīs; just as we also forgive our debtors;

et nē indūcās nōs in temptātiōnem, and lead us not into temptation,

sed līberā nōs ā malō. Amen. but deliver us from evil. Amen.

Songs and Hymns

Magister: Cantēmus "Christus vincit."   Let's sing "Christ Conquers."

Chri - stus vin - cit, Chris - tus rē - gnat, Chri - tus, Chris - tus _ im - per - at.

Magister: Cantēmus "Glōria Patrī."   Let's sing "Glory be to the Father."

Glō - ri - a Pa - trī et Fī - li - ō et Spī - ri - tu - ī San - ctō

2

si - cut _ e - rat in prīn - ci - pi - ō et nunc et sem - per

3

et in _ sae - cu - la sae - cu - lō - rum. A - - - - men.

Magister: Grātiās, discipulī. Sedēte.   Thank you, students. Sit down.

SCHOLA LATINA I

by Ken Stephenson

revised by Ruth Baldwin
& Thomas Caucutt

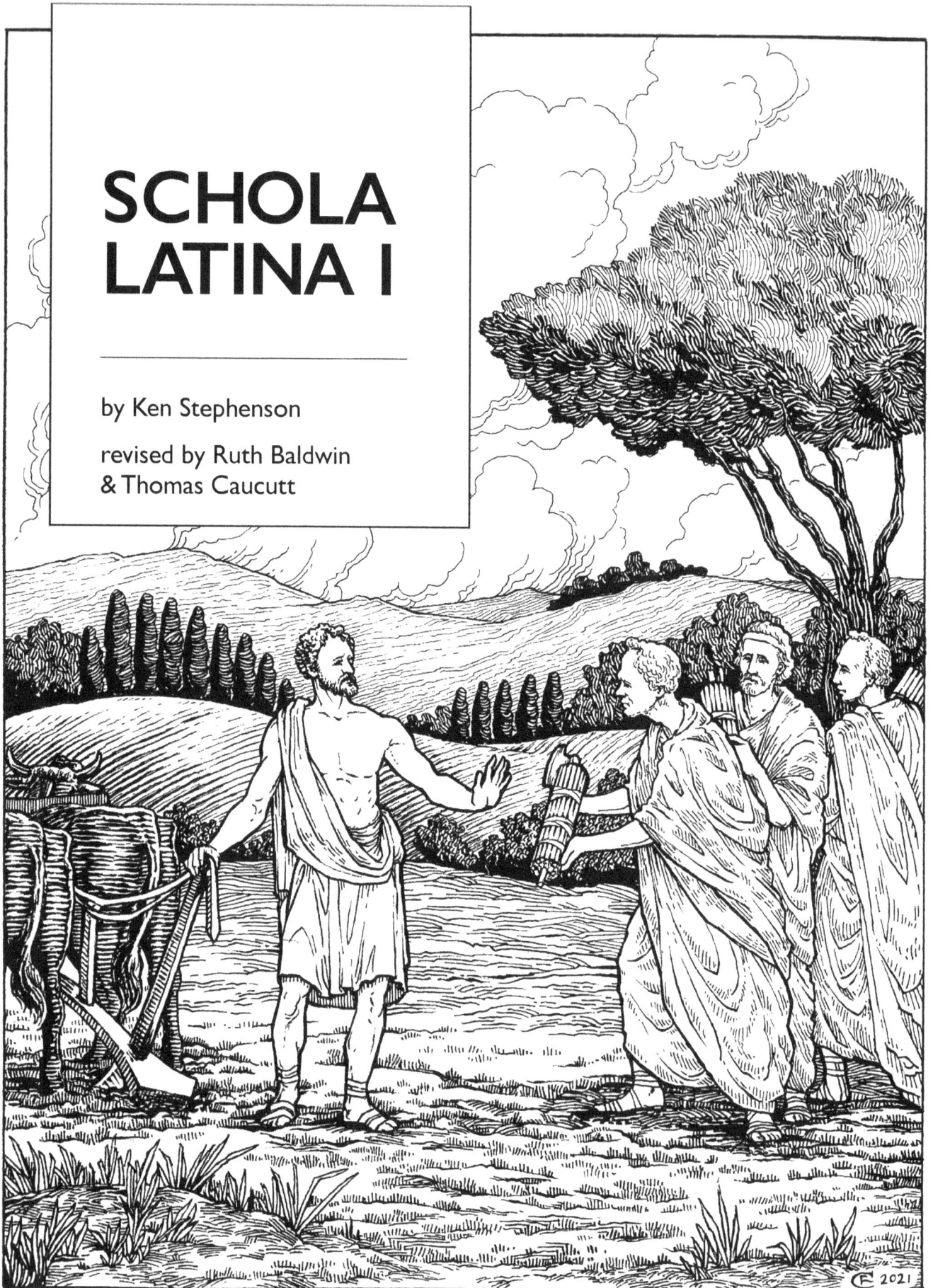

Disciplīna (Lesson) I – ūnus   **VERBS**

I. Dictum (1. Saying)

Crēdō in ūnum Deum.   *I believe in one God.*

II. Colloquium (2. Conversation)

	Latīnē (in Latin)	*Anglicē* (in English)
Magistra:	Salvēte discipulī!	Good morning, students!
Discipulī:	Salvē magistra!	Good morning, teacher!
Magistra:	Valēte discipulī!	Good-bye, students!
Discipulī:	Valē magistra!	Good-bye, teacher!

III. Verba (3. Words or Vocabulary)

Latīnē (in Latin)	*Anglicē* (in English)	*Scrībe tōtum verbum Latīnum.* (Write the whole Latin word.)	*Dērīvātī* (Derivatives)
ambulō, ambulāre	to walk	*ambulō, ambulāre*	*ambulance*
amō, amāre	to love, to like	*amō, amāre*	*amorous*
cantō, cantāre	to sing	*cantō, cantāre*	*canticle*
pugnō, pugnāre	to fight	*pugnō, pugnāre*	*pugnacious*

1. How are these Latin *verba* alike? *They all end with -ō and -āre.*

2. How are the English translations alike? *They all begin with "to".*

3. What kind of *verba* are these? *They are all verbs or action words.*

4. Latin verb forms that end in *–āre* are called *infinitives*

IV. Grammatica (4. Grammar)
Read this paradigm (pattern or example) aloud, by column, and memorize it.

am**ō**	amā**mus**
amā**s**	amā**tis**
ama**t**	ama**nt**

1. A complete sentence normally includes a _____*subject*_____ and a _____*verb*_____.

2. A verb is a word that expresses _____*action*_____ or _____*being*_____.

3. The subject of a sentence tells who or what is _____*doing the action or being.*_____

4. In English, a complete sentence usually has at least how many words? _____*two.*_____

5. In Latin, just one word often forms a _____*complete*_____ _____*sentence.*_____

6. A list of the forms of a verb is called a _*conjugation.*_

7. What does each word in this Latin conjugation mean?

am**ō**	*I love.*	am**āmus**	*We love.*
am**ās**	*You love.*	am**ātis**	*You all love.*
ama**t**	*He, she, it loves.*	ama**nt**	*They love.*

V. Historia (5. History; from *Famous Men of Rome*, Chapter I, Parts I and II)

Amulius, king of the Latins, has banished his brother, the rightful king, and has placed his brother's daughter Sylvia in service at the temple of Vesta so she can never marry. Sylvia secretly marries Mars, the god of war, and has twin sons. Amulius orders that the babies be thrown into the Tiber River, but a kind-hearted servant places them in a basket to save them. They float to the foot of Palatine Hill, where a wolf finds them and nurses them. Then a farmer named Faustulus finds them, and he and his wife, who names them Romulus and Remus, raise the boys.

VI. Dēlēgāta (6. Assignments)

A. *Scrībe* (Write) **the four Latin *verba* from this *disciplīna* and their translations.**

Latīnē	*Anglicē*
1. *ambulō, ambulāre*	1. *to walk*
2. *amō, amāre*	2. *to love, to like*
3. *cantō, cantāre*	3. *to sing*
4. *pugnō, pugnāre*	4. *to fight*

B. *Scrībe* the conjugation of <u>amō, amāre</u> two times.

1.   *amō*   *amāmus*   2.   *amō*   *amāmus*

       amās   *amātis*   *amās*   *amātis*

       amat   *amant*   *amat*   *amant*

C. *Scrībe* the *dictum* from this *disciplīna* and its translation.

       Latīnē: *Crēdō in ūnum Deum.*

       Anglicē: *I believe in one God.*

D. Translate (Write the English meaning of) **these *verba* and phrases.**

1. ūnus   *one*   6. historia   *history*

2. Latīnē   *in Latin*   7. colloquium   *conversation*

3. Anglicē   *in English*   8. dēlēgāta   *assignments*

4. dictum   *a saying*   9. verba   *words / vocabulary*

5. grammatica   *grammar*   10. disciplīna   *lesson*

E. Fill in the blanks.

1. What kind of words are the four *verba*?   *They are verbs*   .

2. What does –**ō** at the end of a Latin verb mean?   *I*

3. A complete sentence normally includes a   *subject*   and a   *verb*   .

4. A verb is a word that expresses   *action*   or   *being*   .

5. The subject of a sentence tells who or what is   *doing the action*   .

6. In English, a complete sentence usually has at least how many words?   *two*

7. In Latin,   *one*   word can be a complete sentence.

8. The letters   *J*   and   *W*   are missing from the Latin alphabet.

9. A list of the forms of a verb is called a   *conjugation*   .

F. *Verbum* **Search.** Each of the *verba* listed below can be found in this grid, reading forward, backward, up, down, or diagonally. Can you find them all? All of the unused letters spell a hidden message when read from left to right, row by row. What is the hidden message?

Hidden message (*Anglicē*):_____ *LEARNING LATIN WILL BE FUN* _____

C	O	L	L	O	Q	U	I	U	M	L
A	L	R	A	N	G	L	I	C	E	D
N	U	E	T	G	R	E	A	R	E	N
T	B	B	I	U	A	I	D	L	A	N
O	M	I	N	P	M	G	E	I	B	S
L	A	T	E	A	M	G	R	A	R	U
S	U	M	E	R	A	O	I	I	E	L
T	I	N	O	T	T	W	V	V	V	U
I	U	N	U	S	I	L	A	L	L	M
B	E	M	I	L	C	O	T	Y	T	O
S	O	H	F	F	A	U	I	S	N	R

AMBULO
AMO
ANGLICE
CANTO
COLLOQUIUM
DELEGATUM
DERIVATI
GRAMMATICA
HISTORIA
LATINE
PUGNO
REMUS
ROMULUS
SYLVIA
TIBER
UNUS
VERBA

G. Dērīvātī. A Latin *derivative* is an English *verbum* that has a Latin root. It must share *both* partial spelling *and* meaning with its Latin root. Complete each sentence with an English *verbum* (derivative) chosen from the following *verba*. The italicized *verbum* in the sentence should help you think of the Latin root.

 amble   amorous   canticle   pugnacious

1. Someone who is often eager to *fight* is ___*pugnacious*___. Latin root:___*pugnō, pugnāre*___

2. Someone who has feelings of *love* is ___*amorous*___. Latin root:___*amō, amāre*___

3. To *walk* slowly is to ___*amble*___. Latin root:___*ambulō, ambulāre*___

4. A *song* in the Bible, such as the prophecy of Zechariah in Luke 1, is sometimes called a

___*canticle*___. Latin root:___*cantō, cantāre*___

H. Historia. Review the history story, and fill in the blanks.

1. Whom does Sylvia secretly marry?___*Sylvia secretly marries Mars.*___

2. Down what river do her sons float in a basket?___*They float down the Tiber.*___

3. Who finds the boys and raises them?___*The shepherd Faustulus raises them.*___

4. What names are Sylvia's sons eventually given?___*They are called Romulus and Remus.*___

Disciplīna II – duo   1st CONJUGATION

I. Dictum

Ōrā et labōrā.   *Pray and work.*

II. Colloquium

	Latīnē	*Anglicē*
Sextus:	Salvē!	Hello!
Iūlia:	Salvē!	Hello!
Sextus:	Quod praenōmen tibi est?	What is your (first) name?
Iūlia:	Nōmen mihi Iūlia est.	My name is Julia.
	Quod nōmen tibi est?	What is your name?
Sextus:	Nōmen mihi Sextus est.	My name is Sextus. (See more names on p. 161)

III. Verba

Latīnē	*Anglicē*	*Scrībe tōtum verbum Latīnum.*	*Dērīvāī*
cēnō, cēnāre	to dine, to eat	*cēnō, cēnāre*	
errō, errāre	to err, to wander, to be mistaken	*errō, errāre*	*error*
festīnō, festīnāre	to hurry	*festīnō, festīnāre*	
iūdicō, iūdicāre	to judge	*iūdicō, iūdicāre*	*judicial*
labōrō, labōrāre	to work	*labōrō, labōrāre*	*laborious*
nāvigō, nāvigāre	to sail	*nāvigō, nāvigāre*	*navigate*
ōrō, ōrāre	to pray, to speak	*ōrō, ōrāre*	*orator*
peccō, peccāre	to sin	*peccō, peccāre*	*impeccable*
tardō, tardāre	to be slow	*tardō, tardāre*	*tardy*

1. What kind of *verba* are these?   *They are all verbs.*

2. The second form of a verb's dictionary entry is called the   *infinitive*

3. These verb forms are always translated   *to*

4. The infinitives of 1st conjugation always end in   *-āre*

IV. Grammatica

Read this paradigm aloud, by column, and memorize it.

		S _ingular_	P _lural_	
__1st__ person	___I___	-ō	-mus	___we___
__2nd__ person	___you___	-s	-tis	___you all___
__3rd__ person	___he, she, it___	-t	-nt	___they___

1. These endings are called <u>personal endings</u>. They indicate the _____person_____ and

    _____number_____ of the subject of the verb. So pronouns are built into Latin verbs!

2. The _____first_____ person is the person *speaking*.

3. The _____second_____ person is the person spoken *to*.

4. The _____third_____ person is the person spoken *about*.

5. The word _____singular_____ refers to one person.

6. The word _____plural_____ refers to more than one person.

Adding each of the personal endings to a verb's stem is called *conjugating*. <u>To find the stem of a verb, drop the –re of the infinitive</u>, but remember that the first form of a 1st conjugation verb in present tense drops the **–ā** of the stem, for example, **cēnō** (*not* **cēnāo).**

Example: **cēnō, cēnāre** (Find the stem by dropping the –re of the inifinitive: **cenā-**)

I dine	cēnō	<u>cēnā</u>**mus**	*we dine*
you dine	<u>cēnā</u>s	<u>cēnā</u>tis	*you all dine*
he/she/it dines	<u>cēna</u>t	<u>cēna</u>nt	*they dine*

V. Historia (*Famous Men of Rome*, Chapter I, Part II)

Romulus and Remus grow up strong, handsome, and pugnacious. One day Remus gets into a fight with a servant of a neighbor, Numitor. Numitor meets the boys, and when he hears of their strange history, he realizes that they are his grandsons. He explains that he is the rightful king. The headstrong boys avenge the injustices King Amulius has committed against their family.

VI. Dēlēgāta

A. *Scrībe* the new Latin *verba* and their translations.

	Latīnē		*Anglicē*
1.	cēnō, cēnāre	1.	to dine, to eat
2.	errō, errāre	2.	to err, to wander, to be mistaken
3.	festīnō, festīnāre	3.	to hurry
4.	iudicō, iudicāre	4.	to judge
5.	labōrō, labōrāre	5.	to work
6.	nāvigō, nāvigāre	6.	to sail
7.	ōrō, ōrāre	7.	to pray, to speak
8.	peccō, peccāre	8.	to sin
9.	tardō, tardāre	9.	to be slow

B. *Scrībe* the personal endings for present tense verbs two times.

1.   -ō   -mus   2.   -ō   -mus

    -s   -tis   -s   -tis

    -t   -nt   -t   -nt

C. *Scrībe* the *dictum* from *Disciplīna II* and its translation.

Latīnē: Ōrā et labōrā.

Anglicē: Pray and work.

D. Translate these *verba* and phrases.

1. ūnus   one   4. Salvēte.   Hello (pl.).

2. duo   two   5. cēnāmus   We eat.

3. Salvē.   Hello.   6. festīnās   You hurry.

7. Valē. _____ *Goodbye.* _____   12. nāvigās. _____ *You sail.* _____

8. tardās. _____ *You are slow.* _____   13. amat. _____ *He, (she, it) loves.* _____

9. ōrant. _____ *They pray.* _____   14. labōrat. _____ *He (she, it) works.* _____

10. peccant. _____ *They sin.* _____   15. peccō. _____ *I sin.* _____

11. nāvigātis. _____ *You all sail.* _____   16. ōrō. _____ *I pray.* _____

17. Quod praenōmen tibi est? _____ *What is your name?* _____

18. Crēdō in ūnum Deum. _____ *I believe in one God.* _____

E. Fill in the blanks.

1. What kind of words are the new *verba*? _____ *They are all verbs.* _____

2. Personal endings indicate the _____ *person* _____ and _____ *number* _____ of the subject of the verb.

3. The 1ˢᵗ person is the person _____ *speaking* _____ .

4. The 2ⁿᵈ person is the person spoken _____ *to* _____ .

5. The 3ʳᵈ person is the person spoken _____ *about* _____ .

6. To find the stem of a verb, drop the _____ *-re* _____ of the _____ *infinitive* _____ .

7. The list of the forms of a verb is called a _____ *conjugation* _____ .

F. Anagrams. Unscramble the letters in each row to form the 1ˢᵗ person singular of one of the new *verba* in this *disciplīna*. Then rearrange the shaded letters to form an important English word from this *disciplīna*. (Hint: one letter I in Latin = J in English.)

ROO	O R O
ROER	E R R O
NCEO	C E N O
COPCE	P E C C O
OTDAR	T A R D O
BOOARL	L A B O R O
GVAONI	N A V I G O
CDIIUO	I U D I C O
ISFOTNE	F E S T I N O
Solution:	C O N J U G A T I O N

G. *Scrībe* the meaning of each verb in the blank next to it. Carefully draw a box around the stem of the verb in the infinitive. Then conjugate each verb in the present tense.

1. tardō, tardāre _____ *to be slow* _____

tardō	*tardāmus*
tardās	*tardātis*
tardat	*tardant*

2. labōrō, labōrāre _____ *to work* _____

labōrō	*labōrāmus*
labōrās	*labōrātis*
labōrat	*labōrant*

3. festīnō, festīnāre _____ *to hurry* _____

festīnō	*festīnāmus*
festīnās	*festīnātis*
festīnat	*festīnant*

4. ōrō, ōrāre _____ *to pray, to speak* _____

ōrō	*ōrāmus*
ōrās	*ōrātis*
ōrat	*ōrant*

5. nāvigō, nāvigāre _____ *to sail* _____

nāvigō	*nāvigāmus*
nāvigās	*nāvigātis*
nāvigat	*nāvigant*

6. iūdicō, iūdicāre _____ *to judge* _____

iūdicō	*iūdicāmus*
iūdicās	*iūdicātis*
iūdicat	*iūdicant*

7. amō, amāre _____ *to love* _____

amō	*amāmus*
amās	*amātis*
amat	*amant*

8. cantō, cantāre _____ *to sing* _____

cantō	*cantāmus*
cantās	*cantātis*
cantat	*cantant*

9. pugnō, pugnāre _____ *to fight* _____

pugnō	*pugnāmus*
pugnās	*pugnātis*
pugnat	*pugnant*

10. ambulō, ambulāre _____ *to walk* _____

ambulō	*ambulāmus*
ambulās	*ambulātis*
ambulat	*ambulant*

H. Dērīvātī

A Latin *derivative* is an English *verbum* with a ___Latin___ root.

English derivatives must share both partial ___spelling___ and ___meaning___. with their Latin roots. A *borrowed word* is a Latin *verbum* that has come directly into English without any change in spelling, e.g., *labor* has **labōrāre** as its root, but the Latin *verbum* for *work* is **labor, labōris, m.**, so *labor* is a borrowed word (as well as a derivative).

Complete each sentence with an English *verbum* chosen from the following *verba*. The italicized *verbum* in the sentence should help you think of the Latin root.

error   judicial   labor   navigate   tardy   impeccable

1. When you *err* or *wander* from the correct way, you make an ___error___.

   Latin root: ___errō, errāre___

2. Physical *work* can be called ___labor___.

   Latin root: ___labōrō, labōrāre___

3. To *sail* a ship is to ___navigate___.

   Latin root: ___nāvigō, nāvigāre___

4. *Judges* make up the ___judicial___ branch of the government.

   Latin root: ___iūdicō, iūdicāre___

5. If you're too *slow*, you'll be ___tardy___.

   Latin root: ___tardō, tardāre___

6. When someone does an ___impeccable___ job, it is nearly perfect or without *sin*.

   Latin root: ___peccō, peccāre___

I. Historia. Review the history story, and fill in the blanks.

1. Who is Romulus's and Remus's grandfather? ___Their grandfather's name is Numitor.___

2. What do the boys do to King Amulius? ___They cut off Amulius' head.___

Disciplīna III – trēs   NOUNS

I. Dictum

Cōgitō ergō sum. (Descartes)   _____ *I think; therefore, I am.* _____

II. Colloquium   *Latīnē*   *Anglicē*

	Latīnē	*Anglicē*
Marcus:	Grātiās tibi agō!	Thank you!
Valeria:	Libenter!	You're welcome!

III. Verba

Latīnē	*Anglicē*	*Scrībe tōtum verbum Latīnum.*	*Dērīvātī*
cōgitō, cōgitāre	to think	*cōgitō, cōgitāre*	*cogitate*
intrō, intrāre	to enter	*intrō, intrāre*	*introduce*
recitō, recitāre	to recite, to read aloud	*recitō, recitāre*	*recitation*
superō, superāre	to overcome, to conquer	*superō, superāre*	*superman*
aqua, -ae, f.	water	*aqua, -ae, f.*	*aquarium*
culīna, -ae, f.	kitchen	*culīna, -ae, f.*	*culinary*
fēmina, -ae, f.	woman	*fēmina, -ae, f.*	*feminine*
furca, -ae, f.	fork	*furca, -ae, f.*	*fork*
Rōma, -ae, f.	Rome	*Rōma, -ae, f.*	*Rome*

1. What kind of *verba* are the first four *verba*?_____ *They are verbs.* _____

2. What kind of *verba* are the last five *verba*?_____ *They are nouns.* _____

3. A noun is a word that names a _____ *person* _____, _____ *place* _____,

   _____ *thing* _____, or _____ *idea* _____

4. Which nouns name places?_____ *culīna, Rōma* _____

5. Which nouns name things?_____ *fēmina, furca, aqua* _____

IV. Grammatica

Read this conjugation aloud, by column, and memorize it.

_____I think._____	cōgit**ō**	cōgitā**mus**	_____We think._____
_____You think._____	cōgitā**s**	cōgitā**tis**	_____You all think._____
He (she, it) thinks.	cōgita**t**	cōgita**nt**	_____They think._____

Translate the verbs in the paradigm into English. This conjugation is in _present tense_. The word _tense_ means _time_. Verbs in the present tense express action occurring in the present (now). They can be translated one of three ways, e.g., **cōgitō** can be translated:

I think   _or_   I am thinking   _or_   I do think

1. What kind of words are _am_ and _do_ above?_____ _They are helping verbs_ _____

   There are _no_ Latin words for _helping verbs_ _____. They are built into the verbs!

2. To find the stem of a Latin verb, drop the __-re__ of the _____ _infinitive_ _____.

3. Each of the translations of the personal endings is a _____ _pronoun_ _____.

4. A pronoun is a word that replaces or takes the place of a _____ _noun_ _____.

5. Underline the personal ending in each of these verbs. Then translate them.

   a. Intrō. _____ _I enter._ _____   d. Tardāmus. _____ _We are slow._ _____

   b. Recitās. _____ _You recite._ _____   e. Iūdicātis. _____ _You judge._ _____

   c. Superat. _____ _She conquers._ _____   f. Cōgitant. _____ _They think._ _____

7. Translate **cōgitāmus** three ways.   8. Translate **ambulō** three ways.

   a. _____ _We think._ _____   a. _____ _I walk._ _____

   b. _____ _We are thinking._ _____   b. _____ _I am walking._ _____

   c. _____ _We do think._ _____   c. _____ _I do walk._ _____

V. Historia (_Famous Men of Rome_, Chapter I, Part III)

753 BC Romulus and Remus decide to build a city on Palatine Hill. They argue about who will be the first king, and Romulus wins. Remus scoffs at Romulus' wall and is killed.

VI. Dēlēgāta

A. *Scrībe* the new Latin *verba* and their meanings.

	Latīnē		*Anglicē*
1.	cōgitō, cōgitāre	1.	to think
2.	intrō, intrāre	2.	to enter
3.	recitō, recitāre	3.	to recite, to read aloud
4.	superō, superāre	4.	to overcome, to conquer
5.	aqua, -ae, f.	5.	water
6.	culīna, -ae, f.	6.	kitchen
7.	fēmina, -ae, f.	7.	woman
8.	furca, -ae, f.	8.	fork
9.	Rōma, -ae, f.	9.	Rome

B. *Scrībe* the meaning of each verb in the blank. Then conjugate each in present tense.

1. intrō, intrāre _____to enter_____

intrō	intrāmus
intrās	intrātis
intrat	intrant

2. superō, superāre _____to overcome_____

superō	superāmus
superās	superātis
superat	superant

3. cōgitō, cōgitāre _____to think_____

cōgitō	cōgitāmus
cōgitās	cōgitātis
cōgitat	cōgitant

4. recitō, recitāre _____to recite_____

recitō	recitāmus
recitās	recitātis
recitat	recitant

C. *Scrībe* the *dictum* and its translation.

Latīnē: _____Cōgitō ergo sum._____   *Anglicē*: _____I think; therefore, I am._____

D. Translate these *verba* and phrases.

1. ūnus _____*one*_____   5. Scrībe. _____*Write.*_____

2. duo _____*two*_____   6. Ōrā et labōrā. _____*Pray and work.*_____

3. trēs _____*three*_____   7. Praenōmen mihi est _____*My name is*_____

4. Grātiās tibi agō. _*Thank you.*_   8. Crēdō in ūnum Deum. _*I believe in one God.*_

E. Fill in the blanks.

1. What kind of words are the last five new *verba*? _____*They are nouns.*_____

2. A noun is a word that names a _____*person*_____, _____*place*_____,

   _____*thing*_____, or _____*idea*_____.

3. A pronoun is a word that takes the place of or replaces a _____*noun*_____.

4. The person spoken *about* is the _____*third*_____ person.

5. The person *speaking* is the _____*first*_____ person.

6. The person spoken *to* is the _____*second*_____ person.

7. The list of the forms of a verb is called a _____*conjugation*_____.

F. Underline the personal ending in these Latin verbs. Then translate each sentence.

1. Tardāmus. _____*We are slow.*_____   9. Amās. _____*You love.*_____

2. Nāvigāmus. _____*We are sailing.*_____   10. Ambulō. _____*I do walk.*_____

3. Peccāmus. _____*We do sin.*_____   11. Iūdicō. _____*I am judging.*_____

4. Cēnant. _____*They eat.*_____   12. Intrō. _____*I enter.*_____

5. Ōrant. _____*They are praying.*_____   13. Errātis. _____*You all are mistaken.*_____

6. Recitant. _____*They read aloud.*_____   14. Labōrātis. _____*You all work.*_____

7. Cantās. _____*You sing.*_____   15. Cōgitātis. _____*You all do think.*_____

8. Festīnās. _____*You are hurrying.*_____   16. Pugnat. _____*He is fighting.*_____

17. Cēnat._____ *It eats.* _____   24. Iūdicātis._____ *You all are judging.* _____

18. Superat._____ *She overcomes.* _____   25. Intrat._____ *It enters.* _____

19. Ambulātis._____ *You all walk.* _____   26. Recitāmus._____ *We are reciting.* _____

20. Nāvigō._____ *I sail.* _____   27. Superant._____ *They conquer.* _____

21. Labōrō._____ *I work.* _____   28. Cantāmus._____ *We are singing.* _____

22. Amant._____ *They love.* _____   29. Errāmus._____ *We wander.* _____

23. Cēnās._____ *You dine.* _____   30. Cantō._____ *I sing.* _____

G. Crossword Puzzle

¹C	²O	G	I	T	³A	M	U	⁴S
	R				M			U
⁵N	A	V	⁶I	G	A	S		P
	N		N		T			E
	T		T					R
			⁷R	E	⁸C	I	T	A	T
			A	■	A			T
⁹F	E	S	T	I	N	A	T	I	S
					T			S
		¹⁰P	U	G	N	A	N	T
					S			

RECTĒ
(across)

1. We think
5. You sail
7. She recites
9. You (all) hurry
10. They fight

DEORSUM
(down)

2. They pray
3. He loves
4. You all overcome
6. It enters
8. You sing

H. Dērīvātī

A Latin derivative is an English *verbum* with a _____*Latin*_____ root.

English derivatives must share both partial ____*spelling*____ and _____meaning____ with their Latin roots.

Complete each sentence with an English *verbum* chosen from the following *verba*.
The italicized *verbum* in the sentence should help you think of the Latin root.

recitation   cogitate   aquarium   culinary   feminine

1. To *think* deeply is to _____*cogitate*_____ . Latin root:_____*cōgitō, cōgitāre*_____

2. Men are masculine; *women* are ____*feminine*____ . Latin root:_____*fēmina, -ae, f.*_____

3. Someone who is good in the *kitchen* has _____*culinary*_____ skill.

   Latin root:_____*culīna, -ae, f.*_____

4. An _____*aquarium*_____ is a large tank of *water* for fish.

   Latin root:_____*aqua, -ae, f.*_____

5. The students will practice *reciting* the poem until their _____*recitation*_____ is perfect.

   Latin root:_____*recitō, recitāre*_____

I. Historia. Review the history story, and fill in the blanks.

1. Where do Romulus and Remus decide to build a city?____*They build it on the Palatine Hill.*____

2. Which brother names the city?_____*Romulus names the city.*_____

3. In what year is it believed that Rome was founded?____*Rome was founded in 753 BC.*____

Disciplīna IV – quattuor   1st DECLENSION

I. Dictum

Ars longa; vīta brevis.   _The art is long; life is short._

II. Colloquium   *Latīnē*   *Anglicē*

Magistra:	Amō, amās, amat. Repetite.	*Amō, amās, amat.* Repeat.
Discipulī:	Amō, amās, amat.	*Amō, amās, amat.*

III. Verba

Latīnē	*Anglicē*	*Scrībe tōtum verbum Latīnum.*	*Dērīvātī*
dubitō, dubitāre	to doubt, to be uncertain	*dubitō, dubitāre*	*dubious*
dūrō, dūrāre	to endure	*dūrō, dūrāre*	*durable*
fenestra, fenestrae, f.	window	*fenestra, fenestrae, f.*	*defenestrate*
Italia, Italiae, f.	Italy	*Italia, Italiae, f.*	*Italy*
lingua, linguae, f.	language, tongue	*lingua, linguae, f.*	*language*
puella, puellae, f.	girl	*puella, puellae, f.*	
ursa, ursae, f.	bear	*ursa, usae, f.*	*Ursa Major*
vīta, vītae, f.	life	*vīta, vītae, f.*	*vitamin*
volō, volāre	to fly	*volō, volāre*	*volatile*

1. Underline the nouns.   Circle the verbs.

2. How can you tell which *verba* are verbs and which are nouns?

3. A noun is a word that names a _____ *person* _____, _____ *place* _____,

   _____ *thing* _____, or _____ *idea* _____

4. Look at each noun. Is it a person, place, thing, or idea?

5. A verb is a word that expresses _____ *action* _____ or _____ *being* _____.

IV. Grammatica

Read this declension aloud, by column, several times.

Singular	_Plural_
ursa	ursae
ursae	ursārum
ursae	ursīs
ursam	ursās
ursā	ursīs

We *conjugate* verbs, but we *decline* nouns. We call a list of all the forms of a noun a declension. In Disciplina V, we will learn how to decline nouns.

1. What do you notice about these forms of **ursa, ursae, f.**?

2. What do you think the stem of the noun is?_____*urs-*_____

3. A paradigm is a _____*pattern*_____ or an _____*example*_____.

There are three kinds or *genders* of Latin nouns. They are *masculine, feminine,* and *neuter*. If a noun names a person, its gender will be masculine or feminine, depending upon whether the noun names a male or a female. However, it is necessary to memorize the gender of all nouns. Later we will learn that sometimes a noun's ending will help us know its gender.

V. Historia (*Famous Men of Rome*, Chapter I, Part IV)

Romulus makes Rome a city of refuge. Since this policy attracts only men, he needs to find another way to attract women to the city. He tricks the Sabines and steals their women. Later, Tarpeia lets King Titus Tatius and the Sabine army into the city, but the women convince him that they are happy now. Romulus establishes the Senate, whose members come from the patricians, or nobles, not from the plebeians, or common people.

VI. Dēlēgāta

A. *Scrībe* the new Latin *verba* and their meanings.

	Latīnē		*Anglicē*
1.	dubitō, dubitāre	1.	to doubt, to be uncertain
2.	dūrō, dūrāre	2.	to endure
3.	fenestra, fenestrae, f.	3.	window
4.	Italia, Italiae, f.	4.	Italy
5.	lingua, linguae, f.	5.	language, tongue
6.	puella, puellae, f.	6.	girl
7.	ursa, ursae, f.	7.	bear
8.	vīta, vītae, f.	8.	life
9.	volō, volāre	9.	to fly

B. *Scrībe* the declension of <u>ursa, ursae, f.</u> two times.

1			2.	
ursa	ursae		ursa	ursae
ursae	ursārum		ursae	ursārum
ursae	ursīs		ursae	ursīs
ursam	ursās		ursam	ursās
ursā	ursīs		ursā	ursīs

C. *Scrībe* the *dictum* and its translation.

Latīnē: _____ Ars longa; vīta brevis. _____

Anglicē: _____ The art is long; life is short. _____

D. Translate these *verba* and phrases.

1. ūnus _____ one _____   2. Scrībe. _____ Write. _____

3. quattuor _____*four*_____   7. Repetite. _____*Repeat.*_____

4. disciplīna _____*lesson*_____   8. Praenōmen mihi est _*My name is*_

5. Ōrā et labōrā. ___*Pray and work.*___   9. colloquium_____*conversation*_____

6. Cōgitō ergō sum._*I think; therefore, I am.*_ 10. Crēdō in unum Deum._*I believe in one God.*_

E. Fill in the blanks.

1. A list of all of the forms of a verb is called a _____*conjugation.*_____

2. A list of all of the forms of a noun is called a _____*declension.*_____

3. Verb endings are called ___*personal*___ ___*endings.*___

F. *Scrībe* the meaning of each verb in the space. Then conjugate each in present tense.

1. dubitō, dubitāre_____*to doubt*_____   2. volō, volāre_____*to fly*_____

___*dubitō*___ ___*dubitāmus*___   ___*volō*___ ___*volāmus*___

___*dubitās*___ ___*dubitātis*___   ___*volās*___ ___*volātis*___

___*dubitat*___ ___*dubitant*___   ___*volat*___ ___*volant*___

3. dūrō, dūrāre_____*to endure*_____   4. peccō, peccāre_____*to sin*_____

___*dūrō*___ ___*dūrāmus*___   ___*peccō*___ ___*peccāmus*___

___*dūrās*___ ___*dūrātis*___   ___*peccās*___ ___*peccātis*___

___*dūrat*___ ___*dūrant*___   ___*peccat*___ ___*peccant*___

G. Underline the personal ending in these Latin verbs. Then translate each sentence.

1. Dūrāmus. ___*We endure.*___   6. Cōgitat. ___*She thinks.*___

2. Dubitāmus. ___*We are uncertain.*___   7. Ambulāmus. ___*We are walking.*___

3. Volant. ___*They fly.*___   8. Intrant. ___*They enter.*___

4. Amant. ___*They love.*___   9. Pugnātis. ___*You all fight.*___

5. Cantātis. ___*You all sing.*___   10. Peccās. ___*You sin.*___

11. Cēnātis. _You all are dining._

12. Festīnō. _I do hurry._

13. Iūdicō. _I judge._

14. Tardās. _You are slow._

15. Recitās. _You recite._

16. Volat. _He flies._

17. Intrō. _I am entering._

18. Dubitat. _He doubts._

19. Volātis. _You all fly._

20. Peccāmus. _We sin._

21. Ōrō. _I read aloud._

22. Labōrant. _They work._

23. Errāmus. _We are mistaken._

24. Superātis. _You all are conquering._

25. Nāvigat. _It is sailing._

26. Errant. _They do wander._

27. Cēnās. _You eat._

28. Volō. _I am flying._

29. Tardant. _They are slow._

30. Pugnās. _You do fight._

H. *Verbum* **Search.** Each of the *verba* listed below can be found in this grid reading forward, backward, up, down, or diagonally. Can you find them all? All of the unused letters spell a hidden message when read from left to right, row by row. What is the hidden message?

Hidden message (*Anglicē*): _ITS GETTING HARDER BUT WERE HAVING FUN!_

P	I	D	U	B	I	T	O	T	S
U	R	S	A	T	I	V	G	E	D
E	E	A	A	S	T	O	T	U	G
L	T	L	E	E	I	L	R	R	N
L	I	U	G	N	H	O	A	A	A
A	T	T	R	I	O	T	D	I	U
E	E	A	R	B	I	M	E	B	G
U	P	T	T	A	W	P	E	E	N
R	E	I	S	S	R	E	H	N	I
A	R	O	V	A	I	N	G	F	L
U	A	R	T	S	E	N	E	F	N

DUBITO
DURO
FENESTRA
GRATIAS
ITALIA
LINGUA
PRAENOMEN
PUELLA
REPETITE
SABINES
SALUTATIO
TARPEIA
URSA
VITA
VOLO

I. Dērīvātī.

A Latin derivative is an English *verbum* with a __Latin__ root.

English derivatives must share both partial __spelling__ and __meaning__ with their Latin roots.

Complete each sentence with an English *verbum* chosen from the following *verba*. The italicized *verbum* in the sentence should help you think of the Latin root.

durable sublingual vital duration vitamin

1. Something that lasts or *endures* is _____durable_____.

Latin root: _____durō, dūrāre_____

2. Organs of your body that are necessary for *life* are called _____vital_____ organs.

Latin root: _____vīta, vītae, f._____

3. A _____sublingual_____ pill is taken under the *tongue*.

Latin root: _____lingua, linguae, f._____

4. A _____vitamin_____ is a daily pill made up of the nutrients necessary for *life*.

Latin root: _____vīta, vītae, f._____

5. The _____duration_____ of an illness is how long it lasts or *endures*.

Latin root: _____dūrō, dūrāre_____

J. Historia. Review the history story, and fill in the blanks.

1. How does Romulus get women to Rome? _____He steals them from the Sabines._____

2. Who lets the Sabine army into Rome? _____Tarpeia lets them in._____

3. What do the women tell the Sabine army? _____They tell them to stop fighting._____

4. What are the Roman nobles called? _____Roman nobles are called patricians._____

5. What are the Roman common people called? _____Common people are called plebeians._____

Disciplīna V – quīnque   CASES

I. Dictum

et cētera   (abbreviation: _etc._)   _and the rest_

II. Colloquium

                       Latīnē   _Anglicē_

Claudia:	Quomodō tē habēs?	How are you today?
Publius:	Bene, grātiās tibi agō.	Well, thank you.
	Et tū?	And you?
	(See more responses on p. 161)	

III. Verba

Latīnē	_Anglicē_	_Scrībe tōtum verbum Latīnum._	_Dērīvātī_
aquila, aquilae, f.	eagle	_aquila, aquilae, f._	_aquiline_
charta, chartae, f.	paper	_charta, chartae, f._	_chart_
corōna, corōnae, f.	crown	_corōna, corōnae, f._	_coronation_
Gallia, Galliae, f.	Gaul (France)	_Gallia, Galliae, f._	_Gaul_
imperō, imperāre	to rule, to order	_imperō, imperāre_	_imperative_
pecūnia, pecūniae, f.	money	_pecūnia, pecūniae, f._	_pecuniary_
rēgīna, rēgīnae, f.	queen	_rēgīna, rēgīnae, f._	_regal_
stō, stāre	to stand	_stō, stāre_	_status_
victōria, victōriae, f.	victory	_victōria, victōriae, f._	_victory_

1. Underline the nouns. Circle the verbs.

2. Look at each noun. Is it a person, place, thing, or idea?

IV. Grammatica

We _conjugate_ verbs, and verb endings are called _personal endings._ We _decline_ nouns, and noun endings are called _case endings._ There are _____ six _____ cases of Latin nouns.

Read the paradigm in the shaded box, and <u>memorize it</u>.

		Singular	*Plural*
Nominative	(Nom.):	**-a**	**-ae**
Genitive	(Gen.):	**-ae**	**-ārum**
Dative	(Dat.):	**-ae**	**-īs**
Accusative	(Acc.):	**-am**	**-ās**
Ablative	(Abl.):	**-ā**	**-īs**

(The sixth case of Latin nouns, which we will rarely use, is the *vocative* case. It is used for *direct address*—when one person speaks directly to another person.)

Noun Cases Chant

The cases of a Latin noun tell what a noun can do.
Let's say them now, and we'll see how.
It's fun to learn things new.

Nominative tells what the subject is.
Genitive shows possession
Dative gives the indirect object.
Now learn this Latin lesson.
Accusative is the direct object.
Ablative's lots of fun—
Means, manner, place, and time,
Object of a preposition.

Nominative,
Genitive,
Dative,
Accusative,
And finally the **Ablative**.
These are the cases of a Latin noun—
Latin's a great way to live! (But don't forget the vocative!)

The two cases we will use the most in this book are the *nominative* and the *genitive* cases.

The sixth Latin noun case, used for direct address, is the _____ *vocative* _____ case.

And now we have a use for the –ae that we've seen in all of our nouns. There are five declensions of Latin nouns. We've only learned nouns from 1ˢᵗ declension so far. Nearly all nouns in 1ˢᵗ declension are feminine in gender. The *genitive singular case ending* of a noun shows to which of the five declensions a noun belongs. **All** nouns in 1ˢᵗ declension have –ae for their *genitive singular ending.*

To find the stem of a Latin noun, drop the case ending from the genitive singular form of the noun. (In 1ˢᵗ declension, we can also find the noun stem by dropping the –a from the *nominative* singular form of the noun.) So the stem for **charta, chartae, f.** is **chart-**.

V. Historia (Famous Men of Rome, Chapter II)

Romulus dies. The Senate elects Numa Pompilius as king. He establishes many good laws. He also gives public lands to all poor Romans since farming is considered the only reputable occupation besides being a soldier.

VI. Dēlēgāta

A. *Scrībe* the new Latin *verba* and their meanings.

	Latīnē		*Anglicē*
1.	aquila, aquilae, f.	1.	eagle
2.	charta, chartae, f.	2.	paper
3.	corōna, corōnae, f.	3.	crown
4.	Gallia, Galliae, f.	4.	Gaul
5.	imperō, imperāre	5.	to rule; to order
6.	pecūnia, pecūniae, f.	6.	money
7.	rēgīna, rēgīnae, f.	7.	queen
8.	stō, stāre	8.	to stand
9.	victōria, victōriae, f.	9.	victory

B. *Scrībe* the *dictum* and its translation.

Latīnē: et cētera

Anglicē: and the rest

25

C. *Scrībe* the case endings for 1st declension three times.

1.	-a	-ae	2.	-a	-ae	3.	-a	-ae
	-ae	-ārum		-ae	-ārum		-ae	-ārum
	-ae	-īs		-ae	-īs		-ae	-īs
	-am	-ās		-am	-ās		-am	-ās
	-ā	-īs		-ā	-īs		-ā	-īs

D. Translate these *verba* and phrases.

1. quīnque _____ *five* _____   6. Scrībe. _____ *Write.* _____

2. quattuor _____ *four* _____   7. Repetite. _____ *Repeat.* _____

3. verba _____ *words* _____   8. et cētera _____ *and the rest* _____

4. trēs _____ *three* _____   9. grammatica _____ *grammar* _____

5. Ars longa. _____ *Art is long.* _____   10. Vīta brevis. _____ *Life is short.* _____

E. Fill in the blanks.

1. Case endings tell the _____ *case* _____ and _____ *number* _____ of a noun.

2. Latin dictionaries list the _____ *nominative* _____ form of a noun, the _____ *genitive* _____ _____ *singular* _____ case ending, and the _____ *gender* _____.

3. The nominative case is used for the _____ *subject* _____ of a sentence.

4. To find the stem of a <u>verb</u>, drop the _____ *-re* _____ of the _____ *infinitive* _____

5. To find the stem of a <u>noun</u>, drop the _____ *genitive* _____ *singular* case ending.

F. Underline the personal ending in these Latin verbs. Then translate each sentence.

1. Stat. _____ *She stands.* _____   4. Imperātis. _____ *You all rule.* _____

2. Stāmus. _____ *We stand* _____   5. Peccāmus. _____ *We sin.* _____

3. Imperant. _____ *They rule.* _____   6. Ōrātis. _____ *You all are praying.* _____

7. Labōrās. *You are working.*   12. Recitātis. *You all are reciting.*

8. Tardō. *I am slow.*   13. Errō. *I am wandering.*

9. Superat. *He overcomes.*   14. Dūrāmus. *We are enduring.*

10. Intrāmus. *We are entering.*   15. Volant. *They are flying.*

11. Nāvigant. *They are sailing.*   16. Dubitās. *You are uncertain.*

G. *Scrībe* the meaning of each noun in the space provided. **Then decline it.**

1. rēgīna, rēgīnae, f. *queen*   2. corōna, corōnae, f. *crown*

rēgīna	*rēgīnae*	*corōna*	*corōnae*
rēgīnae	*rēgīnārum*	*corōnae*	*corōnārum*
rēgīnae	*rēgīnīs*	*corōnae*	*corōnīs*
rēgīnam	*rēgīnās*	*corōnam*	*corōnās*
rēgīnā	*rēgīnīs*	*corōnā*	*corōnīs*

3. puella, puellae, f. *girl*   4. ursa, ursae, f. *bear*

puella	*puellae*	*ursa*	*ursae*
puellae	*puellārum*	*ursae*	*ursārum*
puellae	*puellīs*	*ursae*	*ursīs*
puellam	*puellās*	*ursam*	*ursās*
puellā	*puellīs*	*ursā*	*ursīs*

H. Dērīvātī. Complete each sentence with an English *verbum* chosen from the following *verba*. The italicized *verbum* in the sentence should help you think of the Latin root.

coronation   pecuniary   victorious   imperious   imperative

1. Someone who likes to give *orders* can be called _____ *imperious* _____.

   Latin root: *imperō, imperāre*

2. An ___ *imperative* ___ sentence gives a *command*. Latin root: *imperō, imperāre*

3. A _____*coronation*_____ is a ceremony in which a king or queen is *crowned*.

    Latin root:_____*corōna, corōnae, f.*_____

4. The winning team experiences *victory* or is _____*victorious*_____.

    Latin root:_____*victōria, victōriae, f.*_____

5. Do you have trouble with *money*? If you do, you have ____*pecuniary*____ difficulties.

    Latin root:_____*pecūnia, pecūniae, f.*_____

I. Alphabet Code. (1) Place some of the *verba* from this *disciplīna* in the following blanks, letter by letter. Some letters are given to help you get started. (2) The letters *under* the blanks represent a code. For example, *e* stands for *S* in the code, since *e* is under the *S* in the first *verbum*. Use the code to decipher the longer English message in the shaded box.

```
S  T  O            R  E  G  I  N  A
e  y  d            t  q  o  v  x  j

G  A  L  L  I  A      I  M  P  E  R  O
o  j  k  k  v  j      v  u  a  q  t  d

C  H  A  R  T  A      P  E  C  U  N  I  A
i  w  j  t  y  j      a  q  i  f  x  v  j

C  O  R  O  N  A      V  I  C  T  O  R  I  A
i  d  t  d  x  j      z  v  i  y  d  t  v  j

A  Q  U  I  L  A      R  E  G  I  N  A
j  n  f  v  k  j      t  q  o  v  x  j
```

```
I  T  S      G  R  E  A  T      T  O      L  E  A  R  N
v  y  e      o  t  q  j  y      y  d      k  q  j  t  x

G  R  A  M  M  A  R      E  T      C  E  T  E  R  A  !
o  t  j  u  u  j  t      q  y      i  q  y  q  t  j
```

I. Historia. Review the history story, and fill in the blanks.

1. Who is the second king of Rome?_____*The 2ⁿᵈ king was Numa Pompilius.*_____

2. For what is he most often remembered?__*Numa brings peace to Rome.*__

3. What are the only two jobs which the Romans considered honorable?

    _____*Only soldiers' and farmers' occupations were considered honorable.*_____

Disciplīna VI – sex   SUM, ESSE

I. Dictum

terra incognita   _____*unknown land*_____

II. Colloquium   *Latīnē*   *Anglicē*

Tiberius:	Quid est hoc?	What is this?
Cassia:	Hoc est mēnsa.	This is a table.

III. Verba

Latīnē	*Anglicē*	*Scrībe tōtum verbum Latīnum.*	*Dērīvātī*
culpa, culpae, f.	fault, blame	*culpa, culpae, f.*	*culpable*
ecclēsia, ecclēsiae, f.	church	*ecclēsia, ecclēsiae, f.*	*Ecclesiastes*
fīlia, fīliae, f.	daughter	*fīlia, fīliae, f.*	*filial*
gallīna, gallīnae, f.	chicken	*gallīna, gallīnae, f.*	*gallinaceous*
Hispānia, Hispaniae, f.	Spain	*Hispania, Hispaniae, f.*	*Hispanic*
lūna, lūnae, f.	moon	*lūna, lūnae, f.*	*lunar*
mēnsa, mēnsae, f.	table	*mēnsa, mēnsae, f.*	*mesa*
silva, silvae, f.	forest	*silva, silvae, f.*	*Pennsylvania*
terra, terrae, f.	land, earth	*terra, terrae, f.*	*terrestrial*
sum, esse	to be	*sum, esse*	*essential*

1. Which nouns are persons? _____*fīlia*_____

2. Which nouns are places? _____*Hispania, terra, lūna, ecclēsia, silva*_____

3. Which nouns are things? _____*gallīna, terra, lūna, ecclēsia, mēnsa*_____

4. Which nouns are ideas? _____*culpa*_____

5. The letters ___*J*___ and ___*W*___ are missing from the Latin alphabet.

IV. Grammatica. Read the conjugation in the shaded box, and <u>memorize it</u>.

_I am_	**sum**	**sumus**	_We are_
You are	**es**	**estis**	_You all are_
He (she, it) is	**est**	**sunt**	_They are_

The verb **sum, esse** is a (_state of_) _being_ verb. Because its stem changes, <u>it is an _irregular verb_</u>. Look at the personal endings in this conjugation of present tense. How are they similar to or different from the present tense personal endings you already know for 1ˢᵗ conjugation verbs?

Because **sum, esse** is an irregular verb, we must memorize its forms.

<u>**sum, esse**</u> is also a _linking_ verb, so we can write a new kind of sentence. The noun after the verb in each of the examples below is called a _predicate nominative_. It is not the subject of the sentence, but it uses the nominative form of the noun, because a linking verb is linking two nouns (or a pronoun and a noun) that refer to the same thing. A form of **sum, esse** _links_ the subject with the predicate nominative, which is another word for the subject.

Very often Latin verbs occur at the end of the sentence. However, forms of **sum, esse** usually occur at the beginning or in the middle of the sentence. At the beginning of a sentence, the 3ʳᵈ person form may mean _there is_ / _there are_. For example:

Est porcus.	There is a pig. / It is a pig.
Sunt puellae.	There are girls. / They are girls.

Notice something very important. <u>Latin has no words for the article adjectives, _a_, _an_, and _the_</u>. However, always use them as necessary when translating Latin sentences into English.

Examples:	**Sum fīlia.**	I am <u>a</u> daughter.
	Es puella.	You are <u>a</u> girl.
	Est fēmina.	She is <u>a</u> woman.
	Est ursa.	It is <u>a</u> bear.

V. Historia (_Famous Men of Rome_, Chapter III)

The third king, Tullus Hostilius, leads the Roman army against Alba. He and the Alban king, Mettius, decide to have only the three best warriors of each city fight. The Romans select the Horatii, and the Albans select the Curiatii. After problems early in the battle, the last Horatius wins.

VI. Dēlēgāta

A. *Scrībe* the new Latin *verba* and their meanings.

	Latīnē		*Anglicē*
1.	culpa, culpae, f.	1.	fault, blame
2.	ecclēsia, ecclēsiae, f.	2.	church
3.	fīlia, fīliae f.	3.	daughter
4.	gallīna, gallīnae, f.	4.	chicken
5.	Hispania, Hispaniae, f.	5.	Spain
6.	lūna, lūnae, f.	6.	moon
7.	mēnsa, mēnsae, f.	7.	table
8.	silva, silvae, f.	8.	forest
9.	terra, terrae, f.	9.	land, earth
10.	sum, esse	10.	to be

B. *Scrībe* the conjugation of <u>sum, esse</u> in the present tense two times.

1.			2.		
sum	sumus		sum	sumus
es	estis		es	estis
est	sunt		est	sunt

C. *Scrībe* the *dictum* and its translation.

Latīnē: terra incognita

Anglicē: unknown land

D. Translate these *verba* and phrases.

1. Quid est hoc? *What is this?*   3. et cetēra   *and the rest*

2. quattuor   *four*   4. bene   *well*

E. Fill in the blanks.

1. A verb is a *verbum* that expresses _____*action*_____ or _____*being*_____.

2. The nominative case is used for the _____*subject*_____ of a sentence.

3. To find the stem of a noun, drop the ___*genitive*___ ___*singular*___ case ending.

4. The person spoken *about* is _____*third*_____ person.

5. Because the stem of **sum, esse** changes, it is called an _____*irregular*_____ verb.

6. Sometimes a form of **sum, esse** *links* the _____*subject*_____ to a predicate nominative.

F. Translate each sentence. (*Scrībe* Latin sentences *Anglicē* and English sentences *Latīnē*.)

1. Est lūna. *It is the moon.*   9. Sum puella. *I'm a girl.*

2. You are a woman. *Es fēmina.*   10. Est silva. *It is a forest.*

3. Est gallīna. *It's a chicken.*   11. It is a church. *Est ecclēsia.*

4. Labōrātis. *You all are working.*   12. Peccāmus. *We sin.*

5. We are slow. *Tardāmus.*   13. Recitant. *They are reciting.*

6. Superātis. *You all overcome.*   14. It flies. *Volat.*

7. Dubitās. *You doubt.*   15. They walk. *Ambulant.*

8. I stand. *Stō.*   16. We pray. *Ōrāmus.*

G. *Scrībe* the meaning of each noun in the space provided. Then decline it.

1. gallīna, gallīnae, f. _____*chicken*_____   2. mēnsa, mēnsae, f. _____*table*_____

gallīna	*gallīnae*	*mēnsa*	*mēnsae*
gallīnae	*gallīnārum*	*mēnsae*	*mēnsārum*
gallīnae	*gallīnīs*	*mēnsae*	*mēnsīs*
gallīnam	*gallīnās*	*mēnsam*	*mēnsās*
gallīnā	*gallīnīs*	*mēnsā*	*mēnsīs*

3. culpa, culpae, f. _____ *fault* _____   4. aquila, aquilae, f. _____ *eagle* _____

culpa	*culpae*	*aquila*	*aquilae*
culpae	*culpārum*	*aquilae*	*aquilārum*
culpae	*culpīs*	*aquilae*	*aquilīs*
culpam	*culpās*	*aquilam*	*aquilās*
culpā	*culpīs*	*aquilā*	*aquilīs*

5. ecclēsia, ecclēsiae, f. _____ *church* _____   6. lūna, lūnae, f. _____ *moon* _____

ecclēsia	*ecclēsiae*	*lūna*	*lūnae*
ecclēsiae	*ecclēsiārum*	*lūnae*	*lūnārum*
ecclēsiae	*ecclēsiīs*	*lūnae*	*lūnīs*
ecclēsiam	*ecclēsiās*	*lūnam*	*lūnās*
ecclēsiā	*ecclēsiīs*	*lūnā*	*lūnīs*

H. Crossword Puzzle

Crossword grid:

Row 1: ¹F, ²H I S ³P A N ⁴I A
Row 2: I, E, M
Row 3: L, ⁵C U L P A
Row 4: ⁶S I L ⁷V A, U, E
Row 5: A, ■, I, N, R
Row 6: ⁸E C C ⁹L E S I A, A
Row 7: T, U, A, M
Row 8: O, N, U
Row 9: ¹⁰T E R R A, ¹¹M E N S A
Row 10: I
Row 11: ¹²G A L L I N A

RECTE

2. Spain
5. fault
6. forest
8. church
10. earth, land
11. table
12. chicken

DEORSUM

1. daughter
3. money
4. We order.
7. victory
9. moon

I. *Scrībe* the meaning of each verb in the blank. Then conjugate each in present tense.

1. errō, errāre _____ *to err* _____
errō	*errāmus*
errās	*errātis*
errat	*errant*

2. cogitō, cogitāre _____ *to think* _____
cōgitō	*cōgitāmus*
cōgitās	*cōgitātis*
cōgitat	*cōgitant*

3. cantō, cantāre _____ *to sing* _____
cantō	*cantāmus*
cantās	*cantātis*
cantat	*cantant*

4. ōrō, ōrāre _____ *to pray* _____
ōrō	*ōrāmus*
ōrās	*ōrātis*
ōrat	*ōrant*

J. Dērīvātī. Complete each sentence with an English *verbum* chosen from the following *verba*. The italicized *verbum* in the sentence should help you think of the Latin root.

filial   culpable   lunatic   Pennsylvania   terrestrial

1. William Penn's *forest* is called _____ *Pennsylvania* _____.

   Latin root: _____ *silva, silvae, f.* _____

2. A _____ *lunatic* _____ was thought to suffer from the influence of the *moon*.

   Latin root: _____ *lūna, lūnae, f.* _____

3. Something from *earth* is _____ *terrestrial* ___. Latin root: _____ *terra, terrae, f.* _____

4. When someone is at *fault*, he is _____ *culpable* _____. Latin root: _____ *culpa, culpae, f.* _____

5. A *daughter* has _____ *filial* _____ love for her parents. Latin root: _____ *fīlia, fīliae, f.* _____

K. Historia. Review the history story, and fill in the blanks.

1. Who is the third king of Rome? _____ *The third king of Rome is Tullus Hostilius.* _____

2. What brothers fight for Rome against the Albans? _____ *The Horatii fight for Rome.* _____

3. What brothers fight for Alba against the Romans? _____ *The Curiatii fight for Alba.* _____

Disciplīna VII – septem　　　2ⁿᵈ CONJUGATION

I. Dictum

Rīdent stolidī verba Latīna.　(Ovid)　　_Fools laugh at the Latin language._

II. Colloquium

	Latīnē	_Anglicē_
Aemelia:	Quomodō tē habēs hodiē?	How are you today?
Titus:	Male! Caput mihi dolet.	Bad! My head aches.
Aemelia:	Mē paenitet!	I'm sorry!

III. Verba

Latīnē	_Anglicē_	_Scrībe tōtum verbum Latīnum._	_Dērīvātī_
doleō, dolēre	to ache	_doleō, dolēre_	_dolorous_
fleō, flēre	to weep, to cry	_fleō, flēre_	
gaudeō, gaudēre	to rejoice	_gaudeō, gaudēre_	_gaudy_
maneō, manēre	to remain, to stay	_maneō, manēre_	_permanent_
misereō, miserēre	to be sorry	_misereō, miserēre_	_miserable_
moveō, movēre	to move	_moveō, movēre_	_movable_
rīdeō, rīdēre	to laugh	_rīdeō, rīdēre_	_ridiculous_
salveō, salvēre	to be well	_salveō, salvēre_	_salvo_
sedeō, sedēre	to sit	_sedeō, sedēre_	_sedentary_

1. What kind of _verba_ are these?　_They are all verbs._

2. How can you tell?　_The principal parts end with -ō and -ēre._

3. In what way are these _verba_ alike?　_They are all 2ⁿᵈ conjugation verbs._

4. How are 1ˢᵗ conjugation verbs different from these verbs?　_1ˢᵗ conj. infinitives end in -āre._

5. A verb is a _verbum_ that expresses ___action___ or ___being___.

35

IV. Grammatica. Read the conjugation in the shaded box, and translate it.

<u> *I stay.* </u>	**mane̅ō**	**mane̅mus**	<u> *We stay.* </u>
<u> *You stay.* </u>	**mane̅s**	**mane̅tis**	<u> *You all stay.* </u>
<u>*He (she, it) stays.*</u>	**manet**	**manent**	<u> *They stay.* </u>

All of the verbs we have had so far (except for **sum, esse**) are 1st conjugation verbs. We know a verb's conjugation by the vowel in the infinitive. The infinitives of all 1st conjugation verbs end in –**āre**.

The verbs in this *disciplīna* are 2nd conjugation verbs. Their infinitives *always* end in –**ēre**.

We find the stem of 2nd conjugation verbs the same way we find the stem of 1st conjugation verbs: drop the –**re** of the infinitive. Notice that the whole stem of the verb, including the stem vowel **ē**, is present in all six forms in 2nd conjugation.

1. Conjugating a verb means adding <u> *personal* </u> <u> *endings* </u> to the verb's <u> *stem* </u>.

2. Infinitives of 1st conjugation verbs always end in <u> *-āre* </u>.

3. Infinitives of 2nd conjugation verbs always end in <u> *-ēre* </u>.

4. To find the stem of a 1st- or 2nd conjugation verb, drop the <u> *-re* </u> of the <u> *infinitive* </u>.

V. Historia (*Famous Men of Rome*, Chapter IV, Parts I-III)

The fourth king, Ancus Marcius, builds the seacoast of Ostia. During his reign, a man from the town of Tarquinii in Etruria comes to Rome. Known as Tarquin, he is popular with the people and is elected to be the fifth king of Rome. He builds the Temple of Jupiter, known as the Capitol because a head (**caput**) was found on the site. Tarquin also builds the Forum and the Circus Maximus. Then he also establishes the lictors, the king's chiefs of police, who punish criminals with the fasces.

VI. Dēlēgāta

A. *Scrībe* the new Latin *verba* and their meanings.

	Latīnē		*Anglicē*
1.	doleō, dolēre	1.	to ache
2.	fleō, flēre	2.	to weep, to cry
3.	gaudeō, gaudēre	3.	to rejoice
4.	maneō, manēre	4.	to remain, to stay
5.	misereō, miserēre	5.	to be sorry
6.	moveō, movēre	6.	to move
7.	rīdeō, rīdēre	7.	to laugh
8.	salveō, salvēre	8.	to be well
9.	sedeō, sedēre	9.	to sit

B. *Scrībe* the conjugation of <u>maneō, manēre</u> two times.

1.

maneō	manēmus
manēs	manētis
manet	manent

2.

maneō	manēmus
manēs	manētis
manet	manent

C. *Scrībe* the *dictum* and its translation.

Latīnē: Rīdent stolidī verba Latīna.

Anglicē: Fools laugh at the Latin language.

D. Translate these *verba* and phrases.

1. Quid est hoc?   *What is this?*

2. Caput mihi dolet.   *My head hurts.*

3. sex   *six*

4. How are you?   *Quomodō tē habēs?*

5. ūnus   *one*

6. I think; therefore, I am.   *Cōgitō ergo sum.*

7. septem _____seven_____   9. terra incognita_____unknown land_____

8. duo_____two_____   10. quīnque _____five_____

E. Fill in the blanks.

1. A verb is a *verbum* that expresses ____action____ or ____being____.

2. All 1st conjugation infinitives end in ____-āre____.

3. All 2nd conjugation infinitives end in ____-ēre____.

4. What is the last letter in the *stem* of every *1st conjugation* verb?_____ā_____

5. What is the last letter in the *stem* of every *2nd conjugation* verb?_____ē_____

6. Because the stem of **sum, esse** changes, it is called an _____irregular_____ verb.

7. To find the stem of a *noun*, drop the ____genitive____ ____singular____ case ending.

F. *Scrībe* the meaning of each verb in the blank. Then conjugate it in present tense.

1. doleō, dolēre_____to ache_____   2. rīdeō, rīdēre _____to laugh_____

_____doleō_____ _____dolēmus_____   _____rīdeō_____ _____rīdēmus_____

_____dolēs_____ _____dolētis_____   _____rīdēs_____ _____rīdētis_____

_____dolet_____ _____dolent_____   _____rīdet_____ _____rīdent_____

3. gaudeō, gaudēre _____to rejoice_____   4. misereō, miserēre _____to be sorry_____

_____gaudeō_____ _____gaudēmus_____   _____misereō_____ _____miserēmus_____

_____gaudēs_____ _____gaudētis_____   _____miserēs_____ _____miserētis_____

_____gaudet_____ _____gaudent_____   _____miseret_____ _____miserent_____

5. sedeō, sedēre_____to sit_____   6. moveō, movēre _____to move_____

_____sedeō_____ _____sedēmus_____   _____moveō_____ _____movēmus_____

_____sedēs_____ _____sedētis_____   _____movēs_____ _____movētis_____

_____sedet_____ _____sedent_____   _____movet_____ _____movent_____

38

G. Translate each sentence.

1. Miseret.   *He is sorry.*   13. Est mēnsa.   *It is a table.*

2. Dolent.   *They ache.*   14. Est pecūnia.   *It is money.*

3. Gaudēmus.   *We rejoice.*   15. Sum fēmina.   *I am a woman.*

4. Salvētis.   *You all are well.*   16. Es puella.   *You are a girl.*

5. Sedēs.   *You sit.*   17. Nāvigāmus.   *We are sailing.*

6. Flēmus.   *We weep.*   18. Tardant.   *They are slow.*

7. I stay.   *Maneō.*   19. You speak.   *Ōrās.*

8. You all move.   *Movētis.*   20. He endures.   *Dūrat.*

9. They laugh.   *Rīdent.*   21. We stand.   *Stāmus.*

10. You all sin.   *Peccātis.*   22. You enter.   *Intrās.*

11. I doubt.   *Dubitō*   23. They do overcome.   *Superant.*

12. They are walking.   *Ambulant.*   24. They are slow.   *Tardant.*

H. Anagrams. Unscramble the letters in each row to form one of the *verba* in this *disciplīna*. (Hint: Each answer is the first-person singular form of the verb. Therefore, every *verbum* will end with the letter __O__.) *Scrībe* each *verbum* in the spaces given. Then take all of the shaded letters and rearrange them to complete the English sentence at the end of the puzzle.

OLFE	F L E O
OENMA	M A N E O
DEEOS	S E D E O
EDROI	R I D E O
EODLO	D O L E O
VMOEO	M O V E O
AEGDUO	G A U D E O
VLEOSE	S A L V E O
OMRIESE	M I S E R E O

Solution: S O M E DAY F O O L S WILL LAUGH NO LONGER!

I. Conjugate <u>sum, esse</u> in present tense two times.

1. _sum_   _sumus_   2. _sum_   _sumus_

   _es_   _estis_   _es_   _estis_

   est   _sunt_   _est_   _sunt_

J. Dērīvātī. Complete each sentence with an English _verbum_ chosen from the following _verba_. The italicized _verbum_ in the sentence should help you think of the Latin root.

miserable   movable   ridiculous   sedentary

1. One feels _sorry_ for someone in a _____ _miserable_ _____ situation.

   Latin root: _misereō, miserēre_

2. Someone who _sits_ most of the time is _____ _sedentary_ _____.

   Latin root: _sedeō, sedēre_

3. Something deserving of _laughter_ may be _____ _ridiculous_ _____.

   Latin root: _rīdeō, rīdēre_

4. If something can be _moved_, it is _____ _movable_ _____.

   Latin root: _moveō, movēre_

K. Historia. Review the history story, and fill in the blanks.

1. Who is the fifth king of Rome?_____ _The fifth king of Rome is Tarquin._

2. What is another name for the temple of Jupiter?_ _The temple is called the Capitol._

3. What else does the fifth king build?_____ _He builds the Circus Maximus._

4. What are his chiefs of police called?_____ _They are called lictors._

5. What are the lictors' weapons called?_____ _The lictors' weapons are called fasces._

Disciplīna VIII – octō   SUBJECTS and VERBS

I. Dictum

Hominēs dum docent discunt. (Seneca)   _People learn while they teach._

II. Colloquium   _Latīnē_   _Anglicē_

	Latīnē	_Anglicē_
Lūcius:	Quot annōs nāta es?	How old are you?
Cornelia:	Novem annōs nāta sum.	I am nine years old.
	(if asking a boy, ask, "Quot annōs nātus es?")	
Lūcius:	Quid est hoc?	What is this?
Cornelia:	Est gallīna.	It's a chicken.
Lūcius:	Gallīna mihi placet!	I like the chicken.
	(lit., The chicken is pleasing to me.)	

III. Verba

Latīnē	_Anglicē_	_Scrībe tōtum verbum Latīnum._	_Dērīvātī_
doceō, docēre	to teach	_doceō, docēre_	_docent_
iānua, iānuae, f.	door	_iānua, iānuae, f._	_January_
lūceō, lūcēre	to shine	_lūceō, lūcēre_	_translucent_
pateō, patēre	to be open	_pateō, patēre_	_patio_
placeō, placēre	to please	_placeō, placēre_	_placebo_
sileō, silēre	to be silent	_sileō, silēre_	_silent_
stella, stellae, f.	star	_stella, stellae, f._	_constellation_
timeō, timēre	to fear, to be afraid	_timeō, timēre_	_timid_
valeō, valēre	to be strong, to have power	_valeō, valēre_	_valor_

1. Which _verba_ are nouns?   _ianua, stella_

2. To what conjugation do the verbs belong?   _They are from 2nd conjugation._

3. How can you tell?   _The infinitives end with -ēre._

IV. Grammatica

In this *disciplīna*, we are going to learn how to write a new kind of sentence – one with a subject noun and a verb. So far we have written and translated many sentences with just one Latin word. That's possible because pronouns are built into Latin verbs.

A pronoun is a word that replaces a _____*noun*_____. This is easy to see in 3rd person. Sometimes we say *she* instead of naming the person we're talking about. Or we may say *it* instead of naming the thing we're talking about. In English, these pronouns are separate words. In Latin, these pronouns are *not* separate words because they are built into the ends of the verbs as personal endings. What if we want to *name* the subject of the sentence? In Latin, you just say a noun and a third-person verb, and you have a two-word sentence!

Example:	Rēgīna ambulat.	The queen walks.

Here are three important things to remember:

First, remember that there are no Latin words for article adjectives. When translating into English, you'll have to add *a, an,* and *the* according to common sense and context. **Rēgīna ambulat** could mean *A queen walks* or ***The** queen walks.* Always translate using good English.

Second, we have been translating **ambulat** as *She walks.* However, it would be incorrect English to say *The queen she walks.* When there is a subject noun in a sentence, do not translate the pronoun built into the verb.

Third, since the nouns we use for subjects name a person, place, thing, or idea we're talking *about* (not ourselves, the person[s] *speaking* –1st person; or the person we're speaking *to* – 2nd person), **all of these sentences must use 3rd-person verbs.** Latin subjects and verbs must agree in person and in number. For now we will use only *singular* subject nouns, so that means using –**t** as an ending (-**t** is the 3rd-person singular personal ending). (In *Disciplīna X*, we'll learn to use plural subject nouns and verbs.) **Always** use a 3rd-person verb when there is a subject noun in a sentence. And remember: Only the _____*nominative*_____ case is used for subject nouns.

Translate these sentences:

1. Stella lūcet.   3. Iānua patet.   5. Ursa valet.   7. Puella est rēgīna.

2. Lūna lūcet.   4. Fenestra patet.   6. Ecclēsia valet.   8. Fēmina ōrat.

V. Historia (*Famous Men of Rome*, Chapter IV, Part IV)

The sixth king, Servius Tullius, establishes the census. Tarquin's son, known as Tarquinius Superbus (Tarquin the Proud), kills Servius Tullius and becomes the seventh king. During his reign, a sibyl offers special fortune-telling books known as the Sibylline Books.

VI. Dēlēgāta

A. *Scrībe* the new Latin *verba* and their meanings.

	Latīnē		*Anglicē*
1.	doceō, docēre	1.	to teach
2.	iānua, iānuae, f.	2.	door
3.	lūceō, lūcēre	3.	to shine
4.	pateō, patēre	4.	to be open
5.	placeō, placēre	5.	to please
6.	sileō, silēre	6.	to be silent
7.	stella, stellae, f.	7.	star
8.	timeō, timēre	8.	to fear, to be afraid
9.	valeō, valēre	9.	to be strong, to have power

B. *Scrībe* the *dictum* and its translation.

Latīnē: Hominēs, dum docent, discunt.

Anglicē: People learn while they teach.

C. Translate these sentences.

1. Lūcet.   *It is shining.*   5. They teach.   *Docent.*

2. Silēmus.   *We are silent.*   6. You all fear.   *Timētis.*

3. Est mēnsa.   *It is a table.*   7. Est corōna.   *It is a crown.*

4. I am a queen.   *Sum rēgīna.*   8. Es fēmina.   *You are a woman.*

D. Translate these *verba* and phrases.

1. historia   *history*   3. eight   *octō*

2. seven   *septem*   4. Quomodō tē habēs?   *How are you?*

5. five _____ *quīnque* _____   8. Est stella. _____ *It's a star.* _____

6. four _____ *quattuor* _____   9. Life is short. _____ *Vīta brevis.* _____

7. one _____ *ūnus* _____   10. Quid est hoc? _____ *What is this?* _____

E. Translate these two-word sentences. Remember that sentences begin with a _____ *capital* _____

_____ *letter* _____ and end with an _____ *end* _____ _____ *mark* _____ .

And remember that present-tense verbs can be translated three different ways.

1. Fēmina cēnat. _____ *The woman dines.* _____

2. Fēmina intrat. _____ *The woman is entering.* _____

3. Fēmina docet. _____ *The woman teaches.* _____

4. Puella cantat. _____ *The woman does sing.* _____

5. Puella sedet. _____ *The girl sits.* _____

6. Puella silet. _____ *The girl is silent.* _____

7. Silva silet. _____ *The forest is silent.* _____

8. Aquila silet. _____ *The eagle is silent.* _____

9. Rēgīna iūdicat. _____ *The queen judges.* _____

10. Rēgīna imperat. _____ *The queen is ruling.* _____

11. Rēgīna valet. _____ *The queen is strong.* _____

12. Ursa valet. _____ *The bear is strong.* _____

13. Italia valet. _____ *Italy has power.* _____

14. Mensa valet. _____ *The table is strong.* _____

15. Stella lūcet. _____ *The star shines.* _____

16. Iānua patet. _____ *The door is open.* _____

17. Fīlia gaudet. _____ *The girl rejoices.* _____

18. Lūna lūcet. _____ *The moon is shining.* _____

F. *Scrībe* the meaning of each *verbum* in the space provided. Then decline each one.

1. stella, stellae, f. _____ *star* _____

stella	*stellae*
stellae	*stellārum*
stellae	*stellīs*
stellam	*stellās*
stellā	*stellīs*

2. iānua, iānuae, f. _____ *door* _____

iānua	*iānuae*
iānuae	*iānuārum*
iānuae	*iānuīs*
iānuam	*iānuās*
iānuā	*iānuīs*

G. *Scrībe* the meaning of each verb in the blank. Then conjugate each in present tense.

1. doceō, docēre _____ *to teach* _____

doceō	*docēmus*
docēs	*docētis*
docet	*docent*

2. timeō, timēre _____ *to fear* _____

timeō	*timēmus*
timēs	*timētis*
timet	*timent*

H. *Verbum* **Search.** Each of the *verba* listed below can be found in this grid, reading forward, backward, up, down, or diagonally. Try to find them all. The unused letters will spell a hidden message when read from left to right, row by row. What is the hidden message?

(*Anglicē*): _WE LEARN AS WE TEACH, SO SHOW YOUR PAL SOME LATIN_

I	W	E	L	D	O	C	E	O	E
A	O	A	R	O	N	A	S	E	W
N	E	E	E	E	T	S	N	M	E
U	A	C	L	C	C	I	S	I	H
A	U	S	O	A	L	L	E	T	S
L	O	S	H	L	V	E	R	O	U
W	Y	E	Y	P	O	O	V	U	S
R	P	B	T	A	L	S	I	O	N
M	I	E	L	A	A	T	U	I	E
S	U	B	R	E	P	U	S	N	C

CENSUS
DOCEO
IANUA
LUCEO
PATEO
PLACEO
SERVIUS
SIBYLLINE
SILEO
STELLA
SUPERBUS
TIMEO
VALEO

I. *Scrībe* the meaning of each verb in the blank. Then conjugate each in present tense.

1. lūceō, lūcēre_____*to shine*_____   2. sum, esse_____*to be*_____

_____*lūceō*_____	_____*lūcēmus*_____
_____*lūcēs*_____	_____*lūcētis*_____
_____*lūcet*_____	_____*lūcent*_____

_____*sum*_____	_____*sumus*_____
_____*es*_____	_____*estis*_____
_____*est*_____	_____*sunt*_____

J. Dērīvātī. Complete each sentence with an English *verbum* chosen from the following *verba*. The italicized *verbum* in the sentence should help you think of the Latin root.

January   constellation   timid   valor   translucent

1. A group of *stars* is a _____*constellation*_____.

   Latin root:_____*stella, stellae, f.*_____

2. Someone who is often *afraid* is ____*timid*____. Latin root:_____*timeō, timēre*_____

3. A _____*translucent*_____ substance is one that lets light *shine* through (or *across*).

   Latin root:_____*lūceō, lūcēre*_____

4. Soldiers, who are *strong*, are men of great ___*valor*___. Latin root:___*valeō, valēre*___

5. _____*January*_____, the first month of the year, is the *door* to the new year.

   Latin root:_____*iānua, iānuae, f.*_____

K. Historia. Review the history story, and fill in the blanks.

1. Who is the sixth king of Rome?_____*Servius Tullius is the sixth king of Rome.*_____

2. What governmental tradition does the sixth king establish?____*He orders a census.*____

3. What is the Latin name of the man who kills the sixth king?____*Tarquinius Superbus*____

4. How is his name translated?_____*His name means Tarquin the proud.*_____

5. What are female fortune tellers called?_____*They are called sibyls.*_____

6. What does a fortune teller sell to Tarquinius Superbus?__*She sells the Sibylline books.*__

Disciplīna IX – novem   2nd DECLENSION (masculine)

I. Dictum

Agnus Deī quī tollis peccāta mundī   *Lamb of God who takes away the sins of the world.*

II. Colloquīum   *Latīnē*   *Anglicē*

	Latīnē	*Anglicē*
Antonia:	Loquerisne Latīnē?	Do you speak Latin?
Claudius:	Ita. Loquor Latīnē.	Yes. I speak Latin.

III. Verba

Latīnē	*Anglicē*	*Scrībe tōtum verbum Latīnum.*	*Dērīvātī*
agnus, agnī, m.	lamb	*agnus, agnī, m.*	*Agnes*
Christus, Christī, m.	Christ	*Christus, Christī, m.*	*Christ*
Deus, Deī, m.	God	*Deus, Deī, m.*	*deity*
fīlius, fīliī, m.	son	*fīlius, fīliī, m.*	*filial*
gladius, gladiī, m.	sword	*gladius, gladiī, m.*	*gladiator*
mundus, mundī, m.	world	*mundus, mundī, m.*	*mundane*
nimbus, nimbī, m.	cloud	*nimbus, nimbī, m.*	*cumulonimbus*
oculus, oculī, m.	eye	*oculus, oculī, m.*	*binoculars*
porcus, porcī, m.	pig	*porcus, porcī, m.*	*pork*

1. What kind of *verba* are these?___*They are all nouns.*___

2. How are they different from the other nouns you've learned?

3. What *verbum* is similar to another *verbum* you have learned?___*The word fīlius is like fīlia.*

4. How many cases do Latin nouns have?___*Latin nouns have 6 cases.*

5. Name all the cases of a Latin noun.

6. Which case is used for the subject noun?___*Nominative tells what the subject is.*

IV. Grammatica. Read the declension in the shaded box.

	Singular	Plural
Nominative	nimb<u>us</u>	nimb<u>ī</u>
Genitive	nimb<u>ī</u>	nimb<u>ōrum</u>
Dative	nimb<u>ō</u>	nimb<u>īs</u>
Accusative	nimb<u>um</u>	nimb<u>ōs</u>
Ablative	nimb<u>ō</u>	nimb<u>īs</u>

All of the nouns we have learned so far are in 1st declension (there are five noun declensions in Latin). **Nimbus, -ī, m.** is a 2nd declension noun. Nearly all nouns in 2nd declension are masculine or neuter in gender. These are the case endings for 2nd -declension *masculine* nouns. Nearly all 2nd declension masculine nouns end in **–us** in the nominative singular.

1. What is the stem of **nimbus, nimbī, m.**? _____ *nimb –*

2. Which case endings are the same as 1st declension case endings? _____ *dat. and abl. plural*

<u>All</u> nouns in <u>1st</u> declension have a genitive singular case ending of –ae. <u>All</u> nouns in <u>2nd</u> declension have a genitive singular case ending of –ī. Finding the stem is the same for all Latin nouns in every declension: Take off the genitive singular case ending.

Remember that Latin nouns have one of three genders: masculine, feminine, or neuter. Nouns that name people are masculine or feminine in gender, depending upon whether the person is male or female. <u>We must memorize the gender of *all* Latin nouns.</u>

Note: Because the dative and ablative plural of **fīlia, fīliae, f.** might be confused with the dative and ablative plural of **fīlius, fīliī, m.**, the Romans used the ending –**ābus** for those cases of **fīlia** and –**īs** for those cases of **fīlius**. Otherwise, **fīlia** declines like any other 1st declension noun.

V. Historia (*Famous Men of Rome*, Chapter V, Parts I and II)

510 BC Everyone thinks Tarquīnius Superbus' nephew Junius Brutus is an idiot. Sextus, the oldest son of Tarquīnius, attacks Lucretia, the wife of his cousin, Lucius Collatinus. Junius Brutus reveals that he is of sound mind and leads a revolt against the kings. The people establish a republic to be led by two consuls, elected each year. Brutus and Collatinus are the first two consuls of the Roman Republic.

VI. Dēlēgāta

A. *Scrībe* the new Latin *verba* and their meanings.

Latīnē		*Anglicē*	
1.	agnus, agnī, m.	1.	lamb
2.	Deus, Deī, m.	2.	God
3.	Christus, Christī, m.	3.	Christ
4.	fīlius, fīliī, m.	4.	son
5.	gladius, gladiī, m.	5.	sword
6.	mundus, mundī, m.	6.	world
7.	nimbus, nimbī, m.	7.	cloud
8.	oculus, oculī, m.	8.	eye
9.	porcus, porcī, m.	9.	pig

B. *Scrībe* the declension of **nimbus, nimbī, m.** two times.

1.			2.		
nimbus	nimbī		nimbus	nimbī
nimbī	nimbōrum		nimbī	nimbōrum
nimbō	nimbīs		nimbō	nimbīs
nimbum	nimbōs		nimbum	nimbōs
nimbō	nimbīs		nimbō	nimbīs

C. *Scrībe* the *dictum* and its translation.

Latīnē: Agnus Deī quī tollit peccāta mundī

Anglicē: Lamb of God who takes away the sins of the world

D. Translate these *verba* and phrases.

1. Loquerisne Latīnē? *Do you speak Latin?*   2. five   *quīnque*

3. and the rest _____*et cētera*_____   7. unknown land _____*terra incognita*_____

4. novem _____*nine*_____   8. one _____*ūnus*_____

5. four _____*quattuor*_____   9. seven _____*septem*_____

6. eight _____*octō*_____   10. disciplīna _____*lesson*_____

E. Fill in the blanks.

1. A _____*noun*_____ is a word that names a person, place, thing, or idea.

2. The genitive singular case ending for 1st declension nouns is _____*-ae*_____.

3. The genitive singular case ending for 2nd declension nouns is _____*-ī*_____.

4. Verb endings are called _____*personal*_____ endings.

5. Noun endings are called _____*case*_____ endings.

6. We _____*conjugate*_____ verbs; we _____*decline*_____ nouns.

7. To find the stem of a noun, drop the _____*genitive*_____ _____*singular*_____ case ending.

8. Sentences that have subject nouns must have a _____*third*_____-person verb.

9. Derivatives must share both partial _____*spelling*_____ and _____*meaning*_____ with their Latin roots.

F. *Scrībe* the meaning of each verb in the blank. Then conjugate it in present tense.

1. iūdicō, iūdicāre _____*to judge*_____

iūdicō	*iūdicāmus*
iūdicās	*iūdicātis*
iūdicat	*iūdicant*

2. pugnō, pugnāre _____*to fight*_____

pugnō	*pugnāmus*
pugnās	*pugnātis*
pugnat	*pugnant*

3. sum, esse _____*to be*_____

sum	*sumus*
es	*estis*
est	*sunt*

4. rīdeō, rīdēre _____*to laugh*_____

rīdeō	*rīdēmus*
rīdēs	*rīdētis*
rīdet	*rīdent*

G. Translate these sentences (from Latin to English or from English to Latin).

1. Agnus timet. _____ *The lamb is afraid.* _____

2. Deus iūdicat. _____ *God judges.* _____

3. Mundus gaudet. _____ *The world rejoices.* _____

4. Oculus valet. _____ *The eye is strong.* _____

5. Fīlius flet. _____ *The son weeps.* _____

6. Porcus sedet. _____ *The pig sits.* _____

7. Christus docet. _____ *Christ teaches.* _____

8. Gladius superat. _____ *The sword does conquer.* _____

9. Nimbus movet. _____ *The cloud moves.* _____

10. Fēmina silet. _____ *The woman is silent.* _____

11. Ursa manet. _____ *The bear stays.* _____

12. Puella ridet. _____ *The girl laughs.* _____

13. Christus est Agnus. _____ *Christ is the Lamb.* _____

14. A cloud is water. _____ *Nimbus est aqua.* _____

15. The moon is moving. _____ *Lūna movet.* _____

16. The queen thinks. _____ *Rēgīna cōgitat.* _____

17. A son is sinning. _____ *Fīlius peccat.* _____

18. A woman is singing. _____ *Fēmina cantat.* _____

19. The bear sits. _____ *Ursa sedet.* _____

20. Christ is life. _____ *Christus est vīta.* _____

21. Christ is God. _____ *Christus est Deus.* _____

22. The bear does fight. _____ *Ursa pugnat.* _____

H. Alphabet Code. (1) Place *verba* from this *disciplīna* in the following blanks. The first letter of each is given to help you get started. (2) The letters *under* the blanks represent a code. Use the code to decipher the longer English message below the vocabulary list.

D E U S
q k w n

F I L I U S
a v o v w n

A G N U S
z p b w n

O C U L U S
g l w o w n

M U N D U S
i w b q w n

G L A D I U S
p o z q v w n

P O R C U S
x g h l w n

C H R I S T U S
l y h v n c w n

N I M B U S
j v i f w n

I P R A I S E T H E L A M B O F G O D
v x h z v n k c y k o z i f g a p g q

I. Dērīvātī. Complete each sentence with an English *verbum* chosen from the following *verba*. The italicized *verbum* in the sentence should help you think of the Latin root.

pork   binoculars   gladiator   fīlial

1. We use _____ *binoculars* _____ to view distant objects with both (two) *eyes*.

   Latin root: _____ *oculus, oculī, m.* _____

2. A _____ *gladiator* _____ fights with a *sword*. Latin root: _____ *gladius, gladiī, m.*

3. A *son* has _____ *filial* _____ love for his father and mother. Latin root: _____ *fīlius, fīliī, m.*

4. _____ *Pork* _____ is meat that comes from a *pig*. Latin root: _____ *porcus, porcī, m.*

J. Historia. Review the history story, and fill in the blanks.

1. In what year is the Roman Republic founded? _____ *Rome was founded in 753 BC*

2. What nephew of Tarquinius Superbus leads a revolution? _____ *Junius Brutus leads the revolt.*

3. What is the title of the two chief officers of the Republic? _____ *The leaders are called consuls.*

4. How often are they elected? _____ *New consuls are elected every year.*

Disciplīna X – decem   **PLURAL SENTENCES**

I. Dictum

Glōria in excelsīs Deō! (from Luke 2:14)   *Glory to God in the highest!*

II. Colloquium   *Latīnē*   *Anglicē*

Antonia:	Fēlīcem nātālem tibi!	Happy birthday (to you)!
Claudius:	Grātiās tibi agō.	Thank you.

III. Verba

Latīnē	*Anglicē*	*Scrībe tōtum verbum Latīnum.*	*Dērīvātī*
calamus, calamī, m.	pen	*calamus, calamī, m.*	*calamari*
digitus, digitī, m.	finger, toe	*digitus, digitī, m.*	*digit*
equus, equī, m.	horse	*equus, equī, m.*	*equestrian*
glōria, glōriae, f.	glory	*glōria, glōriae, f.*	*glorious*
Maria, Mariae, f.	Mary	*Maria, Mariae, f.*	*Mary*
puteus, puteī, m.	well	*puteus, puteī, m.*	*pit*
sella, sellae, f.	chair	*sella, sellae, f.*	
servus, servī, m.	slave, servant	*servus, servī, m.*	*servant*
stilus, stilī, m.	pencil	*stilus, stilī, m.*	*style*

1. What kind of *verba* are these? _____ *They are nouns.* _____

2. Which *verba* are from 1st declension? _____ *glōria, Maria, sella* _____

3. Which *verba* are from 2nd declension? _____ *calamus, digitus, equus, puteus, servus, stilus* _____

4. Which *verba* would you find in school? _____ *calamus, stilus, sella* _____

5. Which *verbum* is an idea? _____ *glōria* _____

IV. Grammatica. Read the paradigm in the shaded box, and <u>memorize it</u>.

<u>Nominative</u>	**-us**	**-ī**
<u>Genitive</u>	**-ī**	**-ōrum**
<u>Dative</u>	**-ō**	**-īs**
<u>Accusative</u>	**-um**	**-ōs**
<u>Ablative</u>	**-ō**	**-īs**

These are the <u>case endings for 2nd declension masculine nouns</u>. <u>All</u> 2nd declension nouns have a genitive singular ending of –ī. To find the stem of all nouns, take off the genitive singular ending. For example, the genitive singular of **servus, servī, m.** is **servī**. So the stem is **serv-**.

<u>serv</u>**us**   <u>serv</u>**ī**
<u>serv</u>**ī**   <u>serv</u>**ōrum**
<u>serv</u>**ō**   <u>serv</u>**īs**
<u>serv</u>**um**   <u>serv</u>**ōs**
<u>serv</u>**ō**   <u>serv</u>**īs**

In a Latin sentence, <u>the subject noun must agree with the verb in person and in number</u>. **Remember:** If a sentence has a subject noun, the verb *must* be third person because someone or something is being talked about) *If the subject noun is singular*, the verb must be third-person *singular*. For example:

Puell<u>a</u> ambula<u>t</u>.   The girl walks. (The girl is walking. The girl does walk.)

If the subject noun is plural, the verb must be third-person plural so the ending must be *-nt*.

Puell<u>ae</u> ambula<u>nt</u>.   The girls walk. (The girls are walking. The girls do walk.)

Remember: In Latin sentences, subject nouns and verbs must agree in ___*person*___ and ___*number*___.

There are no Latin words for ___*article*___ ___*adjectives*___ or ___*helping*___ ___*verbs*___ !

V. Historia (*Famous Men of Rome*, Chapter V, Parts III)

Tarquin sends people to Rome to retrieve his personal goods. While in the city, they plan a secret revolution, but the plan is discovered. Two sons of Brutus, Titus and Tiberius, are among the traitors, and Brutus sentences them to death by the fasces. In a later battle with Tarquin's army from Etruria, Brutus is killed. But the Etruscans hear a voice in the night, and they believe it to be Jupiter's voice. The voice warns them that the Romans will win the war, so they break camp and go home.

VI. Dēlēgāta

A. *Scrībe* the new Latin *verba* and their meanings.

Latīnē		*Anglicē*	
1.	calamus, calamī, m.	1.	pen
2.	digitus, digitī, m.	2.	finger, toe
3.	equus, equī, m.	3.	horse
4.	glōria, glōriae, f.	4.	glory
5.	Maria, Mariae, f.	5.	Mary
6.	puteus, puteī, m.	6.	well
7.	sella, sellae, f.	7.	chair
8.	servus, servī, m.	8.	servant, slave
9.	stilus, stilī, m.	9.	pencil

B. *Scrībe* the case endings for 2nd declension masculine nouns three times.

1.	-us	-ī	2.	-us	-ī	3.	-us	-ī
	-ī	-ōrum		-ī	-ōrum		-ī	-ōrum
	-ō	-īs		-ō	-īs		-ō	-īs
	-um	-ōs		-um	-ōs		-um	-ōs
	-ō	-īs		-ō	-īs		-ō	-īs

C. *Scrībe* the *dictum* and its translation.

Latīnē: Glōria in excelsīs Deō!

Anglicē: Glory to God in the highest!

D. Translate these *verba* and phrases.

1. Agnus Deī   Lamb of God   2. decem   ten

3. scrībe	*write*	7. five	*quīnque*
4. four	*quattuor*	8. Grātiās tibi agō.	*Thank you.*
5. Quid est hoc?	*What is this?*	9. grammatica	*grammar*
6. nine	*novem*	10. seven	*septem*

E. *Scrībe* the meaning of each *verbum* in the space provided. Then decline it.

1. servus, servī, m. *servant, slave*

servus	*servī*
servī	*servōrum*
servō	*servīs*
servum	*servōs*
servō	*servīs*

2. equus, equī, m. *horse*

equus	*equī*
equī	*equōrum*
equō	*equīs*
equum	*equōs*
equō	*equīs*

3. stilus, stilī, m. *pencil*

stilus	*stilī*
stilī	*stilōrum*
stilō	*stilīs*
stilum	*stilōs*
stilō	*stilīs*

4. digitus, digitī m. *finger, toe*

digitus	*digitī*
digitī	*digitōrum*
digitō	*digitīs*
digitum	*digitōs*
digitō	*digitīs*

5. sella, sellae, f. *chair*

sella	*sellae*
sellae	*sellārum*
sellae	*sellīs*
sellam	*sellās*
sellā	*sellīs*

6. calamus, calamī, m. *pen*

calamus	*calamī*
calamī	*calamōrum*
calamō	*calamīs*
calamum	*calamōs*
calamō	*calamīs*

F. Translate these sentences (from Latin to English or from English to Latin). Remember the three ways present tense can be translated.

1. Servus labōrat.   *The servant is working.*

2. Servī labōrant.   *The servants are working.*

3. Equus stat.   *The horse stands.*

4. Equī stant.   *The horses stand.*

5. Oculī movent.   *The eyes do move.*

6. Mēnsae valent.   *The tables are strong.*

7. Aquilae volant.   *The eagles fly.*

8. Puellae cōgitant.   *The girls think.*

9. The stars are shining.   *Stellae lūcent.*

10. The church rejoices.   *Ecclēsia guadet.*

11. The churches rejoice.   *Ecclēsiae gaudent.*

12. The bear is moving.   *Ursa movet.*

13. The bears move.   *Ursae movent.*

14. The women hurry.   *Fēminae festīnant.*

15. The doors are open.   *Iānuae patent.*

16. The sons wander.   *Fīliī errant.*

G. *Scrībe* the meaning of the *verba* in the space provided. Then conjugate them.

1. sum, esse   *to be*   2. valeō, valēre *to be strong, to have power*

sum	*sumus*	*valeō*	*valēmus*
es	*estis*	*valēs*	*valētis*
est	*sunt*	*valet*	*valent*

H. Crossword Puzzle (Note: All *verba* in the puzzle are in the nominative case.)

				¹M	U	N	D	I	
²S	E	L	L	A					
T			R			³P			
I		⁴D	I	G	I	T	U	S	
L	⁵P	A			T				
I	O		⁶N		E				
R	⁷G	I	U						
⁸C	L	M	S						
⁹D	U	O	B						
E	¹⁰S	E	R	V	U	S			
U	I	S							
¹¹S	I	L	V	A	E				

RECTĒ

1. worlds
2. chair
4. finger, toe
8. pen
10. slave
11. forests

DEORSUM

1. Mary
2. pencils
3. (a) well
5. pig
6. cloud
7. glory
9. God

I. Dērīvātī. Complete each sentence with an English *verbum* chosen from the following *verba*. The italicized *verbum* in the sentence should help you think of the Latin root.

digits   glorious   equestrian

1. _____*Equestian*_____ events at the Olympics involve *horses*.

   Latin root:_____*equus, equī, m.*_____

2. Since *fingers* were among the first symbols for numbers, we still call symbols such as 1 and 2

   _____*digits*_____. Latin root:_____*digitus, digitī, m.*_____

3. God is full of *glory*, so He is _____*glorious*_____.

   Latin root:_____*glōria, glōriae, f.*_____

J. Historia. Review the history story, and fill in the blanks.

1. Whom does Brutus sentence to death? _*Brutus sentences his sons Titus and Tiberius.*_

2. For what crime are they executed? _____*They plotted to restore Tarquin to the throne.*_

3. Whom do the Etruscans think they hear in the night? ____*They think they hear Jupiter.*_

Disciplīna XI – ūndecim   2nd DECLENSION (neuter)

I. Dictum

In prīncipiō erat Verbum . . .   _In the beginning was the Word..._
(Secundum Ioānnem 1:1a)   (John 1:1a)

II. Colloquium   _Latīnē_   _Anglicē_

	Latīnē	_Anglicē_
Magistra:	Quaenam est tempestās hodiē?	What is the weather today?
Discipulus:	Sōl (nōn) lūcet.	The sun is (not) shining.
	Pluit.	It's raining.
	Frīgidum (calidum) est.	It's cold (warm).
Magistra:	Quōmodō hoc Latīnē dīcitur?	How do you say this in Latin?
Discipula:	Brācchium	_Brācchium_

III. Verba

Latīnē	_Anglicē_	_Scrībe tōtum verbum Latīnum._	_Dērīvātī_
brācchium, brācchiī, n.	arm	_bracchium, brācchiī, n._	_embrace_
caelum, caelī, n.	sky, heaven	_caelum, caelī, n._	_celestial_
dōnum, dōnī, n.	gift	_dōnum, dōnī, n._	_donation_
gaudium, gaudiī, n.	joy	_gaudium, gaudiī, n._	_gaudy_
oppidum, oppidī, n.	town	_oppidum, oppidī, n._	
peccātum, peccātī, n.	sin	_peccātum, peccātī, n._	_peccadillo_
rēgnum, rēgnī, n.	kingdom	_rēgnum, rēgnī, n._	_reign_
solum, solī, n.	floor	_solum, solī, n._	_sole (of the foot)_
verbum, verbī, n.	word	_verbum, verbī, n._	_verbal_

1. What kind of _verba_ are these? _They are nouns._

2. How are they different from other nouns you have learned? _They are neither m. nor f._

3. Are they from 1st or 2nd declension? _They are from 2nd declension._

IV. Grammatica. Read the declension in the shaded box several times.

Nominative	**dōn<u>um</u>**	**dōn<u>a</u>**
Genitive	**dōn<u>ī</u>**	**dōn<u>ōrum</u>**
Dative	**dōn<u>ō</u>**	**dōn<u>īs</u>**
Accusative	**dōn<u>um</u>**	**dōn<u>a</u>**
Ablative	**dōn<u>ō</u>**	**dōn<u>īs</u>**

1. Latin nouns have three genders: ___*masculine*___, ___*feminine*___, and ___*neuter*___.

2. *Neuter* is a <u>borrowed word</u> from Latin that means _____. Therefore, *neuter* nouns are *neither* masculine nor feminine.

3. Nearly all 2nd declension nouns (*all* that *we* will learn) are either _____*m*_____ or _____*f*_____

4. Almost all 2nd declension masculine nouns end in _____*-us*_____ in the nominative singular.

5. **All** 2nd declension *neuter* nouns end in ____*-um*_____ in the nominative singular.

6. The genitive singular case ending for **all** 2nd declension nouns is _____*-ī*_____.

7. The declension of **dōnum, dōnī, n.** above shows the case endings for 2nd declension *neuter* nouns. Circle the three case endings (in the gray box above) that are different from the case endings for 2nd declension masculine nouns.

8. We must ___*memorize*_____ the gender of every noun so we *don't* confuse their endings.

V. Historia (*Famous Men of Rome*, Chapter VI)

Popular consul Publius Valerius, known as Publicola (which means "the people's friend"), frequently fights Tarquinius Superbus and the Etruscans. Once Tarquinius comes with an ally named Lars Porsena. Only the Tiber River stands between Porsena and Rome, and the Sublician Bridge offers his army a way to cross. Horatius Cocles defends the bridge against the whole Etruscan army while other Romans destroy the bridge's foundations.

VI. Dēlēgāta

A. *Scrībe* the new Latin *verba* and their meanings.

Latīnē	*Anglicē*
1. bracchium, brācchī, n.	1. arm
2. caelum, caelī, n.	2. heaven, sky,
3. dōnum, dōnī, n.	3. gift
4. gaudium, gaudiī, n.	4. joy
5. oppidum, oppidī, n.	5. town
6. peccātum, peccātī, n.	6. sin
7. rēgnum, rēgnī, n.	7. kingdom
8. solum, solī, n.	8. floor
9. verbum, verbī, n.	9. word

B. *Scrībe* the declension of <u>dōnum, dōnī, n.</u> two times.

1.		2.	
dōnum	dōna	dōnum	dōna
dōnī	dōnōrum	dōnī	dōnōrum
dōnō	dōnīs	dōnō	dōnīs
dōnum	dōna	dōnum	dōna
dōnō	dōnīs	dōnō	dōnīs

C. *Scrībe* the *dictum* and its translation.

Latīnē: In prīncipiō erat Verbum. . .

Anglicē: In the beginning was the Word. . .

D. Translate these *verba* and phrases.

1. Salvēte discipulī. *Hello, students.*   2. ūndecim *eleven*

3. Ōrā et labōrā. *Pray and work.*   7. four   *quattuor*

4. Agnus Deī *Lamb of God.*   8. et cētera   *and the rest*

5. Grātiās tibi agō. *Thank you.*   9. Libenter. *You're welcome.*

6. ten   *decem*   10. quīnque   *five*

11. Glōria in excelsīs Deō!   *Glory to God in the highest!*

E. Fill in the blanks.

1. *Scrībe* the nominative singular and plural case endings for these declensions.

	S	P
a. 1st declension	*-a*	*-ae*
b. 2nd declension masculine (M)	*-us*	*-ī*
c. 2nd declension neuter (N)	*-um*	*-a*

2. Latin sentences with subject nouns <u>always</u> use *third* person verbs.

3. It is necessary to *memorize* the gender of each Latin noun.

4. In Latin sentences, a subject noun must agree with its verb in *person* and *number* .

F. *Scrībe* the meaning of each verb in the blank. Then conjugate each in present tense.

1. cōgitō, cōgitāre *to think*   2. doleō, dolēre *to ache*

cōgitō	*cōgitāmus*	*doleō*	*dolēmus*
cōgitās	*cōgitātis*	*dolēs*	*dolētis*
cōgitat	*cōgitant*	*dolet*	*dolent*

G. Translate these sentences (from Latin to English or from English to Latin). Remember the three ways present tense can be translated.

1. Gallīnae pugnant. *The chickens are fighting.*

2. Rēgna pugnant. *The kingdoms fight.*

3. Oppida pugnant. *The towns do fight.*

4. Caelum gaudet. *Heaven rejoices.*

5.　Rēgnum valet.　　　　　　　*The kingdom is strong.*

6.　Rēgna valent.　　　　　　　*The kingdoms do have power.*

7.　Rōma dūrat.　　　　　　　*Rome endures.*

8.　Maria flet.　　　　　　　*Maria is crying.*

9.　Ursae cēnant.　　　　　　　*The bears do eat.*

10.　Fīliī cōgitant.　　　　　　　*The sons are thinking.*

11.　Equus est dōnum.　　　　*The horse is a gift.*

12.　Equī sunt dōna.　　　　　*The horses are gifts.*

13.　The gift is open.　　　　　*Dōnum patet.*

14.　The gifts are open.　　　　*Dōna patent.*

H. *Verbum* **Search.** Each of the *verba* listed below can be found in this grid, reading forward, backward, up, down, or diagonally. Try to find them all. The unused letters will spell a hidden message when you read from left to right, row by row. What is the hidden message?

hidden message (*Anglicē*):　*And the word became flesh and dwelled among us*

L	A	S	U	I	T	A	R	O	H	N	D
A	A	T	R	E	B	I	T	H	E	B	Q
T	W	R	M	U	L	O	S	O	R	R	U
I	R	G	S	D	P	B	E	A	E	S	O
N	E	A	C	P	E	C	C	A	T	U	M
E	G	U	I	H	O	C	A	M	U	B	O
E	N	D	F	M	H	R	L	E	E	L	D
S	U	I	O	I	U	H	S	A	N	I	O
M	M	U	U	N	N	B	D	E	D	C	W
E	L	M	L	E	U	D	R	A	N	I	M
O	C	A	E	L	U	M	N	E	G	A	U
O	I	P	I	C	N	I	R	P	V	N	S

BRACCHIUM
CAELUM
DONUM
GAUDIUM
HOC
HORATIUS
LARS PORSENA
LATINE
NEUTER
OPPIDUM
PECCATUM
PRINCIPIO
QUOMODO
REGNUM
SOLUM
SUBLICIAN
TIBER
VERBUM

I. Dērīvātī. Complete each sentence with an English *verbum* chosen from the following *verba*. The italicized *verbum* in the sentence should help you think of the Latin root.

donation   verbal   embrace   celestial   reign

1. To hold someone in your *arms* is to _____ *embrace* _____ him/her.

   Latin root:_____ *bracchium, brācchiī, n.* _____

2. The moon and stars are _____ *celestial* _____ creations; they are in the *sky*.

   Latin root:_____ *caelum, caelī, n.* _____

3. To rule a *kingdom* is to _____ *reign* _____. Latin root:_____ *rēgnum, rēgnī, n.* _____

4. A *gift* to a charity is a _____ *donation* _____. Latin root:_____ *dōnum, dōnī, n.* _____

5. Someone who is good with *words* has admirable _____ *verbal* _____ skills.

   Latin root:_____ *verbum, verbī, n.* _____

J. Historia. Review the history story, and fill in the blanks.

1. What is the common nickname of Publius Valerius? ____ *He is nicknamed Publicola.* ____

2. What Etruscan ally does Tarquinius bring south in this story? ____ *He brings Lars Porsena.* ____

3. What bridge do the Etruscans need to cross to attack Rome? ____ *The Sublician Bridge* ____

4. Who defends the bridge while its foundations are being cut? ____ *Horatius Cocles defends*

   ____ *the Sublician bridge and prevents the Etruscans from entering Rome.* ____

Disciplīna XII – duodecim   **PRESENT TENSE**

I. Dictum

Annō Dominī (abbreviation: <u>AD</u>)   <u>*In the year of our Lord*</u>

II. Colloquium   *Latīne*   *Anglicē*

	Latīne	*Anglicē*
Fābius:	Fēlīcem nātālem Christī!	Merry Christmas!
Maria:	Fēlīcem annum novum!	Happy new year!

III. Verba

Latīne	*Anglicē*	*Scrībe tōtum verbum Latīnum.*	*Dērīvātī*
agricola, agricolae, m.	farmer	*agricola, agricolae, m.*	*agriculture*
annus, annī, m.	year	*annus, annī, m.*	*annual*
arō, arāre	to plow	*arō, arāre*	*arable*
cubiculum, cubiculī, n.	bedroom	*cubiculum, cubiculī, n.*	*cubicle*
dominus, dominī, m.	lord, master	*dominus, dominī, m.*	*dominate*
nauta, nautae, m.	sailor	*nauta, nautae, m.*	*nautical*
patella, patellae, f.	plate	*patella, patellae, f.*	*patella*
rēgnō, rēgnāre	to reign	*rēgnō, rēgnāre*	*reign*
vīnum, vīnī, n.	wine	*vīnum, vīnī, n.*	*wine*

1. Which *verba* are verbs? <u>*Arāre and rēgnāre are verbs.*</u> Which conjugation? <u>*1st*</u>

2. How are **agricola** and **nauta** different from other 1st declension nouns? <u>*They are masculine.*</u>

3. Which nouns are 2nd declension masculine? <u>*annus, dominus*</u>

4. Which nouns are 2nd declension neuter? <u>*cubiculum, vīnum*</u>

5. What detail identifies a noun's declension? <u>*The gen. s. ending tells the declension.*</u>

6. Which *verba* name people? <u>*agricola, dominus, nauta*</u>

IV. Grammatica. Read the paradigm in the shaded box, and <u>memorize it</u>.

<u>Nominative</u>	-um	-a
<u>Genitive</u>	-ī	-ōrum
<u>Dative</u>	-ō	-īs
<u>Accusative</u>	-um	-a
<u>Ablative</u>	-ō	-īs

These are <u>case endings for 2nd declension *neuter* nouns</u>. As always, find the noun's stem by dropping the genitive singular ending. For example, **verbum, verbī, n.**: The stem is **verb-.**

verb**um**	verb**a**
verb**ī**	verb**ōrum**
verb**ō**	verb**īs**
verb**um**	verb**a**
verb**ō**	verb**īs**

It is important to learn that with **all** neuter nouns in **all** five declensions, the nominative and accusative singular endings are the same (*-um* in 2nd declension), *and* the plural nominative and accusative endings are **always –a**.

All of our conjugations so far have been present tense. <u>Present tense</u> expresses action or being that is occurring in the present (now). The present tense can be translated three ways. For example:

Agricola arat.	The farmer plows.
	The farmer is plowing.
	The farmer does plow.

In the example above, *is* and *does* are _____*helping*_____ verbs. We must remember that there are no helping verbs in Latin. And we must not confuse helping and linking verbs. **Sum, esse** is a linking verb and should **never** be used as a helping verb. It can *only* be a *linking* verb. So far, our sentences have only one verb in them – either an action verb *or* a linking verb. Look at these sentences:

Fēmina ambulat.	The woman *is* walking.
	(*is* is a helping verb; it's "helping" the verb *walking*.)
Fēmina est rēgīna.	The woman *is* a queen.
	(*is* is a linking verb; it links *woman* and *queen*.)

V. Historia. There is no new history lesson in this *disciplīna*!

VI. Dēlēgāta

A. *Scrībe* the new Latin *verba* and their meanings.

	Latīnē		*Anglicē*
1.	agricola, agricōlae, m.	1.	farmer
2.	annus, annī, m.	2.	year
3.	arō, arāre	3.	to plow
4.	cubiculum, cubiculī, n.	4.	bedroom
5.	dominus, dominī, m.	5.	lord, master
6.	nauta, nautae, m.	6.	sailor
7.	patella, patellae, f.	7.	plate
8.	rēgnō, rēgnāre	8.	to reign
9.	vīnum, vīnī, n.	9.	wine

B. *Scrībe* the case endings for 2nd declension neuter nouns three times.

1.		2.		3.	
-um	-a	-um	-a	-um	-a
-ī	-ōrum	-ī	-ōrum	-ī	-ōrum
-ō	-īs	-ō	-īs	-ō	-īs
-um	-a	-um	-a	-um	-a
-ō	-īs	-ō	-īs	-ō	-īs

C. *Scrībe* the *dictum* and its translation.

Latīnē: annō Dominī (AD)

Anglicē: in the year of our Lord

D. Translate these *verba* and phrases.

1. ten   decem   2. twelve   duodecim

3. Fēlicem nātālem Christī!_____   *Merry Christmas!*

4. In principiō erat Verbum._____   *In the beginning was the Word.*

5. Quaenam est tempestās hodiē?_____   *What is the weather today?*

6. Quot annōs nātus (nāta) es?_____   *How old are you?*

E. *Scrībe* **the meaning of these** *verba* **in the space provided. Then decline them.**

1. dōnum, dōnī, n.____*gift*_____   2. oppidum, oppidī, n.____*town*_____

dōnum	*dōna*	*oppidum*	*oppida*
dōnī	*dōnōrum*	*oppidī*	*oppidōrum*
dōnō	*dōnīs*	*oppidō*	*oppidīs*
dōnum	*dōna*	*oppidum*	*oppida*
dōnō	*dōnīs*	*oppidō*	*oppidīs*

3. vīnum, vīnī, n._____*wine*_____   4. rēgnum, rēgnī, n._____*kingdom*____

vīnum	*vīna*	*rēgnum*	*rēgna*
vīnī	*vīnōrum*	*rēgnī*	*rēgnōrum*
vīnō	*vīnīs*	*rēgnō*	*rēgnīs*
vīnum	*vīna*	*rēgnum*	*rēgna*
vīnō	*vīnīs*	*rēgnō*	*rēgnīs*

5. verbum, verbī, n.___*word*_____   6. peccātum, peccātī, n.____*sin*_____

verbum	*verba*	*peccātum*	*peccāta*
verbī	*verbōrum*	*peccātī*	*peccātōrum*
verbō	*verbīs*	*peccātō*	*peccātīs*
verbum	*verba*	*peccātum*	*peccāta*
verbō	*verbīs*	*peccātō*	*peccātīs*

F. Translate each sentence three different ways.

1. Agricolae arant.   a. *The farmers are plowing.*

   b. *The farmers plow.*   c. *The farmers do plow.*

2. Nautae nāvigant.   a. *The sailors are sailing.*

   b. *The sailors sail.*   c. *The sailors do sail.*

3. Dominus rēgnat.   a. *The Lord is reigning.*

   b. *The Lord reigns.*   c. *The Lord does reign.*

G. Translate these sentences (from Latin to English or from English to Latin). Remember the three ways present tense can be translated.

1. Dominī gaudent.   *The masters are rejoicing.*

2. Rēgīnae intrant.   *The queens enter.*

3. Rēgīnae rīdent.   *The queens laugh.*

4. Aquila cēnat.   *An eagle eats.*

5. Oculī movent.   *Eyes do move.*

6. Oppida pugnant.   *Towns are fighting.*

7. Puellae ambulant.   *The girls are walking.*

8. The women are singing.   *Fēminae cantant.*

9. The queen is a girl.   *Rēgīna est puella.*

10. The plate is a gift.   *Patella est dōnum.*

11. The plates are gifts.   *Patellae sunt dōna.*

12. The sailor is praying.   *Nauta ōrat.*

13. Chickens do fight.   *Gallīnae pugnant.*

14. The forest is a kingdom. *Silva est rēgnum.*

15. The queen is reigning.   *Rēgīna rēgnat.*

H. Misspelled *Verba*. Each of these *verba* has one extra letter. Mark out the extra letter, and *scrībe* it in the space to the left of the *verbum*. When you have finished, the letters in the blanks should spell a message. What is the message?

Message (*Anglicē*): _____ *GOD IS HELPING US LEARN THE LATIN LANGUAGE* _____

G	DIGGITUS	U	FENESTURA	T	GLORITA
O	AGORICOLA	S	INSTRO	I	REGINO
D	OPPIDDUM	L	OCULLUS	N	VINNUM
I	DOMINIUS	E	STEO	L	CAELLUM
S	MISSEREO	A	ROAMA	A	HISAPANIA
H	BRACCHHIUM	R	DOLERO	N	DONNUM
E	PATELLEA	N	ITALIAN	G	IAGNUA
L	SOLLUM	T	CUBICTULUM	U	NAUVIGO
P	PATEPO	H	HARO	A	SALAVEO
I	NIMIBUS	E	TARDEO	G	CEGNO
N	ANNNUS	L	PLUTEUS	E	MOEVEO
G	PECUGNIA	A	REGANO		

I. Dērīvātī. Complete each sentence with an English *verbum* chosen from the following *verba*. The italicized *verbum* in the sentence should help you think of the Latin root.

agriculture   patella   annual   arable

1. Land that can be *plowed* is _____*arable*_____. Latin root: _____*arō, arāre*_____

2. Something that happens every *year* is _____*annual*_____. Latin root: _____*annus, annī, m.*_____

3. The knee bone is shaped like a *plate* and is called the _____*patella*_____.

   Latin root: _____*patella, patellae, f.*_____

4. A *farmer* is an expert in _____*agriculture*_____. Latin root: _____*agricola, agricolae, f.*_____

J. Historia. Review the history stories from *Disciplīnae* VII through XI, and fill in the blanks.

1. Who is the last king of Rome? _____*The last king of Rome is Tarquinius Superbus.*_____

2. In what year does the Roman Republic begin? _____*The Roman Republic begins in 510 BC*_____

3. Who are the first two consuls? _*The consuls are Junius Brutus and Lucius Collatinus.*_

4. Who defends the Sublician Bridge? _____*Horatius defends the Sublician Bridge.*_____

Disciplīna XIII – tredecim   **ADJECTIVES**

I. Dictum

Nihil sub sōle novum est.
(Liber Ecclesiastes 1:10a)

<u>*There is nothing new under the sun.*</u>
(Ecclesiastes 1:10a)

II. Colloquium   *Latīnē*   *Anglicē*

	Latīnē	*Anglicē*
Magistra:	Quaenam est tempestās hodiē?	What is the weather today?
Discipulus:	Nūbilum est.	It's cloudy.
	Ventōsum est.	It's windy.
	Nebulōsum est.	It's foggy.

III. Verba

Latīnē	*Anglicē*	*Scrībe tōtum verbum Latīnum.*	*Dērīvātī*
aeternus, -a, -um	eternal	*aeternus, -a, -um*	eternal
angustus, -a, -um	narrow	*angustus, -a, -um*	anguish
antīquus, -a, -um	old, ancient	*antīquus, -a, -um*	antique
bonus, -a, -um	good	*bonus, -a, -um*	bonus
lātus, -a, -um	wide	*lātus, -a, -um*	latitude
magnus, -a, -um	large, great	*magnus, -a, -um*	magnitude
malus, -a, -um	bad, wicked	*malus, -a, -um*	malicious
novus, -a, -um	new	*novus, -a, -um*	novice
parvus, -a, -um	small	*parvus, -a, -um*	
sanctus, -a, -um	holy	*sanctus, -a, -um*	sanctify

1. What kind of *verba* are these? <u>*They are all adjectives.*</u>

2. An adjective is a *verbum* that <u>*modifies*</u> or <u>*describes*</u> a noun or a pronoun.

3. Why are there three forms for each adjective? <u>*There is one form for each gender.*</u>

71

IV. Grammatica. Read the declensions in the shaded box. Why are there three?

_____ m. _____		_____ f. _____		_____ n. _____	
bon**us**	bon**ī**	bon**a**	bon**ae**	bon**um**	bon**a**
bon**ī**	bon**ōrum**	bon**ae**	bon**ārum**	bon**ī**	bon**ōrum**
bon**ō**	bon**īs**	bon**ae**	bon**īs**	bon**ō**	bon**īs**
bon**um**	bon**ōs**	bon**am**	bon**ās**	bon**um**	bon**a**
bon**ō**	bon**īs**	bon**ā**	bon**īs**	bon**ō**	bon**īs**

The adjectives in this lesson are called *adjectives of the 1st and 2nd declension* because they take the case endings of those declensions.

In Latin, an adjective **must** agree with the noun it modifies in _____ *case* _____,

_____ *number* _____, and _____ *gender* _____.

Use 1st declension endings if the noun is feminine; use the appropriate 2nd declension endings if the noun is masculine or neuter. (Be careful with **agricola, -ae, m.** and **nauta, -ae, m.**)

In this *disciplina*, we'll write a new kind of Latin sentence. Each sentence will use a form of **sum, esse** and a predicate adjective. Because the predicate adjective modifies or describes the

subject of the sentence, it must be written in the case for subject nouns, the _*nominative*_ case. For example:

1. **Sella est lāta.**   The chair is wide.
2. **Equus est bonus.**   The horse is good.
3. **Oppidum est antīquum.**   The town is old.

4. **Oppida sunt antīqua.**   _*The towns are old.*_

5. **Nauta est malus.**   _*The sailor is bad*_

6. **Sum parvus.**   _*I am small*_

V. Historia (*Famous Men of Rome*, Chapter VII)

Lars Porsena besieges Rome. The Roman Caius Mucius marches into the enemy camp to kill Porsena, but he kills a secretary by mistake. Porsena threatens to burn Mucius, but Mucius thrusts his right hand into the fire and lets it be roasted. Porsena is terrified by this display of Roman bravery, and he makes peace with Rome.

VI. Dēlēgāta

A. *Scrībe* the new Latin *verba* and their meanings.

	Latīnē		*Anglicē*
1.	aeternus, -a, -um	1.	eternal
2.	angustus, -a, -um	2.	narrow
3.	antīquus, -a, -um	3.	old, ancient
4.	bonus, -a, -um	4.	good
5.	lātus, -a, -um	5.	wide
6.	magnus, -a, -um	6.	large
7.	malus, -a, -um	7.	bad, wicked
8.	novus, -a, -um	8.	new
9.	parvus, -a, -um	9.	small
10.	sanctus, -a, -um	10.	holy

B. *Scrībe* the declension of <u>novus, -a, -um</u>.

1. novus	novī	2. nova	novae	3. novum	nova
novī	novōrum	novae	novārum	novī	novōrum
novō	novīs	novae	novīs	novō	novīs
novum	novōs	novam	novās	novum	nova
novō	novīs	novā	novīs	novō	novīs

C. *Scribe* the *dictum* and its translation.

Latīnē: Nihil sub sōle novum est.

Anglicē: There is nothing new under the sun.

D. Translate these *verba* and phrases.

1. ten _____*decem*_____   6. eleven _____*ūndecim*_____

2. twelve _____*duodecim*_____   7. thirteen_____*tredecim*_____

3. Annō Dominī _*in the year of our Lord.*_   8. Quid est hoc? _*What is this?*_

4. Grātiās tibi agō. _*Thank you.*_   9. Valēte. _____*Goodbye.*_____

5. Frīgidum est. ___*It is cold.*___   10. Sōl lūcet. ___*The sun is shining.*___

11. Quaenam est tempestās hodiē?_____*What is the weather today?*_____

12. Lamb of God who takes away the sins of the world _*Agnus Deī quī tollis peccāta mundī.*_

E. Fill in the blanks.

1. *Scrībe* the nominative singular and plural case endings for these declensions.

	S	**P**
a. 1st declension	*-a*	*-ae*
b. 2nd declension masculine (M)	*-us*	*-ī*
c. 2nd declension neuter (N)	*-um*	*-a*

2. An adjective is a *verbum* that _____*modifies*_____ or _____*describes*_____ a noun or a pronoun.

3. In Latin sentences, an adjective must agree with the noun it modifies in _____*case*_____, _____*number*_____, and _____*gender*_____.

4. In Latin sentences, a subject noun must agree with its verb in __*person*__ and __*number*__.

F. *Scribe* the meaning of these *verba* in the space provided. Then conjugate them.

1. volō, volāre _____*to fly*_____   2. sedeō, sedēre_____*to sit*_____

volō	*volāmus*	*sedeō*	*sedēmus*
volās	*volātis*	*sedēs*	*sedētis*
volat	*volant*	*sedet*	*sedent*

G. Translate these sentences.

1. Deus est aeternus.   _God is eternal._

2. Christus est sanctus.   _Christ is holy._

3. Cubiculum est angustum.   _The bedroom is narrow._

4. Aqua est bona.   _Water is good._

5. Fenestrae sunt magnae.   _The windows are large._

6. Peccāta sunt mala.   _Sins are bad._

7. Lūna est antīqua.   _The moon is ancient._

8. Charta est lāta.   _The paper is wide._

9. Stilī sunt parvī.   _The pencils are small._

10. Gladius est novus.   _The sword is new._

11. Life is good.   _Vīta est bona._

12. The kingdom is ancient.   _Rēgnum est antīquum._

13. The pigs are large.   _Porcī sunt magnī._

14. The farmer is good.   _Agricola est bonus._

15. The eagles are large.   _Aquilae sunt magnae._

16. The sailor is great.   _Nauta est magnus._

17. The daughters are good.   _Fīliae sunt bonae._

18. The kitchen is narrow.   _Culīna est angusta._

H. Dērīvātī.
Complete each sentence with an English _verbum_ chosen from the following _verba_. The italicized _verbum_ in the sentence should help you think of the Latin root.

antiques   malicious   magnify   sanctify   novice

1. To make something _larger_ is to ___*magnify*___ it. Latin root: ___*magnus, -a, -um*___

2. A ___*novice*___ is someone who is _new_ at doing something. Latin root: ___*novus, -a, -um*___

3. *Old* collectible items are _____*antiques*_____ . Latin root: _*antīquus, -a, -um*_

4. To _____*sanctify*_____ is to make *holy*. Latin root: _____*sanctus, -a, -um*_____

5. _____*Malicious*_____ words are *bad* words. Latin root: _____*malus, -a, -um*_____

I. Crossword Puzzle. (Note: All adjectives are in the nominative case. Pay attention to gender and number!)

¹S	T	²A	N	T		³R	⁴E	G	N	⁵A	T		
		D			⁶P		Q			■		⁷L	
		J			A		U		⁸N	O	V	A	
	⁹A	E	T	E	R	N	U	M				T	
		C			V	■	S			¹⁰F		U	
¹¹A	N	T	I	Q	U	I		¹²M	A	L	U	S	
N		I		M				U	■	E			
G		V			¹³M		¹⁴C	E	N	A	¹⁵S		
U		E			A		I		T		E		
S					G		U				D		
T			¹⁶B	O	N	U	S		¹⁷O		E		
U					A			¹⁸E	R	R	O		
¹⁹S	A	N	C	T	A	E			O				

RECTĒ
1. They are standing.
3. She reigns.
8. new (n. pl.)
9. eternal (n. sing.)
11. ancient (m. pl.)
12. bad (m. sing.)
14. You eat.
16. good (m. sing.)
18. I wander.
19. holy (f. pl.)

DEORSUM
2. describes or modifies a noun
4. horse
5. I plow.
6. small (n. sing.)
7. wide (m. sing.)
10. They weep.
11. narrow (m. sing.)
12. left-handed Roman
13. great (f. pl.)
15. I sit.
17. I pray.

J. Historia. Review the history story, and fill in the blanks.

1. Who attacks Rome again in this story? _*Lars Porsena, the Etruscan king, attacks Rome.*_

2. Which hand does Mucius hold in the fire? _____*Mucius burns his right hand in the fire.*_____

Disciplīna XIV – quattuordecim   MORE ADJECTIVES

I. Dictum

Ūsus est magister optimus.   _Experience is the best teacher._

II. Colloquium

	Latīnē	_Anglicē_
Flāvius:	Ignōsce mihi, quaesō.	Please, excuse me.
Marcia:	Ō! Digitus meus!	Oh! My toe!
Flāvius:	Mea culpa! Mē paenitet!	My fault! I'm sorry!

III. Verba

Latīnē	_Anglicē_	_Scrībe tōtum verbum Latīnum._	_Dērīvātī_
altus, -a, -um	high, deep	altus, -a, -um	altitude
bellus, -a, -um	pretty	bellus, -a, -um	belle
meus, -a, -um	my	meus, -a, -um	my
multus, -a, -um	much, many	multus, -a, -um	multitude
optimus, -a, -um	best	optimus, -a, -um	optimist
prīmus, -a, -um	first	prīmus, -a, -um	primary
secundus, -a, -um	second	secundus, -a, -um	second
tōtus, -a, -um	whole	tōtus, -a, -um	total
tūtus, -a, -um	safe	tūtus, -a, -um	tutor
tuus, -a, -um	your (singular)	tuus, -a, -um	

1. What kind of _verba_ are these? _They are adjectives._

2. Why do Latin dictionaries and vocabulary lists give three endings for these _verba_?

   There is one ending for each of the three genders.

3. In what three ways must Latin adjectives agree with the nouns they modify?

   Adjectives must agree in case, number, and gender with the nouns they modify.

77

IV. Grammatica. Read the paradigm in the shaded box, and <u>memorize it</u>.

-bō	**-bimus**
-bis	**-bitis**
-bit	**-bunt**

These are <u>personal endings for the *future tense*</u> for 1st- and 2nd conjugation verbs. The future tense expresses action that has not yet happened.

Latin adjectives may be written directly before or after the noun they modify. However, it is customary to write adjectives that describe _____*number*_____ or _____*size*_____

before the noun and all other adjectives *after* the noun.

A Latin adjective must agree with the noun it modifies or describes in ___*case*___

_____*number*_____, and _____*gender*_____.

Examples:
Multa rēgna **pugnant.**	Many kingdoms are fighting.
Prīma ecclēsia **est magna.**	The first church is large.
Equus meus **tardat.**	My horse is slow.

V. Historia (*Famous Men of Rome*, Chapter VIII, Parts I and II)

5th century BC Caius Marcius bravely leads the attack on the Volscian city of Corioli and is given the new name *Coriolanus*. Coriolanus objects to the establishment of the tribunes, a new plebeian office with veto power. The people turn against him, and he flees to the city of the Volscians.

VI. Dēlēgāta

A. *Scrībe* the new Latin *verba* and their meanings.

	Latīnē		*Anglicē*
1.	altus, -a, -um	1.	high, deep
2.	bellus, -a, -um	2.	pretty
3.	meus, -a, -um	3.	my
4.	multus, -a, -um	4.	much, many
5.	optimus, -a, -um	5.	best
6.	prīmus, -a, -um	6.	first
7.	secundus, -a, -um	7.	second
8.	tōtus, -a, -um	8.	whole
9.	tūtus, -a, -um	9.	safe
10.	tuus, -a, -um	10.	your (singular)

B. *Scrībe* the future tense personal endings three times.

1.	-bō	-bimus	2.	-bō	-bimus	3.	-bō	-bimus
	-bis	-bitis		-bis	-bitis		-bis	-bitis
	-bit	-bunt		-bit	-bunt		-bit	-bunt

C. *Scrībe* the *dictum* and its translation.

Latīnē: Ūsus est optimus magister.

Anglicē: Experience is the best teacher.

D. Translate these *verba* and phrases.

1. mea culpa   my fault   3. quattuordecim   fourteen

2. Crēdō in ūnum Deum.   I believe in one God.   4. Agnus Deī   Lamb of God

5. duodecim _____*twelve*_____   9. et cētera _____*and the rest*_____

6. thirteen _____*tredecim*_____   10. ten _____*decem*_____

7. five _____*quīnque*_____   11. Nūbilum est. _*It is cloudy.*_

8. Ventōsum est. ___*It is windy.*___   12. eleven _____*ūndecim*_____

13. Nihil sub sōle novum est. _____*There is nothing new under the sun.*_____

14. Glory to God in the highest! _____*Glōria in excelsīs Deō!*_____

15. In the beginning was the Word. _____*In prīncipiō erat Verbum.*_____

16. Ūsus est magister optimus. _____*Experience is the best teacher.*_____

E. Fill in the blanks.

1. List the cases of Latin nouns. *nominative, genitive, dative, accusative, ablative, vocative.*

2. The _____*nominative*_____ case is used for subject nouns.

3. Sentences that have subject nouns *must* use _____*3ʳᵈ*_____ -person verbs.

4. A verb must agree with the subject in _____*person*_____ and in _____*number*_____.

5. Adjectives that describe _____*number*_____ or _____*size*_____ usually *precede* the noun they modify.

6. Adjectives must agree with the nouns they modify in _____*case*_____, _____*number*_____

   and _____*gender*_____.

F. *Scrībe* the meaning of these *verba* in the space provided. Then decline them.

1. gallīna, gallīnae, f. *chicken*   2. rēgnum, rēgnī, n. *kingdom*

gallīna	*gallīnae*	*rēgnum*	*rēgna*
gallīnae	*gallīnārum*	*rēgnī*	*rēgnōum*
gallīnae	*gallīnīs*	*rēgnō*	*rēgnīs*
gallīnam	*gallīnās*	*rēgnum*	*rēgna*
gallīnā	*gallīnīs*	*rēgnō*	*rēgnīs*

G. Translate these sentences.

1. Prīmus equus est magnus. _The first horse is large._

2. Secundus equus est parvus. _The second horse is small._

3. Parvum oppidum est tūtum. _The small town is safe._

4. Silvae antīquae sunt bellae. _The ancient forests are pretty._

5. Deus sanctus iūdicat. _A holy God judges._

6. Tōtus mundus gaudet. _The whole world rejoices._

7. Puella bella cantat. _The pretty girl is singing._

8. Cubiculum meum patet. _My bedroom is open._

9. Puteī optimī sunt altī. _The best wells are deep._

10. Many bears are eating. _Multae ursae cēnant._

11. Your queen is afraid. _Rēgīna tua timet._

12. Eternal life is a gift. _Vīta aeterna est dōnum._

13. Many chickens are flying. _Multae gallīnae volant._

14. My sins are many. _Peccāta mea sunt multa._

15. Your victory is great. _Victōria tua est magna._

16. The small woman sits. _Parva fēmina sedet._

H. _Scribe_ these adjective-noun phrases in the nominative case.

1. large church _magna ecclēsia_

2. great victory _magna victōria_

3. pretty daughter _fīlia bella_

4. wide papers _chartae lātae_

5. narrow kitchen _culīna angusta_

6. safe kingdom _rēgnum tūtum_

7. your fork _furca tua_

8. good sailor _nauta bonus_

9. my money _pecūnia mea_

10. many stars _multae stellae_

I. Alphabet Code. (1) Place some of the *verba* from this *disciplīna* in the following blanks. Some letters are given to help you get started. (2) The letters *under* the blanks represent a code. Use the code to decipher the longer English message below the vocabulary list.

M E U S
c v p w

M U L T U S
c p x z p w

T U U S
z p p w

P R I M U S
y k q c p w

A L T U S
t x z p w

B E L L U S
u v x x p w

T O T U S
z j z p w

O P T I M U S
j y z q c p w

T U T U S
z p z p w

S E C U N D U S
w v b p f h p w

C O R I O L A N U S   C O U L D   C O N T R O L
b j k q j x t f p w   b j p x h   b j f z k j x

S O L D I E R S   B U T   N O T   P R I D E
w j x h q v k w   u p z   f j z   y k q h v

J. Dērīvātī. Complete each sentence with an English *verbum* chosen from the following *verba*. The italicized *verbum* in the sentence should help you think of the Latin root.

altimeter   optimal   multitude   primary

1. The ___optimal___ time to do something is the *best* time. Latin root:___optimus, -a, -um___

2. Something of *first* importance is ___primary___. Latin root:___prīmus, -a, -um___

3. A ___multitude___ is a group of *many* people. Latin root:___multus, -a, -um___

4. An ___altimeter___ tells how *high* a plane is flying. Latin root:___altus, -a, -um___

K. Historia. Review the history story, and fill in the blanks.

1. What is the capital city of the Volscians?___Corioli was the Volscian capital city.___

2. What nickname is given to Caius Marcius?___He was given the name Coriolanus.___

3. What officers had veto power over laws passed by the Senate?___the tribunes___

Disciplīna XV – quīndecim   ADVERBS / FUTURE TENSE

I. Dictum

semper fīdēlis   _always faithful_

II. Colloquium   _Latīnē_   _Anglicē_

Fābia:	Loquerisne Latīnē?	Do you speak Latin?
Quīntus:	Ita. Latīnē parum loquor.	Yes. I speak Latin a little.

III. Verba

Latīnē	_Anglicē_	_Scrībe tōtum verbum Latīnum._	_Dērīvātī_
bene	well	_bene_	_benevolent_
hīc	here	_hīc_	
ibi	there	_ibi_	
male	badly, wickedly	_male_	_malevolent_
multum	a lot	_multum_	_multiply_
numquam	never	_numquam_	
nunc	now	_nunc_	
parum	a little	_parum_	
saepe	often	_saepe_	
semper	always	_semper_	

1. What kind of _verba_ are these? _They are adverbs._

2. An adverb is a word that modifies a _verb_, an _adjective_, or

   another _adverb_.

3. Adverbs cannot be _declined_ or _conjugated_.

4. This means that adverbs have no _endings_!

IV. Grammatica. Read the conjugation in the shaded box, and translate it.

I will love	**amā<u>bō</u>**	**amā<u>bimus</u>**	_We will love_
You will love	**amā<u>bis</u>**	**amā<u>bitis</u>**	_You all will love_
He (she, it) will love	**amā<u>bit</u>**	**amā<u>bunt</u>**	_They will love_

This is the model for the _future tense_ in 1st conjugation. Simply add the endings, one by one, to the stem of the verb.

The _future tense_ expresses action or being in a future time. The main helping verb for future

tense is _____ _will_ _____. It is also correct to use _____ _shall_ _____ for first person.

Examples:
Fīlia mea ambula<u>t</u>. My daughter _is_ walking (walks, does walk).
Fīlia mea ambulā<u>bit</u>. My daughter _will_ walk.
Nautae labōra<u>nt</u>. The sailors work (are working, do work).
Nautae labōrā<u>bunt</u>. The sailors _will_ work.

Remember: The subject noun of a sentence must agree with the verb in _____ _person_ _____

and _____ _number_ _____.

<u>Adverbs</u> can be placed anywhere in a Latin sentence, but most often they go right before the verb (which is usually last in a Latin sentence). Examples:

Rēgīna <u>numquam</u> rīdet. The queen never laughs.
Aquilae <u>bene</u> volant. Eagles fly well.

Because the declensions of **fīlia, -ae, f.** and **fīlius, -ī, m.** could be confused in the dative and ablative plurals, the Romans declined them this way:

fīlia	fīliae		fīlius	fīliī
fīliae	fīliārum		fīliī	fīliōrum
fīliae	fīliā**bus**		fīliō	fīliī**s**
fīliam	fīliās		fīlium	fīliōs
fīliā	fīliā**bus**		fīliō	fīliī**s**

V. Historia (_Famous Men of Rome_, Chapter VIII, Part III)

Coriolanus marches on Rome with a Volscian army. His mother, Veturia, comes out of the city to meet Coriolanus and reminds him that by attacking Rome, he will be killing his mother, his wife, and his children. Coriolanus relents and tells her, "Mother, you have saved Rome, but you have ruined your son."

VI. Dēlēgāta

A. *Scrībe* the new Latin *verba* and their meanings.

	Latīnē		*Anglicē*
1.	bene	1.	well
2.	hīc	2.	here
3.	ibi	3.	there
4.	male	4.	badly
5.	multum	5.	a lot
6.	numquam	6.	never
7.	nunc	7.	now
8.	parum	8.	a little
9.	saepe	9.	often
10.	semper	10.	always

B. *Scrībe* the conjugation of <u>amō, amāre</u> in future tense two times.

1.	amābō	amābimus	2.	amābō	amābimus
	amābis	amābitis		amābis	amābitis
	amābit	amābunt		amābit	amābunt

C. *Scrībe* the *dictum* and its translation.

Latīnē: semper fīdēlis   *Anglicē*:   always faithful

D. Translate these *verba* and phrases.

1. ten   decem   4. ūndecim   eleven

2. Ignosce mihi!   Excuse me!   5. five   quīnque

3. fourteen   quattuordecim   6. et cētera   and the rest

7. In the beginning was the Word. _____ *In prīncipiō erat Verbum.* _____

E. *Scrībe* the meaning of each verb in the blank. Then conjugate each in future tense.

1. iūdicō, iūdicāre _____ *to judge* _____

iūdicābō	*iūdicābimus*
iūdicābis	*iūdicābitis*
iūdicābit	*iūdicābunt*

2. dūrō, dūrāre _____ *to endure* _____

dūrābō	*dūrābimus*
dūrābis	*dūrābitis*
dūrābit	*dūrābunt*

3. rēgnō, rēgnāre _____ *to reign* _____

rēgnābō	*rēgnābimus*
rēgnābis	*rēgnābitis*
rēgnābit	*rēgnābunt*

4. peccō, peccāre _____ *to sin* _____

peccābō	*peccābimus*
peccābis	*peccābitis*
peccābit	*peccābunt*

F. *Scrībe* the correct Latin form of these *verba* in the blank. Then decline them.

1. word _____ *verbum, verbī, n.* _____

verbum	*verba*
verbī	*verbōrum*
verbō	*verbīs*
verbum	*verba*
verbō	*verbīs*

2. son _____ *fīlius, fīliī, m.* _____

fīlius	*fīliī*
fīliī	*fīliōrum*
fīliō	*fīliīs*
fīlium	*fīliōs*
fīliō	*fīliīs*

3. woman _____ *fēmina, fēminae, f.* _____

fēmina	*fēminae*
fēminae	*fēminārum*
fēminae	*fēminīs*
fēminam	*fēminās*
fēminā	*fēminīs*

4. daughter _____ *fīlia, fīliae, f.* _____

fīlia	*fīliae*
fīliae	*fīliārum*
fīliae	*fīliābus*
fīliam	*fīliās*
fīliā	*fīliābus*

G. Translate these sentences (from Latin to English or from English to Latin).

1. Dūrābō. _____ *I will endure.* _____

2. Dūrābimus. _____ *We will endure.* _____

3. Superābunt. _____ *They will overcome.* _____

4. Ambulābis. _____ *You will walk.* _____

5. Recitābitis. _____ *You all will recite.* _____

6. Recitābit. _____ *He will read aloud.* _____

7. Volābit. _____ *It will fly.* _____

8. Ōrābimus. _____ *We will pray.* _____

9. Puella bene recitābit. _____ *The girl will recite well.* _____

10. Saepe peccāmus. _____ *We often sin.* _____

11. Deus semper amābit. _____ *God will always love.* _____

12. Fīlius meus nunc festīnat. _____ *My son hurries now.* _____

13. Pecūnia hīc manēbit. _____ *The money will stay here.* _____

14. Fēminae ibi labōrābunt. _____ *The women will work there.* _____

15. Lingua tua numquam silet! _____ *Your tongue is never silent!* _____

16. The bad slaves think a little. _____ *Servī malī parum cōgitant.* _____

17. The church will sing a lot. _____ *Ecclēsia multum cantābit.* _____

18. The old farmer sails badly. _____ *Agricola antīquus male nāvigat.* _____

19. The towns will fight. _____ *Oppida pugnābunt.* _____

20. The farmer will plow. _____ *Agricola arābit.* _____

21. The church will pray. _____ *Ecclēsia ōrābit.* _____

22. Many churches will pray now. _____ *Multae ecclēsiae nunc ōrābunt.* _____

23. The large horses never fight. _____ *Magnī equī numquam pugnant.* _____

24. The horses will never fight. _____ *Equī numquam pugnābunt.* _____

25. The small girls often sing. _____ *Parvae puellae saepe cantant.* _____

26. The girls are always singing. _____ *Puellae semper cantant.* _____

H. Anagrams. Unscramble the letters in each row to form one of the *verba* from this *discipīna*. *Scrībe* each *verbum* in the spaces given. Then write all the sheded letters in the margin on the right and unscramble them to form the name of an organization (*Anglicē*) that might be interested in Disciplina XV.

HCI   H̲ I̲ C̲

IIB   I̲ B̲ I̲

CNNU   N̲ U̲ N̲ C̲

EMLA   M̲ A̲ L̲ E̲

NBEE   B̲ E̲ N̲ E̲

PAESE   S̲ A̲ E̲ P̲ E̲

RPUMA   P̲ A̲ R̲ U̲ M̲

MLUUTM   M̲ U̲ L̲ T̲ U̲ M̲

MSEERP   S̲ E̲ M̲ P̲ E̲ R̲

UUQMANM   N̲ U̲ M̲ Q̲ U̲ A̲ M̲

SOLUTION: T̲ H̲ E̲   M̲ A̲ R̲ I̲ N̲ E̲ S̲

I. Dērīvātī. Complete each sentence with an English *verbum* chosen from the following *verba*. The italicized *verbum* in the sentence should help you think of the Latin root.

benevolent   malefactor

1. Someone who wishes you *well* or wants to be kind is _____*benevolent*_____.

   Latin root: _____*bene*_____

2. A _____*malefactor*_____ does *wicked* deeds. Latin root:_____*male*_____

J. Historia. Review the history story, and fill in the blanks.

1. What is the name of Coriolanus's mother?_____*Coriolanus' mother was Veturia.*_____

2. What does Coriolanus say to his mother?_____

   _____*He says: "Mother, you have saved Rome, but you have ruined your son."*_____

Disciplīna XVI – sēdecim   MORE FUTURE TENSE

I. Dictum

antebellum   _before the war_

II. Colloquium   _Latīnē_   _Anglicē_

Catō:	Hic est amīcus meus Sextus.	This is my friend Sextus.
Porcia:	Salvē Sexte.	Hello, Sextus.
Sextus:	Salvē. Quid agis?	Hello. What are you up to?

III. Verba

Latīnē	_Anglicē_	_Scrībe tōtum verbum Latīnum._	_Dērīvātī_
amīcus, amīcī, m.	friend	_amīcus, amīcī, m._	_amiable_
bellum, bellī, n.	war	_bellum, bellī, n._	_bellicose_
focus, focī, m.	fireplace, family	_focus, focī, m._	_focus_
hōra, hōrae, f.	hour	_hōra, hōrae, f._	_hour_
īnsula, īnsulae, f.	island	_īnsula, īnsulae, f._	_insulation_
nōn	not	_nōn_	_non-_
patria, patriae, f.	country, fatherland	_patria, patriae, f._	_patriot_
praemium, praemiī, n.	reward	_praemium, praemiī, n._	_premium_
tēlum, tēlī, n.	weapon	_tēlum, tēlī, n._	

1. Which _verbum_ is not a noun? _nōn_ What kind of _verbum_ is it? _an adverb_

2. Which _verba_ are 1st declension nouns? _hōra, īnsula, patria_

3. Which _verba_ are 2nd declension masculine nouns? _amīcus, focus_

4. Which _verba_ are 2nd declension neuter nouns? _bellum, praemium, tēlum_

5. An _adjective_ must agree with the _noun_ it modifies in gender, number, and case.

IV. Grammatica. Read the conjugation in the shaded box, and translate it.

I will stay	**manēbō**	**manēbimus**	_We will stay_
You will stay	**manēbis**	**manēbitis**	_You all will stay_
He, she, it will stay	**manēbit**	**manēbunt**	_They will stay_

This is the model for the _future tense_ in 2ⁿᵈ conjugation. As with 1ˢᵗ conjugation, simply add the endings, one by one, to the stem of the verb.

When **nōn** modifies a verb:
     a. It is placed _before_ the verb it modifies.
     b. It is usually translated with a helping verb such as _do_, _does_, _is_, or _are_. For example:

         Aquila volat.   The eagle flies (is flying, does fly).
         Aquila nōn volat.   The eagle does _not_ fly (is _not_ flying).

From the colloquium: Note that when addressing someone with a 2ⁿᵈ declension name that ends in –**us**, the nominative ending –**us** is replaced with the vocative ending –**e**. For example:

Sextus becomes **Sexte**.

Marcus becomes **Marce**.

When addressing someone with a 2ⁿᵈ declension name that ends in -**ius**, the nominative ending –**ius** is replaced with the vocative ending –**ī**.

Fabius becomes **Fabī**

Tarquinius becomes **Tarquinī**

V. Historia (_Famous Men of Rome_, Chapter IX)

Rome is at war with the Veientians. The Fabii are a powerful family in Rome. Marcus Fabius and Caeso Fabius are popular consuls who take the side of the plebeians in many issues. Threatened by the patricians, the Fabii offer to build a new town close to Veii, the capital city of the Veientians, and to carry on the war at no cost to Rome. They succeed for a while, but the Veientians attack on the day of the annual religious festival and destroy the city of the Fabii.

VI. Dēlēgāta

A. *Scrībe* the new Latin *verba* and their meanings.

Latīnē	*Anglicē*
1. amīcus, amīcī, m.	1. friend
2. bellum, bellī, n.	2. war
3. focus, focī, m.	3. fireplace, family
4. hōra, hōrae, f.	4. hour
5. īnsula, īnsulae, f.	5. island
6. nōn	6. not
7. patria, patriae, f.	7. country, fatherland
8. praemium, praemiī, n.	8. reward
9. tēlum, tēlī, n.	9. weapon

B. *Scrībe* the conjugation of <u>maneō, manēre</u> in future tense two times.

manēbō	manēbimus	manēbō	manēbimus
manēbis	manēbitis	manēbis	manēbitis
manēbit	manēbunt	manēbit	manēbunt

C. *Scrībe* the *dictum* and its translation.

Latīnē: antebellum   *Anglicē*: before the war

D. Translate these *verba* and phrases.

1. sēdecim   sixteen

2. fourteen   quattuordecim

3. semper fidēlis   always faithful

4. tredecim   thirteen

5. Quid agis?   What are you up to?

6. Hic est amīcus meus.   This is my friend.

7. Fēlīcem annum novum!   Happy new year!

E. *Scrībe* the meaning of each verb in the blank. Then conjugate each in future tense.

1. timeō, timēre _____ *to fear* _____

timēbō	*timēbimus*
timēbis	*timēbitis*
timēbit	*timēbunt*

2. placeō, placēre _____ *to please* _____

placēbō	*placēbimus*
placēbis	*placēbitis*
placēbit	*placēbunt*

3. misereō, miserēre _____ *to be sorry* _____

miserēbō	*miserēbimus*
miserēbis	*miserēbitis*
miserēbit	*miserēbunt*

4. rīdeō, rīdēre _____ *to laugh* _____

rīdēbō	*rīdēbimus*
rīdēbis	*rīdēbitis*
rīdēbit	*rīdēbunt*

F. *Scrībe* the correct Latin form of these *verba* in the blank. Then decline them.

1. friend _____ *amīcus, amīcī, m.* _____

amīcus	*amīcī*
amīcī	*amīcōrum*
amīcō	*amīcīs*
amīcum	*amīcōs*
amīcō	*amīcīs*

2. war _____ *bellum, bellī, n.* _____

bellum	*bella*
bellī	*bellōrum*
bellō	*bellīs*
bellum	*bella*
bellō	*bellīs*

G. Translate these sentences (from Latin to English or from English to Latin).

1. Hispania valēbit.   *Spain will be strong.*

2. Patria valēbit.   *The fatherland will be strong.*

3. Patria semper valēbit.   *The country will always be strong.*

4. Patria nōn semper valēbit.   *The country will not always be strong.*

5. Iēsus est amīcus optimus.   *Jesus is the best friend.*

6. Iēsus est amīcus meus.   *Jesus is my friend.*

7. Amīcus meus manēbit. *My friend will stay.*

8. Amīcus meus ibi manēbit. *My friend will stay there.*

9. Multae iānuae patēbunt. *Many doors will be open.*

10. Magnae fenestrae patēbunt. *The large windows will be open.*

11. Mundus silēbit. *The world will be silent.*

12. Ecclēsia gaudet. *The church rejoices.*

13. Ecclēsia multum gaudēbit. *The church will rejoice a lot.*

14. Tēlum meum dūrat. *My weapon endures.*

15. Magna bella nōn sunt bona. *Large wars are not good.*

16. Īnsula est angusta. *The island is narrow.*

17. The island is not narrow. *Īnsula nōn est angusta.*

18. The fireplace is wide. *Focus est lātus.*

19. The country is wide. *Patria est lāta.*

20. A crown is a reward. *Corōna est praemium.*

21. Life is a gift. *Vīta est dōnum.*

22. Eternal life is a gift. *Vīta aeterna est dōnum.*

23. The well is deep. *Puteus est altus.*

24. The sword is a weapon. *Gladius est tēlum.*

25. Many sons will laugh. *Multī fīliī rīdēbunt.*

26. The daughters will not laugh. *Fīliae nōn rīdēbunt.*

27. The hour is now. *Hōra est nunc.*

28. God is great! *Deus est magnus!*

29. I love to work! *Amō labōrāre!*

H. *Verbum* Search. Each of the *verba* listed below can be found in this grid reading forward, backward, up, down, or diagonally. All the unused letters will spell a hidden message when read from left to right, row by row. What is the hidden message (*Latīnē*)?

Hidden message: _____ *INSULA GILLIGANIS EST PARVA* _____

I	N	A	R	O	H	S	U
L	A	B	E	L	L	U	M
F	A	B	I	I	G	U	I
A	L	U	S	N	I	L	L
I	M	T	I	M	F	E	G
R	A	I	E	N	O	I	V
T	S	A	C	L	C	E	S
A	R	T	P	U	U	A	R
P	V	N	O	N	S	M	A

AMICUS
BELLUM
FABII
FOCUS
HORA
INSULA
NON
PATRIA
PRAEMIUM
TELUM
VEII

I. Dērīvātī. Complete each sentence with an English *verbum* chosen from the following *verba*. The italicized *verbum* in the sentence should help you think of the Latin root.

amiable   insulation   bellicose   patriot

1. A ____*patriot*____ is devoted to his *country*. Latin root:_____*patria, patriae, f.*_____

2. A *friendly* person is _____*amiable*_____. Latin root:_____*amīcus, amīcī, m.*_____

3. _____*Insulation*_____ helps make your house an *island* of warm air in the winter

  and an *island* of cool air in the summer. Latin root:_____*īnsula, īnsulae, f.*_____

4. A ____*bellicose*____ person likes to fight (is *war*-like). Latin root:_____*bellum, bellī, n.*_____

J. Historia. Review the history story, and fill in the blanks.

1. Who is at war with Rome in this story?_____*The Veientians are at war with Rome.*_____

2. Who builds a town close to Veii?____*Caeso and Marcus Fabius build a city near Veii.*____

3. How do the Veientians conquer the city of the Fabii?____*They conquer the city of the Fabii*

  _____*by attacking during a religious holiday when no one expects an attack.*_____

Disciplīna XVII – septendecim   POSSUM, POSSE

I. Dictum

Errāre hūmānum est. (Terence)   <u>*To err is human.*</u>

II. Colloquium   *Latīnē*   *Anglicē*

Marcia:	Haec est amīca mea Iūlia.	This is my friend Julia.
Porcia:	Salvē Iūlia.	Hello, Julia.
Iūlia:	Salvē.	Hello.

III. Verba

Latīnē	*Anglicē*	*Scrībe tōtum verbum Latīnum.*	*Dērīvātī*
capillus, capillī, m.	(a) hair	*capillus, capillī, m.*	*capillary*
discipula, disicpulae, f.	student (female)	*discipula, discipulae, f.*	*discipline*
discipulus, discipulī, m.	student (male)	*discipulus, discipulī, m.*	*disciple*
exedrium, exedriī, n.	living room	*exedrium, exedriī, n.*	
herba, herbae, f.	plant, herb	*herba, herbae, f.*	*herbal*
mūrus, mūrī, m.	wall	*mūrus, mūrī, m.*	*mural*
pōculum, pōculī, n.	cup	*pōculum, pōculī, n.*	
signum, signī, n.	sign, standard	*signum, signī, n.*	*sign*
taurus, taurī, m.	bull	*taurus, taurī, m.*	*taurine*
via, viae, f.	road, way	*via, viae, f.*	*viaduct*
possum, posse	to be able, can	*possum, posse*	*possible*

1. Which *verbum* is not a noun?<u> *possum, posse* </u> What kind of *verbum* is it? <u>*It is a verb.*</u>

2. Which *verba* are 1ˢᵗ declension nouns?<u>   *discipula, herba, via*   </u>

3. Which *verba* are 2ⁿᵈ declension masculine nouns? <u>*capillus, discipulus, mūrus, taurus*</u>

4. Which *verba* are 2ⁿᵈ declension neuter nouns?<u>   *exedrium, pōculum, signum*   </u>

IV. Grammatica. Read the conjugation in the shaded box, and <u>memorize it</u>.

I am able / can	**possum**	**possumus**	_We are able / can_
You are able / can	**potes**	**potestis**	_You all are able / can_
He (she, it) is able/can	**potest**	**possunt**	_They are able / can_

We cannot find the stem of *possum, posse* in the usual way because *posse* is an irregular verb. The stems of irregular verbs change frequently and so we must memorize them.

To what other irregular verb is **possum, posse** similar? _____ *sum, esse* _____

We have already talked about and used <u>infinitives</u> a lot. The word infinitive comes from the Latin word *in-finītum,* which means "un-limited". The infinive provides the meaning of a verb without being limited by person, number, and tense.

Infinitives are always translated __*to*__ + _____*verb*_____

The infinitives of 1st and 2nd conjugation verbs are used to find the _____*stem*_____ of the verb.

To find the _____*stem*_____ of 1st and 2nd conjugation verbs, drop the _-re_ from the infinitive.

Nearly all forms of **possum, posse** require a *complementary* (completing) *infinitive* in order for them to make sense. For example:

Cantāre possum.	I am able <u>to sing</u>. (*or* I can sing.)
Aquila volāre potest.	The eagle is able <u>to fly</u>. (*or* The eagle can fly.)

V. Historia (*Famous Men of Rome*, Chapter X)

Rome goes to war with the Aequians. The army, led by the consul Minucius, is trapped in a valley, and the Senate decides to appoint a dictator for six months. They choose Lucius Quinctius, called *Cincinnatus* because of his curly hair. They find him plowing the fields of his farm. He leaves his plow and defeats the Aequians, making them pass under a yoke. Then he returns to his farm.

96

VI. Dēlēgāta

A. *Scrībe* the new Latin *verba* and their meanings.

Latīnē	*Anglicē*
1. capillus, capillī, m.	1. (a) hair
2. discipula, discipulae, f.	2. student (female)
3. discipulus, discipulī, m.	3. student (male)
4. exedrium, exedriī, n.	4. living room
5. herba, herbae, f.	5. plant, herb
6. mūrus, mūrī, m.	6. wall
7. pōculum, pōculī, n.	7. cup
8. signum, signī n.	8. sign, standard
9. taurus, taurī, m.	9. bull
10. via, viae, f.	10. road, way
11. possum, posse	11. to be able, can

B. *Scrībe* the conjugation of <u>possum, posse</u> in present tense two times.

possum	possumus		possum	possumus
potes	potestis		potes	potestis
potest	possunt		potest	possunt

C. *Scrībe* the *dictum* and its translation.

Latīnē: Errāre hūmānum est.   *Anglicē*: To err is human.

D. Translate these *verba* and phrases.

1. septendecim   seventeen   3. sixteen   sēdecim

2. antebellum   before the war   4. Haec est amīca mea. This is my friend.

E. *Scrībe* the meaning of these *verba* in the space provided. Then conjugate them in the tense indicated (P – present; F – future).

1. arō, arāre (F)_____*to plow*_____

arābō	*arābimus*
arābis	*arābitis*
arābit	*arābunt*

2. sileō silēre (P)_____*to be silent*_____

sileō	*silēmus*
silēs	*silētis*
silent	*silent*

F. *Scrībe* the Latin dictionary form of these *verba* in the blank. Then decline them.

1. sign_____*signum, signī, n.*_____

signum	*signa*
signī	*signōrum*
signō	*signīs*
signum	*signa*
signō	*signīs*

2. road, way_____*via, viae, f.*_____

via	*viae*
viae	*viārum*
viae	*viīs*
viam	*viās*
viā	*viīs*

G. Translate these sentences (from Latin to English or from English to Latin).

1. Pōculum est magnum. *The cup is large.*

2. Herba est magna. *The plant is large.*

3. Porcus est magnus. *The pig is large.*

4. Iānua patet. *The door is open.*

5. Fenestrae nōn patent. *The windows are not open.*

6. Discipulī nōn sunt antīquī. *The students are not ancient.*

7. Discipulus festīnat. *The student hurries.*

8. Discipulus saepe errat. *The student is mistaken often.*

9. Discipulī nōn gaudēbunt. *The students will not rejoice.*

10. I am able to sing. *Possum cantāre.*

11. You all cannot sing.   *Nōn potestis cantāre.*

12. The student is able to sing.   *Discipula cantāre potest.*

13. I can laugh.   *Possum rīdēre.*

14. You can laugh.   *Rīdēre potes.*

15. We can laugh.   *Rīdēre possumus.*

16. The students are always thinking.   *Discipulī semper cōgitant.*

17. Discipulī bonī multum cōgitant.   *Good students think a lot.*

18. Many women are able to work.   *Multae fēminae possunt labōrāre.*

19. Many girls cannot work.   *Multae puellae labōrāre nōn possunt.*

H. Crossword Puzzle. When the puzzle is finished, the lightly shaded squares will spell a Latin infinitive when read from left to right, top to bottom, and the slashed squares will spell its English translation.   *Latīnē:*____**DUBITARE**____   *Anglicē:*____**TO DOUBT**

¹E			²C		³P	O	T	E	⁴S	T
X		⁵V	I	A	Ø			U		⁶D
E			P		C			M		U
⁷D	I	S	C	I	P	U	L	⁸A		R
R			L		L		⁹M	A	N	E	Ø
I		¹⁰H	L		U		B			
U		E	U		M		U			
¹¹M	U	R	U	S			L		¹²S	
		B		¹³M	¹⁴N	A	V	I	G	O
¹⁵T	A	U	R	U	S	■	R	■	G	
		N			¹⁶R	E	G	N	A	T
		D							U	
17C	U	B	I	C	U	L	U	M		

RECTE
3. He is able.
5. road
7. female student
9. I remain.
11. wall
14. I sail.
15. bull
16. He reigns.
17. bedroom

DEORSUM
1. living room
2. hair
3. cup
4. I am.
6. I endure.
8. to walk
10. plant
12. sign
13. worlds

I. Dērīvātī. Complete each sentence with an English *verbum* chosen from the following *verba*. The italicized *verbum* in the sentence should help you think of the Latin root.

disciple   herbal   mural   capillary   possible

1. A painting done on a *wall* is called a ____*mural*____. Latin root:____*mūrus, mūrī, m.*____

2. You are *able* to do things that are _____*possible*_____. Latin root:____*possum, posse*____

3. A *student* who follows one particular teacher is called a _____*disciple*_____.

    Latin root:_____*discipula, discipulae, f.* or *disicpulus, discipulī, m.*_____

4. _____*Herbal*_____ medicine is from *plants*.

    Latin root:_____*herba, herbae, f.*_____

5. A _____*capillary*_____ is a tiny, *hair*-like blood vessel.

Latin root:_____*capillus, capillī, m.*_____

J. Historia. Review the history story, and fill in the blanks.

1. Who is at war with Rome in this story?__*The Romans and the Aequians are at war.*__

2. Whom does the Roman Senate appoint as dictator?_*The senate chooses Lucius Quinctius.*_

3. What is the dictator's nickname?__*Lucius Quinctius is nicknamed "Cincinnatus".*__

4. What does he do after he defeats the enemy?_____*He goes home to his farm.*_____

Disciplīna XVIII – duodēvīgintī   2ⁿᵈ DECLENSION: M in –er

I. Dictum

ex librīs   *from the books of*

II. Colloquium   *Latīnē*   *Anglicē*

Monica:	Repetitiō māter memoriae.	Repetition is the mother of memory.
Claudius:	Est dictum bonum.	That is a good saying.
Monica:	Grātiās tibi agō.	Thank you.

III. Verba

Latīnē	*Anglicē*	*Scrībe tōtum verbum Latīnum.*	*Dērīvātī*
culter, cultrī, m.	knife	*culter, cultrī, m.*	*cutlery*
et	and	*et*	*etc. / et cetera*
liber, librī, m.	book	*liber, librī, m.*	*library*
magister, magistrī, m.	teacher (male)	*magister, magistrī, m.*	*master, mr.*
puer, puerī, m.	boy	*puer, puerī, m.*	*puerile*

(The plural form, **puerī**, can mean *children*.)

stomachus, stomachī, m.	stomac	*stomachus, -ī, m.*	*stomach*

1. What detail identifies a declension? *The gen. sing. case ending tells the declension.*

2. What is this detail for 1ˢᵗ declension? *-ae*   For 2ⁿᵈ declension? *-ī*

3. We find the stem of a noun by dropping the *genitive* *singular* case ending.

4. What is the stem of **liber, librī, m.**? *libr-*   **puer, puerī, m.**? *puer-*

    magister, magistrī, m.? *magistr-*   **culter, cultrī, m.**? *cultr-*

5. Which word is not a noun? *et*   What kind of word is it? *It is a conjunction.*

6. A *conjunction* is a word that *joins* two or more words or phrases.

7. Can you list three other English conjunctions? _____

IV. Grammatica. Read the declension in the shaded box several times.

Nominative	**liber**	**librī**
Genitive	**librī**	**librōrum**
Dative	**librō**	**librīs**
Accusative	**librum**	**librōs**
Ablative	**librō**	**librīs**

This is a paradigm for 2nd declension masculine nouns that end in **–er**. It is very much like the normal pattern for 2nd declension masculine nouns *except* that the nominative singular ends in **-er** rather than in **–us**.

The stem of a Latin noun is found by dropping the ___genitive___ ___singular___ case ending.

Therefore, the stem of **liber, librī, m.** is _____*libr-*_____.

Notice that when a *consonant* comes before the **–er** ending in the nominative singular, the **e** is normally dropped in the stem. However, in a word like **puer, puerī, m.**, which has a *vowel* before the **–er** ending, the **e** remains in the stem.

puer	**puerī**
puerī	**puerōrum**
puerō	**puerīs**
puerum	**puerōs**
puerō	**puerīs**

V. Historia (*Famous Men of Rome*, Chapter XI, Parts I-III)

Ca. 400 BC Rome is again at war with the Veientians. They appoint a new dictator, Marcus Furius Camillus. Camillus digs a tunnel under the wall of the Veii and attacks the city through the floor of the temple. He defeats the city, but he is accused of keeping more than his share of the spoils. He leaves Rome, praying that some disaster might befall Rome so that he would be called back to save the city.

VI. Dēlēgāta

A. *Scrībe* the new Latin *verba* and their meanings.

	Latīnē		*Anglicē*
1.	culter, cultrī, m.	1.	knife
2.	et	2.	and
3.	liber, librī, m.	3.	book
4.	magister, magistrī, m.	4.	teacher
5.	puer, puerī, m.	5.	boy
6.	stomachus, -ī, m.	6.	stomach

B. Decline <u>liber, librī, m.</u> **(1) and** <u>puer, puerī, m.</u> **(2).**

1.		2.	
liber	librī	puer	puerī
librī	librōrum	puerī	puerōrum
librō	librīs	puerō	puerīs
librum	librōs	puerum	puerōs
librō	librīs	puerīs	puerīs

C. *Scrībe* the *dictum* and its translation.

Latīnē: ex librīs   *Anglicē*:   from the books of

D. Fill in the blanks.

1. The two irregular verbs we have had are ____sum, esse____ and___possum , posse___.

2. Adjectives must agree with the nouns they modify in __case__, __number__, and __gender__.

3. **Possum, posse** requires a complementary ____infinitive____.

4. Latin adjectives usually *follow* the noun they modify except for those that refer to

   ____size____ or _____number_____; these usually *precede* the noun.

E. *Scrībe* the meaning of these *verba* in the space provided. Then conjugate them in the tense indicated (P – present; F – future).

1. arō, arāre (P)_____*to plow*_____   2. lūceō, lūcēre (F)_____*to shine*_____

arō	*arāmus*	*lūcēbō*	*lūcēbimus*
arās	*arātis*	*lūcēbis*	*lūcēbitis*
arat	*arant*	*lūcēbit*	*lūcēbunt*

3. valeō, valēre (F) ___*to have power*___   4. volō, volāre (P)_____*to fly*_____

valēbō	*valēbimus*	*volō*	*volāmus*
valēbis	*valēbitis*	*volās*	*volātis*
valēbit	*valēbunt*	*volat*	*volant*

5. possum, posse (P) _*to be able*_   6. sum, esse (P)_____*to be*_____

possum	*possumus*	*sum*	*sumus*
potes	*potestis*	*es*	*estis*
potest	*possunt*	*est*	*sunt*

F. *Scrībe* the meaning of these *verba* in the space provided. Then decline them.

1. culter, cultrī, m._____*knife*_____   2. magister, magistrī, m._____*teacher*_____

culter	*cultrī*	*magister*	*magistrī*
cultrī	*cultrōrum*	*magistrī*	*magistrōrum*
cultrō	*cultrīs*	*magistrō*	*magistrīs*
cultrum	*cultrōs*	*magistrum*	*magistrōs*
cultrō	*cultrīs*	*magistrō*	*magistrīs*

G. Translate these sentences (from Latin to English or from English to Latin).

1. Culter est magnus.   *The knife is large.*

2. Furca est parva.   *The fork is small.*

3. Liber antīquus patet.   *The old book is open.*

4. Liber novus nōn patet.   *The new book is not open.*

5. Stomachus meus est magnus.   *My stomach is large.*

6. Stomachus tuus est parvus.   *Your stomach is small.*

7. Magister docet.   *The teacher teaches.*

8. Discipulī bene recitant.   *The students recite well.*

9. Puer et puella multum rīdent.   *The boy and girl laugh a lot.*

10. The girl is crying.   *Puella semper flet.*

11. The boy is always sorry.   *Puer semper miseret.*

12. Books often wander.   *Librī saepe errant.*

13. God never wanders.   *Deus numquam errat.*

14. Discipulī nunc timent.   *The students are afraid now.*

15. Disicipulī superābunt.   *The students will overcome.*

16. Magister cantat.   *The teacher sings.*

17. Magistra cantat.   *The teacher sings.*

18. Magistrī cantābunt.   *The teachers will sing.*

19. The boy is able to work.   *Puer potest labōrāre.*

20. The boys can work.   *Puerī labōrāre possunt.*

21. The teacher can sing well.   *Magistra bene cantāre potest.*

22. Many teachers can sing well.   *Multī magristrī possunt bene cantāre.*

23. The boy is thinking.   *Puer cōgitat.*

24. He will think well.   *Bene cōgitābit.*

25. We often recite.   *Saepe recitāmus.*

H. Misspelled *Verba*. Each of the following *verba Latīna* has either a missing letter or an extra letter. In either case, *scribe* the letter in the space to the left of the *verbum*. When you are finished, the letters should spell a Latin message when read column by column. *Scrībe* the hidden Latin message, and then translate it. (Hint: It is two sentences.)

Latin message: ___*Magistri boni bene docent. Pueri et puellae multum laborant.*___

Translation: ___*Good teachers teach well. Boys and girls work a lot.*___

M	SIGNU	O	HRA	A	TAURAUS
A	SEPE	C	STOMACCHUS	E	MAGISTERORUM
G	SANGCTUS	E	PRAMIUM	M	BELLU
I	DISICIPULUS	N	PONCULUM	U	PARM
S	MEUSS	T	LATTUS	L	TELLUM
T	TOTTUS	P	CAPPILLUS	T	BONUST
R	MURRUS	U	ANTIQUS	U	TUS
I	MULITUM	E	PUR	M	AMMO
B	AMBICUS	R	PATIA	L	HILC
O	NOUNC	I	IBII	A	SAECUNDUS
N	BENNE	E	CULTERORUM	B	HERA
I	INISULA	T	INRO	O	NOON
B	VIAB	P	OTIMUS	R	PARRVUS
E	LIBERORUM	U	NOVUUS	A	SAEMPER
N	AGUS	E	PRIMUSE	N	NUNMQUAM
E	ATERNUS	L	MALLE	T	ETT
D	EXEDDRIUM	L	BELUS		

I. Dērīvātī. Complete each sentence with an English *verbum* chosen from the following *verba*. The italicized *verbum* in the sentence should help you think of the Latin root.

puerile   library

1. A room or building with many *books* is called a ___*library*___. Latin root:___*liber, librī, m.*___

2. If a teenager acts like a little *boy*, he is being ___*puerile*___. Latin root:___*puer, puerī, m.*___

J. Historia. Review the history story, and fill in the blanks.

1. Whom does Rome appoint dictator in this story? ___*Marcus Furius Camillus is dictator.*___

2. How does he defeat the city of Veii?___*Camillus has his men dig a tunnel under the city wall and enters through a temple inside the city.*___

3. Of what do the Romans accuse him? ___*They accuse him of taking more than his share.*___

Disciplīna XIX – ūndēvīgintī   3rd DECLENSION (M / F)

I. Dictum

"Ego sum via et vēritās et vīta."
(Secundum Ioānnem 14:6a)

"I am the way and the truth and the life."
(John 14:6a)

II. Colloquium   *Latīnē*   *Anglicē*

	Latīnē	*Anglicē*
Marcus:	Nōnne sūdum est?	Isn't the weather nice?
Cornelia:	Ita. Sūdum est.	Yes, it's nice.

III. Verba

Latīnē	*Anglicē*	*Scrībe tōtum verbum Latīnum.*	*Dērīvātī*
frāter, frātris, m.	brother	*frāter, frātris, m.*	*fraternity*
māter, mātris, f.	mother	*māter, mātris, f.*	*maternal*
pater, patris, m.	father	*pater, patris, m.*	*paternal*
vēritās, vēritātis, f.	truth	*vēritās, vēritātis, f.*	*verify*
virtūs, virtūtis, f.	courage, virtue, manliness	*virtūs, virtūtis, f.*	*virtue*
lectus, -ī, m.	couch, bed	*lectus, -ī, m.*	
mendācium, -ī, n.	lie, falsehood	*mendācium, -ī, n.*	*mendacious*
nuntius, -ī, m.	messenger, message	*nuntius, -ī, m.*	*announce*
vallum, -ī, n.	rampart, wall	*vallum, -ī, n.*	*wall*

1. All of these *verba* are _____ *nouns* _____.

2. A declension can be identified by its ___ *genitive* ___ ___ *singular* ___ case ending.

3. This ending for 1st declension is___ *-ae* ___. 2nd declension? ___ *-ī* ___. 3rd declension? ___ *-is* ___.

4. The last four *verba* are from _____ *second* _____ declension.

5. The gender of each noun must be _____ *memorized* _____.

IV. Grammatica. Read the declension in the shaded box several times.

_____ *Nominative* _____	**pater**	**patrēs**
_____ *Genitive* _____	**patris**	**patrum**
_____ *Dative* _____	**patrī**	**patribus**
_____ *Accusative* _____	**patrem**	**patrēs**
_____ *Ablative* _____	**patre**	**patribus**

This is the declension of <u>a noun from 3rd declension</u>. The genitive singular ending in 3rd declension is always **–is**. When we learn 3rd declension nouns, we must *always* write out the full dictionary form, i.e., (***id est*** means *that is* in Latin) we cannot abbreviate the genitive singular form, because the stem is nearly always different from the nominative singular form.

There are masculine, feminine, and neuter nouns in 3rd declension. There is no easy way to tell the gender for most nouns, so again, we must memorize the gender of each noun. Masculine and feminine nouns in 3rd declension use the same endings. And remember: Adjectives and the nouns they modify must always agree in gender, number, and case. For example:

māter mea	my mother
pater meus	my father
frātrēs meī	my brothers
sorōrēs meae	my sisters

<u>Nōtā bene:</u> Noun dictionary entries are often shortened by listing only the genitive singular *ending* rather than the full genitive singular *form*. So **lectus, lectī, m.** would be written as **lectus, -ī, m.** and **vallum, vallī, n.** would become **vallum, -ī, n.** This seems confusing at first, but you can still see the stem of these nouns in the nominative singular forms **lectus** and **vallum**.

Nouns like **culter, cultrī, m.** and **māter, mātris, f.** will *not* be abbreviated, because their stems cannot be guessed from the nominative singular form.

V. Historia (*Famous Men of Rome*, Chapter XI, Parts III-VI)

390 BC The Gauls, led by Brennus, cross the Alps and attack the Romans. At the river Allia, Marcus Manlius cannot hold the Gauls back. The Romans retreat and hide in the hills, but some patricians, led by Marcus Manlius, lock themselves in the Capitol and send for Camillus to come and help. When Camillus arrives in Rome, he finds the Senate weighing gold to give to Brennus. Camillus says, "We Romans defend our country, not with gold, but with steel," and he drives the Gauls from the city. The Romans call him the *Father of His Country.*

VI. Dēlēgāta

A. *Scrībe* the new Latin *verba* and their meanings.

	Latīnē		*Anglicē*
1.	frāter, frātris, m	1.	brother
2.	māter, matris, f.	2.	mother
3.	pater, patris, m.	3.	father
4.	vēritās, vēritātis, f.	4.	truth
5.	virtūs, virtūtis, f.	5.	courage, virtue, manliness
6.	lectus, -ī, m.	6.	bed, couch
7.	mendācium, -ī, n.	7.	lie, falsehood
8.	nuntius, -ī, m.	8.	messenger; message
9.	vallum, -ī, n.	9.	wall, rampart

B. *Scrībe* the declension of <u>pater, patris, m.</u> two times.

1.			2.		
pater	patrēs		pater	patrēs
patris	patrum		patris	patrum
patrī	patribus		patrī	patribus
patrem	patrēs		patrem	patrēs
patre	patribus		patre	patribus

C. *Scrībe* the *dictum* and its translation.

Latīnē: Ego sum via et vēritās et vīta.

Anglicē: I am the way and the truth and the life.

D. Translate these *verba* and phrases.

1. terra incognita   unknown land   2. mea culpa   my fault

3. semper fidēlis ____always faithful____   5. duodēvīgintī____eighteen____

4. ex librīs ____from the books of____   6. ūndēvīgintī ____nineteen____

7. Quot annōs nātus(a) es? ____How old are you?____

E. *Scrībe* the Latin word for these *verba* in the space provided. Then conjugate them in the tense indicated (P – present; F – future).

1. to stand (P)____stō, stāre____   2. to move (F)____moveō, movēre____

stō	stāmus	movēbō	movēbimus
stās	stātis	movēbis	movēbitis
stat	stant	movēbit	movēbunt

F. *Scrībe* the correct Latin form of these *verba* in the blank. Then decline them.

1. couch____lectus, -ī, m.____   2. gift____dōnum, -ī, n.____

lectus	lectī	dōnum	dona
lectī	lectōrum	donī	donōrum
lectō	lectīs	donō	donīs
lectum	lectōs	donum	dōna
lectō	lectīs	dōnō	dōnīs

3. eagle____aquila, -ae, f.____   4. daughter____fīlia, -ae, f.____

aquila	aquilae	fīlia	fīliae
aquilae	aquilārum	fīliae	fīliārum
aquilae	aquilīs	fīliae	fīliābus
aquilam	aquilās	fīliam	fīliās
aquilā	aquilīs	fīliā	fīliābus

G. Translate these sentences (from Latin to English or from English to Latin).

1. Māter labōrat.   _Mother is working._

2. Pater labōrat.   _Father is working._

3. Māter et pater labōrant.   _Mother and father work._

4. Pater est agricola.   _Father is a farmer._

5. Frāter est nuntius.   _Brother is a messenger._

6. Lectus est lātus.   _The couch is wide._

7. Vallum est lātum et altum.   _The rampart is wide and high._

8. Vēritās est bona.   _Truth is good._

9. Mendācia sunt mala.   _Lies are bad._

10. Gaudium est virtūs.   _Joy is a virtue._

11. Virtūs tua est magna.   _Your courage is great._

12. The mother can sing.   _Māter potest cantāre._

13. She sings well.   _Bene cantat._

14. She sings often.   _Saepe cantat._

15. My father is sailing.   _Pater meus nāvigat._

16. Your father will sail.   _Pater tuus nāvigābit._

17. Iēsus est via et vēritās et vīta.   _Jeus is the way and the truth and the life._

18. The messenger is hurrying.   _Nuntius festinat._

19. Many messengers are hurrying.   _Multī nuntiī festinant._

20. My mother is a queen.   _Mater mea est rēgīna._

21. My mother is not a farmer.   _Mater mea nōn est agricola._

22. The women do not stand.   _Fēminae nōn stant._

H. *Verbum* **Search.** Each of the *verba* listed below can be found in this grid. When read from left to right, the unused letters will tell you where the sign for each declension is. The sign for each declension can be found in... (*Anglicē*) _____ *THE GENITIVE SINGULAR* ____.

V	T	S	I	R	T	A	R	F	L	N
E	M	U	L	L	A	V	E	O	H	O
R	A	U	E	E	I	G	T	E	C	I
I	R	N	I	R	C	I	A	A	S	S
T	C	I	T	C	P	T	M	T	U	N
A	U	U	P	A	A	I	U	I	I	E
T	S	I	C	A	L	D	T	S	L	L
I	V	E	S	L	T	N	N	I	N	C
S	N	G	U	U	U	E	L	E	A	E
A	R	S	U	N	N	E	R	B	M	D

FRATRIS
MATER
PATER
VERITATIS
VIRTUS
LECTUS
NUNTIUS
MENDACIUM
VALLUM
BRENNUS
MARCUS
MANLIUS
CAPITOL
CAMILLUS
DECLENSION

I. Dērīvātī. Complete each sentence with an English *verbum* chosen from the following *verba*. The italicized *verbum* in the sentence should help you think of the Latin root.

paternal   announce   fraternity   maternal

1. A *mother's* desire to care for a child is called _____ *maternal* _____ instinct.

   Latin root: _____ *māter, mātris, f.* _____

2. Members of a ____ *fraternity* ____ are called *brothers*. Latin root: _____ *frāter, frātris, m.* ____

3. To ____ *announce* ____ is to send out or deliver a *message*. Latin root: ____ *nuntius, -ī, m.* ___

4. Your *father's* parents are your _____ *paternal* _____ grandparents.

   Latin root: _____ *pater, patris, m.* _____

J. Historia. Review the history story, and fill in the blanks.

1. Who is the leader of the Gauls at this time? _____ *Brennus leads the Gauls.*

2. What Roman leader is unable to defeat the Gauls? _____ *Marcus Manlius*

3. Where does he lead the patricians for a last defense? _____ *to the Capitoline Hill*

4. Whom do the Romans call upon in this desperate hour? _____ *Marcus Furius Camillus*

5. What do the Romans end up calling Camillus? _____ *"Pater Patriae" (father of his country)*

Disciplīna XX – vīgintī   3ʳᵈ DECLENSION (M / F)

I. Dictum

"Ego sum pāstor bonus."
(Secundum Ioannem 10:11a)

I am the good shepherd.
(John 10:11a)

II. Colloquium   *Latīnē*   *Anglicē*

	Latīnē	*Anglicē*
Claudia:	Pluit.	It's raining.
Iūlius:	Ita, et fulgurat.	Yes, and there's lightning.
Claudia:	Tonat!	It's thundering!

III. Verba

Latīnē	*Anglicē*	*Scrībe tōtum verbum Latīnum.*	*Dērīvātī*
Caesar, Caesaris, m.	Caesar	Caesar, Caesaris, m.	Caesar salad
homō, hominis, m.	person, man, human being	homō, hominis, m.	homo sapiens
imperātor, imperātōris, m.	commander, general	imperātor, imperātōris, m.	imperious
legiō, legiōnis, f.	legion	legiō, legiōnis, f.	legion
lēx, lēgis, f.	law	lēx, lēgis, f.	legal
mīles, mīlitis, m.	soldier	mīles, mīlitis, m.	military
pāstor, pāstōris, m.	shepherd	pastor, pastōris, m.	pastor
rēx, rēgis, m.	king	rēx, rēgis, m.	regal
soror, sorōris, f.	sister	soror, sorōris, f.	sorority

1. All of these *verba* are _____nouns_____ from _____3rd_____ declension.

2. What gender have we not yet seen in 3ʳᵈ declension? _____We've not seen neuter._____

3. What is the genitive singular ending for each declension? 1ˢᵗ __-ae__ ; 2ⁿᵈ __-ī__ ; 3ʳᵈ __-is__ .

4. Which declension has no neuter nouns? _____1ˢᵗ declension has no neuter nouns._____

IV. Grammatica. Read the paradigm in the shaded box, and <u>memorize it</u>.

Nominative	(varies)	-ēs
Genitive	-is	-um
Dative	-ī	-ibus
Accusative	-em	-ēs
Ablative	-e	-ibus

This paradigm shows the <u>case endings for masculine and feminine nouns from 3rd declension</u>. The dictionary form of a noun always gives the first two forms of the declension.

Remember to find the stem of a noun by dropping the <u>genitive</u> <u>singular</u> case ending.

When we say the case endings for 3rd declension, we will say "varies" for the nominative singular (see gray box above), because there is no pattern or predictable ending for this case. It *varies* or changes from word to word.

rēx	rēg<u>ēs</u>
rēg<u>is</u>	rēg<u>um</u>
rēg<u>ī</u>	rēg<u>ibus</u>
rēg<u>em</u>	rēg<u>ēs</u>
rēg<u>e</u>	rēg<u>ibus</u>

V. Historia (*Famous Men of Rome*, Chapter XII)

Titus Manlius, a descendant of Marcus Manlius, defeats a giant from Gaul. He takes the giant's twisted gold collar, called a *torques*, and is given the nickname *Torquatus*. Later Torquatus leads the Roman army against some Latins to the south. He gives orders not to attack the Latins, but his son disobeys. Torquatus must have his son killed for disobeying orders.

VI. Dēlēgāta

A. *Scrībe* the new Latin *verba* and their meanings.

	Latīnē		*Anglicē*
1.	Caesar, Caesaris, m.	1.	Caesar
2.	homō, hominis, m.	2.	person, man, human being
3.	imperātor, imperātōris, m.	3.	commander, general
4.	legiō, legiōnis, f.	4.	legion
5.	lēx, lēgis, f.	5.	law
6.	mīles, mīlitis, m.	6.	soldier
7.	pastor, pastōris, m.	7.	shepherd
8.	rēx, rēgis, m.	8.	king
9.	soror, sorōris, f.	9.	sister

B. *Scrībe* the 3rd declension case endings for masculine and feminine nouns three times.

1. (varies)	-ēs	2. (varies)	-ēs	3. (varies)	-ēs
-is	-um	-is	-um	-is	-um
-ī	-ibus	-ī	-ibus	-ī	-ibus
-em	-ēs	-em	-ēs	-em	-ēs
-e	-ibus	-e	-ibus	-e	-ibus

C. *Scrībe* the *dictum* and its translation.

Latīnē: Ego sum pastor bonus.

Anglicē: I am the good shepherd.

D. Translate these *verba* and phrases.

1. before the war   antebellum   2. vīgintī   twenty

3. Pluit. _____*It is raining.*_____   5. Excuse me._____*Ignōsce mihi.*_____

4. nineteen _____*ūndēvīgintī*_____   6. Sōl lūcet._____*The sun is shining.*_____

7. Repetitiō māter memoriae. _____*Repetition is the mother of memory.*_____

E. *Scrībe* the meaning of these *verba* in the space provided. **Then decline them.**

1. soror, sorōris, f.____*sister*____   2. frāter, frātris, m.____*brother*____

soror	*sorōrēs*	*frāter*	*frātrēs*
sorōris	*sorōrum*	*frātris*	*frātrum*
sorōrī	*sorōribus*	*frātrī*	*frātribus*
sorōrem	*sorōrēs*	*frātrem*	*frātrēs*
sorōre	*sorōribus*	*frātre*	*frātribus*

3. lēx, lēgis, f.____*law*____   4. homō, hominis, m.____*person, man*____

lēx	*lēgēs*	*homō*	*hominēs*
lēgis	*lēgum*	*hominis*	*hominum*
lēgī	*lēgibus*	*hominī*	*hominibus*
lēgem	*lēgēs*	*hominem*	*hominēs*
lēge	*lēgibus*	*homine*	*hominibus*

F. Translate these sentences (from Latin to English or from English to Latin).

1. Caesar imperat et superābit. _____*Caesar commands and will overcome.*_____

2. Rēx numquam timet. _____*The king never fears.*_____

3. Rēx bene iūdicābit. _____*The king will judge well.*_____

4. Soror bene cantāre potest. _____*Sister can sing well.*_____

5. Pāstor cantāre nōn potest. _____*The shepherd cannot sing.*_____

6. Mīlitēs multum pugnant. _____*The soldiers fight a lot.*_____

7. Legiōnēs pugnābunt.   _The legions will fight._

8. Lēx est semper bona.   _The law is always good._

9. Lēx valet et dūrābit.   _The law is strong and will remain._

10. The legions are large.   _Legiōnēs sunt magnae._

11. They are not small.   _Nōn sunt parvae._

12. The kings are sitting.   _Rēgēs sedent._

13. The kings will stand.   _Rēgēs stabunt._

14. The kings will not fight.   _Rēgēs nōn pugnābunt._

15. Jesus is the good Shepherd.   _Iēsus est pastor bonus._

16. He is your friend.   _Amīcus tuus est._

17. The great commander is staying.   _Magnus imperātor manet._

18. The new commander will not move.   _Novus imperātor nōn movēbit._

19. The sisters and brothers are friends.   _Sorōrēs et frātrēs sunt amīcī_

G. Crossword Puzzle Note: All nouns are in the nominative case (singular or plural).

```
¹H          ²P  L  U  I  ³T
O                         O
⁴M  I  L  I  T  E  ⁵S     N
O                   O     A
        ⁶I  M  ⁷P  E  R  A  T  O  ⁸R
            A  ■  O            E
   ⁹C  A  E  S  A  R      ¹⁰L  E  X
            T
¹¹L  E  G  I  O  N  E  S
            R
```

RECTE

2. It's raining.
4. soldiers
6. commander
9. Julius _____
10. law
11. legions

DEORSUM

1. man
3. It's thundering.
5. sister
7. shepherd
8. king

117

H. Dērīvātī. Complete each sentence with an English *verbum* chosen from the following *verba*. The italicized *verbum* in the sentence should help you think of the Latin root.

military   legal   sorority   regal   pastor

1. The _____ *pastor* _____ of a church is like a *shepherd* to the people.

    Latin root:_____ *pastor, pastōris, m.* _____

2. Members of a _____ *sorority* _____ are called *sisters*.

    Latin root:_____ *soror, sorōris, f.* _____

3. It is not _____ *legal* _____ to break the *law*. Latin root:_____ *lēx, lēgis, f.* _____

4. A *king's* robe and crown are _____ *regal* _____. Latin root:_____ *rēx, rēgis, f.* _____

5. *Soldiers* often practice _____ *military* _____ maneuvers.

    Latin root:_____ *mīles, mīlitis, m.* _____

I. Historia. Review the history story, and fill in the blanks.

1. What nickname is given to Titus Manlius?_____ *He is nicknamed "Torquatus".* _____

2. Why is he given this nickname?_____ *He kills a giant Gaul in single combat and* _____

    _____ *takes the giant's golden collar (torques) as a trophy.* _____

3. Why must he have his son killed?_____ *because his son disobeyed orders* _____

Disciplīna XXI – vīgintī ūnus   3rd DECLENSION NEUTER

I. Dictum

"Fīat lūx."
(Liber Genesis 1:3)

"Let there be light."
(Genesis 1:3)

II. Colloquium   *Latīnē*   *Anglicē*

	Latīnē	*Anglicē*
Sextus:	Lūdō lūdāmus.	Let's play a game.
Antonia:	Bene. Quī lūdus?	Okay. Which game?
Sextus:	Tabula aut Mendāx	Tabula or Mendax

III. Verba

Latīnē	*Anglicē*	*Scrībe tōtum verbum Latīnum.*	*Dērīvātī*
bōs, bovis, m./f.	ox, cow	*bōs, bovis, m./f.*	*bovine*
crux, crucis, f.	cross	*crux, crucis, f.*	*crucifix*
lūx, lūcis, f.	light	*lūx, lūcis, f.*	*translucent*
pēs, pedis, m.	foot	*pēs, pedis, m.*	*pedal*
vōx, vōcis, f.	voice	*vōx, vōcis, f.*	*vocal*
corpus, corporis, n.	body	*corpus, corporis, n.*	*corporal*
flūmen, flūminis, n.	river	*flūmen, flūminis, n.*	*flume*
nōmen, nōminis, n.	name	*nōmen, nōminis, n.*	*name*
tempus, temporis, n.	time	*tempus, temporis, n.*	*temporary*

1. All of these *verba* are ___*nouns*___ from ___*3rd*___ declension.

2. What genders are found in each declension? 1st ___*m, f*___ ; 2nd ___*m, f, n*___ ; 3rd ___*m, f, n*___ .

3. What is the genitive singular ending for each declension? 1st ___*-ae*___ ; 2nd ___*-ī*___ ; 3rd ___*-is*___ .

4. Which declension has only a few masculine nouns? ___*1st declension*___

5. To find the stem of a noun, drop the ___*genitive*___ ___*singular*___ case ending.

IV. Grammatica. Read the declension in the shaded box several times.

_____ *Nominative* _____	**flūmen**	**flūmina**
_____ *Genitive* _____	**flūminis**	**flūminum**
_____ *Dative* _____	**flūminī**	**flūminibus**
_____ *Accusative* _____	**flūmen**	**flūmina**
_____ *Ablative* _____	**flūmine**	**flūminibus**

This declension shows a <u>neuter noun from 3rd declension</u>. The case endings are similar to those of masculine and feminine nouns from 3rd declension *except*, as with neuter nouns in

2nd declension, the _____ *nominative* _____ is the same as the _____ *accusative* _____, *and*

the _____ *nominative* _____ and the _____ *accusative* _____ plural end in __ *-a* __.

There are three good reasons to learn the genitive singular for every 3rd declension noun:

1. You'll always know to which _____ *declension* _____ the noun belongs.

2. You'll know how to spell the _____ *stem* _____ of the noun.

3. Most English _____ *derivatives* _____ of Latin nouns are derived from the stem of the noun.

V. Historia (*Famous Men of Rome*, Chapter XIII, Part I)

Appius Claudius is a censor, in charge of the census, taxes, and public works. He builds aqueducts (some are still in use) and the Appian Way, parts of which still exist. During his time, the Greeks in the city of Tarentum attack five Roman ships. Rome sends Lucius Posthumius to negotiate with the Greeks, but they laugh at his poor pronunciation and his Roman toga. Rome declares war on the Greeks.

VI. Dēlēgāta

A. *Scrībe* the new Latin *verba* and their meanings.

	Latīnē		*Anglicē*
1.	bōs, bovis, m./f.	1.	ox, cow
2.	crux, crucis, f.	2.	cross
3.	lūx, lūcis, f.	3.	light
4.	pēs, pedis, m.	4.	foot
5.	vox, vōcis, f.	5.	voice
6.	corpus, corporis, n.	6.	body
7.	flūmen, flūminis, n.	7.	river
8.	nōmen, nōminis, n.	8.	name
9.	tempus, temporis, n.	9.	time

B. *Scrībe* the declension of <u>flūmen, flūminis, n.</u> two times.

1.			2.	
flūmen	flūmina		flūmen	flūmina
flūminis	flūminum		flūminis	flūminum
flūminī	flūminibus		flūminī	flūminibus
flūmen	flūmina		flūmen	flūmina
flūmine	flūminibus		flūmine	flūminibus

C. *Scrībe* the *dictum* and its translation.

Latīnē: Fīat lūx.   *Anglicē*:   Let there be light.

D. Fill in the blanks.

1. To find the stem of a Latin _____ verb _____, drop the **–re** of the _____ infinitive _____

2. To find the _____ stem _____ of a Latin noun, drop the _____ genitive _____ singular case ending.

3. There are no *verba* for ___*article*___ ___*adjectives*___ or ___*helping*___ ___*verbs*___ in Latin.

4. All neuter Latin nouns end in ___*-a*___ in the nominative and accusative plural.

5. List the cases of Latin nouns: *nominative, genitive, dative, accusative, ablative, vocative*

E. *Scribe* **the meaning of these *verba* in the space provided. Then decline them.**

1. lūx, lūcis, f. ___*light*___

lūx	*lūcēs*
lūcis	*lūcum*
lūcī	*lūcibus*
lūcem	*lūcēs*
lūce	*lūcibus*

2. aqua, -ae, f. ___*water*___

aqua	*aquae*
aquae	*aquārum*
aquae	*aquīs*
aquam	*aquās*
aquā	*aquīs*

3. pēs, pedis, m. ___*foot*___

pēs	*pedēs*
pedis	*pedum*
pedī	*pedibus*
pedem	*pedēs*
pede	*pedibus*

4. taurus, -ī, m. ___*bull*___

taurus	*taurī*
taurī	*taurōrum*
taurō	*taurīs*
taurum	*taurōs*
taurō	*taurīs*

5. bōs, bovis, m./f. ___*ox, cow*___

bōs	*bovēs*
bovis	*bovum*
bovī	*bovibus*
bovem	*bovēs*
bove	*bovibus*

6. dōnum, -ī, n. ___*gift*___

dōnum	*dōna*
dōnī	*dōnōrum*
dōnō	*dōnīs*
dōnum	*dōna*
dōnō	*dōnīs*

F. Translate these sentences (from Latin to English or from English to Latin).

1. Pedēs ambulant.   _Feet are walking._

2. Vōx cantat.   _A voice sings._

3. Vōcēs cantant.   _Voices are singing._

4. Vōcēs nunc silent.   _The voices are now silent._

5. Bōs ambulat.   _An ox walks._

6. Bovēs ambulābunt.   _The oxen will walk._

7. Bovēs cēnāre possunt.   _Oxen can eat._

8. Flūmen est lātum.   _The river is wide._

9. Flūmina sunt lāta.   _The rivers are wide._

10. Flūmina nōn sunt angusta.   _The rivers are not narrow._

11. Sisters are girls.   _Sorōrēs sunt puellae._

12. Brothers are boys.   _Frātrēs sunt puerī._

13. My father is a king.   _Pater meus est rēx._

14. My mother is a queen.   _Māter mea est rēgīna._

15. The general will stand.   _Imperātor stabit._

16. A bad general sits a lot.   _Imperātor malus multum sedēt._

17. Christ is the light.   _Christus est lūx._

18. The church is a body.   _Ecclēsia est corpus._

19. Nōmen tuum est novum.   _Your name is new._

20. Multa nōmina sunt antīqua.   _Many names are old._

21. Your voice and my voice sing well.   _Vox tua et vox mea bene cantant._

22. Homō bonus ōrāt et labōrat.   _A good person prays and works._

G. Anagrams. Unscramble the letters in each row to form one of the *verba* from this *disciplīna*. Only the nominative is scrambled, but *scrībe* both the nominative and the genitive singular of each noun. Rearrange the shaded letters to spell something (*Anglicē*) that God made that split into parts. (Hint: See Genesis 2:10.)

XLU	L U X	L U C I S
OXV	V O X	V O C I S
PSE	P E S	P E D I S
OSB	B O S	B O V I S
CXRU	C R U X	C R U C I S
ENMNO	N O M E N	N O M I N I S
MLUEFN	F L U M E N	F L U M I N I S
MPUTSE	T E M P U S	T E M P O R I S
PCROSU	C O R P U S	C O R P O R I S

Solution: G A R D E N   O F   E D E N

H. Dērīvātī. Complete each sentence with an English *verbum* chosen from the following *verba*. The italicized *verbum* in the sentence should help you think of the Latin root.

corporal   temporary   pedal   crucifixion   translucent

1. You push a _____*pedal*_____ with your foot. Latin root:_____*pēs, pedis, m.*_____

2. *Light* shines through (across) _____*translucent*_____ things. Latin root:_____*lūx, lūcis, f.*_____

3. Jesus' _____*crucifixion*_____ was death on a *cross*. Latin root:_____*crux, crūcis, f.*_____

4. A _____*temporary*_____ assignment lasts for only a short *time*. Latin root:_____*tempus, temporis, n.*_____

5. _____*Corporal*_____ punishment is applied to the *body*. Latin root:_____*corpus, corporis, n.*_____

I. Historia. Review the history story, and fill in the blanks.

1. Of what is the Roman *censor* in charge? _____*the taxes, the census, and public works*_____

2. Whom does Rome send to negotiate with the Greek city of Tarentum? _____*Lucius Posthumius*_____

3. Why does Rome declare war on the Greeks? _____*because of the Greeks' insolent reply.*_____

Disciplīna XXII – vīgintī duo   PARTĒS CORPORIS
(Parts of the Body)

I. Dictum

Requiēscat in pāce. (abbreviation: _R.I.P._)   _May he (she, it) rest in peace._

II. Colloquium   *Latīnē*   *Anglicē*

Aemīlia:	Eāmus ad scholam!	Let's go to school!
Catō:	Bene! Eāmus!	Great! Let's go!

III. Verba

Latīnē	*Anglicē*	*Scrībe tōtum verbum Latīnum.*	*Dērīvātī*
auris, auris, f.	ear	_auris, auris, f._	_aural_
caput, capitis, n.	head	_caput, capitis, n._	_capitol_
crūs, crūris, n.	leg	_crūs, crūris, n._	
dēns, dentis, m.	tooth	_dēns, dentis, m._	_dental_
ōs, ōris, n.	mouth	_ōs, ōris, n._	_oral_
pars, partis, f.	part	_pars, partis, f._	_partition_
pax, pācis, f.	peace	_pax, pācis, f._	_pacify_
manus, manūs, f.	hand	_manus, manūs, f._	_manual_
nāsus, -ī, m.	nose	_nāsus, -ī, m._	_nasal_

1. All except two of the *verba nova* are from ___3rd___ declension.

2. We know **nāsus, -ī, m.** is from ___2nd___ declension, because the genitive singular is ___-ī___.

3. **Manus, manūs, f.** is from ___4th___ declension.

4. The genitive singular case ending for 4th declension is ___-ūs___.

5. In 3rd declension, ___masculine___ and ___feminine___ nouns have the same endings.

6. There are ___5___ declensions of Latin nouns.

IV. Grammatica. Read the paradigm in the shaded box, and <u>memorize it</u>.

Case	Sing.	Plur.
Nominative	(varies)	-a
Genitiive	-is	-um
Dative	-ī	-ibus
Accusative	(varies)	-a
Ablative	-e	-ibus

This paradigm shows the case endings for <u>neuter nouns from 3rd declension</u>. They are similar to the case endings for masculine and feminine nouns of 3rd declension *except:*

1. The _____*nominative*_____ case is the same as the ___*accusative*___ case.

2. The _____*nominative*_____ and ____*accusative*____ plural end in __*-a*__.

Find the stem by dropping the ____*genitive*____ ____*singular*____ ending _-is_.

Then copy the nominative singular form, add the endings to the stem, and you're all done!

Example:

ōs	ōr<u>a</u>
ōr<u>is</u>	ōr<u>um</u>
ōr<u>ī</u>	ōr<u>ibus</u>
ōs	ōr<u>a</u>
ōr<u>e</u>	ōr<u>ibus</u>

Note: **Manus, manūs, f.** belongs to 4th declension, which you have not learned yet. **Auris, auris, f.; dēns, dentis, m.;** and **pars, partis, f.** belong to a special group of 3rd declension nouns that you will learn about in *Disciplīna* XXIII.

V. Historia (*Famous Men of Rome*, Chapter XIII, Part II)

The Tarentines, Greeks of Tarentum, send for Pyrrhus to lead them in the war against Rome. Pyrrhus brings elephants to Italy, but he doesn't use them until he has lost many men. The Romans retreat, but the Greeks do not have enough men left to attack again. Today we call a victory a *Pyrrhic victory* when it is so costly that the winner would rather not have fought at all.

VI. Dēlēgāta

A. *Scrībe* the new Latin *verba* and their meanings.

	Latīnē		*Anglicē*
1.	auris, auris, f.	1.	ear
2.	caput, capitis, n.	2.	head
3.	crūs, crūris, n.	3.	leg
4.	dēns, dentis, m.	4.	tooth
5.	ōs, ōris, n.	5.	mouth
6.	pars, partis, f.	6.	part
7.	pax, pācis, f.	7.	peace
8.	manus, manūs, f.	8.	hand
9.	nāsus, -ī, m.	9.	nose

B. *Scrībe* the case endings for 3rd declension neuter nouns three times.

1. varies	-a	2. varies	-a	3. varies	-a
-is	-um	-is	-um	-is	-um
-ī	-ibus	-ī	-ibus	-ī	-ibus
varies	-a	varies	-a	varies	-a
-e	-ibus	-e	-ibus	-e	-ibus

C. *Scrībe* the *dictum* and its translation.

Latīnē: Requiescat in pāce.   *Anglicē*: Rest in peace.

D. Fill in the blanks.

1. Translate **rīdēmus** three ways: a. We are laughing.

    b. We laugh.   c. We do laugh.

2. Helping verbs for future tense are will and shall.

3. The subject of 1ˢᵗ- and 2ⁿᵈ-person verbs is _always_ the ___pronoun___ built into them.

4. <u>All</u> neuter Latin nouns end in ___-a___ in the nominative and accusative plural.

5. The subject of a 3ʳᵈ-person verb can be ___he__ , ___she__ , _____it_____ , or ___they___ OR

   a subject noun that agrees with the ___verb___ in ___person___ and in ___number___ .

E. _Scrībe_ the meaning of these _verba_ in the space provided. Then decline them.

1. flūmen, flūminis, n._____river_____

flūmen	flūmina
flūminis	flūminum
flūminī	flūminibus
flūmen	flūmina
flūmine	flūminibus

2. tempus, temporis, n._____time_____

tempus	tempora
temporis	temporum
temporī	temporibus
tempus	tempora
tempore	temporibus

3. corpus, corporis, n._____body_____

corpus	corpora
corporis	corporum
corporī	corporibus
corpus	corpora
corpore	corporibus

4. homō, hominis, m._____person, man_____

homō	hominēs
hominis	hominum
hominī	hominibus
hominem	hominēs
homine	hominibus

5. nōmen, nōminis, n._____name_____

nōmen	nōmina
nōminis	nōminum
nōminī	nōminibus
nōmen	nōmina
nōmine	nōminibus

6. virtūs, virtūtis, f._____courage_____

virtūs	virtūtēs
virtūtis	virtūtum
virtūtī	virtūtibus
virtūtem	virtūtēs
virtūte	virtūtibus

F. Translate these sentences (from Latin to English or from English to Latin).

1. Manus labōrat.   *The hand works.*

2. Caput cōgitat.   *The head thinks.*

3. Ōs ōrat.   *The mouth prays.*

4. Pax est bona.   *Peace is good*

5. Vīta est bona.   *Life is good.*

6. Prīma pars est lāta.   *The first part is wide.*

7. Secunda pars est angusta.   *The second part is narrow.*

8. My brother is my friend.   *Frāter meus est amīcus meus.*

9. Christ is my best friend.   *Christus est amīcus meus optimus.*

10. The girls work well.   *Puellae bene labōrant.*

11. The boys will work well.   *Puerī bene labōrābunt.*

12. We shall sing now.   *Nunc cantābimus.*

13. You will sing now.   *Nunc cantābis.*

14. Ōs meum est magnum.   *My mouth is large.*

15. Dentēs meī sunt parvī.   *My teeth are small.*

16. Aurēs meae sunt bellae.   *My ears are pretty.*

17. Your nose is small.   *Nāsus tuus est parvus.*

18. Your voice is pretty.   *Vox tua est bella.*

19. My legs are strong.   *Crūra mea valent.*

20. My mouth is not silent.   *Ōs meum nōn silet.*

21. Corpus meum nōn est magnum. *My body is not large.*

22. Christ speaks: "I am the light." *Christus ōrat: "Sum lūx."*

G. *Scrībe* **the parts of the body indicated in these pictures.**

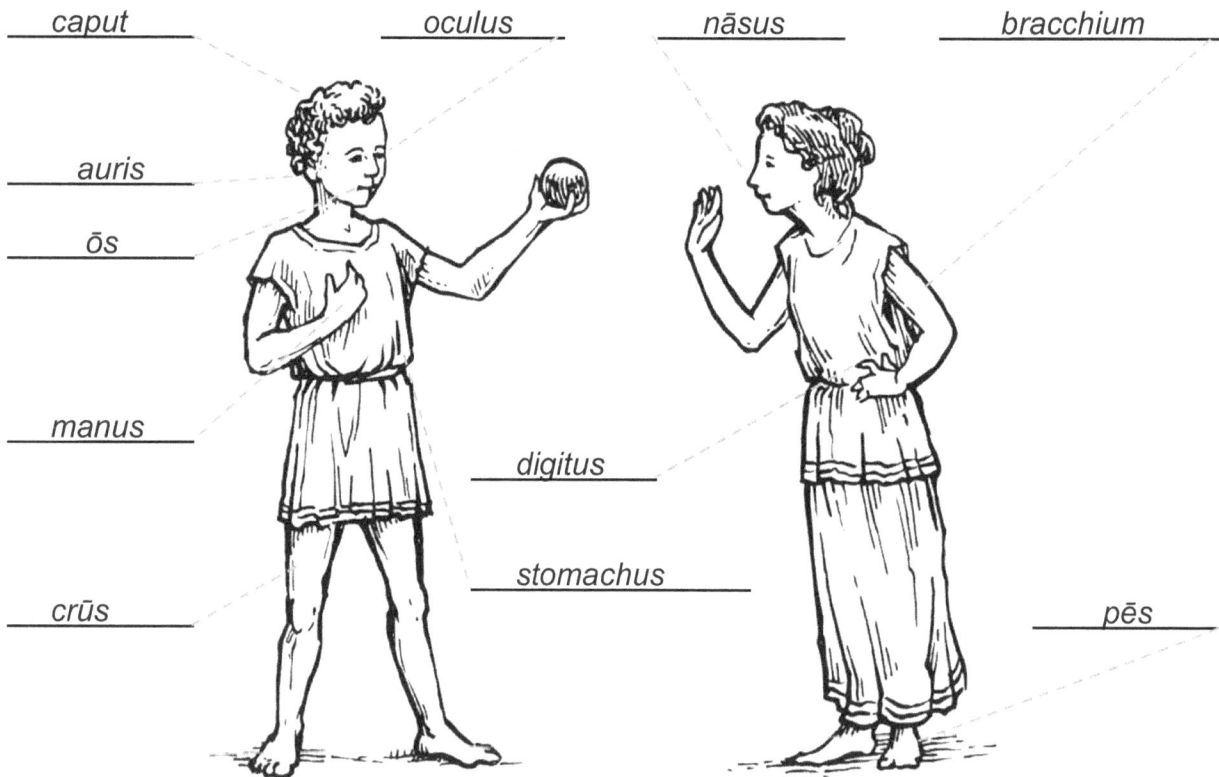

<u> caput </u>   <u> oculus </u>   <u> nāsus </u>   bracchium

<u> auris </u>

<u> ōs </u>

<u> manus </u>

         <u> digitus </u>

         <u> stomachus </u>

<u> crūs </u>   <u> pēs </u>

H. Dērīvātī. Complete each sentence with an English *verbum* chosen from the following *verba*. The italicized *verbum* in the sentence should help you think of the Latin root.

      dental manual nasal oral pacify

1. <u> Dental </u> floss is for the *teeth*. Latin root:<u> dēns, dentis, m. </u>

2. <u> Nasal </u> spray is for the *nose*. Latin root:<u> nāsus, -ī, m. </u>

3. To <u> pacify </u> is to bring *peace*. Latin root:<u> pax, pācis, f. </u>

4. An <u> oral </u> thermometer goes in the *mouth*. Latin root:<u> ōs, ōris, n. </u>

5. <u> Manual </u> labor is done by *hand*. Latin root:<u> manus, manūs, f. </u>

I. Historia. Review the history story, and fill in the blanks.

1. Whom do the Greeks recruit to lead the war against Rome?<u> Pyrrhus </u>

2. What is a *Pyrrhic victory*?<u> A Pyrrhic victory wins the battle but loses the war. </u>

Disciplīna XXIII – vīgintī trēs   ANIMĀLIA

(Animals)

I. Dictum

Cavē canem.   _Beware [of] the dog._

II. Colloquium   _Latīnē_   _Anglicē_

Catō:	Īmus ad scholam.	We're going to school.
Māter:	Bene sit vōbīs!	Have fun!

III. Verba

Latīnē	_Anglicē_	_Scrībe tōtum verbum Latīnum._	_Dērīvātī_
avis, avis, f.	bird	_avis, avis, f._	_aviary_
canis, canis, m./f.	dog	_canis, canis, m./f._	_canine_
collis, collis, m.	hill	_collis, collis, m._	
fēles, fēlis, f.	cat	_fēles, fēlis, f._	_feline_
hostis, hostis, m./f.	enemy	_hostis, hostis, m./f._	_hostile_
ignis, ignis, m.	fire	_ignis, ignis, m._	_ignite_
mors, mortis, f.	death	_mors, mortis, f._	_mortal_
nāvis, nāvis, f.	ship	_nāvis, nāvis, f._	_navy_
serpēns, serpentis, m./f.	snake	_serpēns, serpentis, m./f._	_serpent_

1. All of the _verba_ are from _____3rd_____ declension.

2. What do you notice about some of the _verba_?

3. What genders are included in each declension? 1st? _m./f._   2nd? _m./n._   3rd? _m./f./n._

4. The _____nominative_____ case is used for the subject of a sentence.

5. What noun sometimes has **–ābus** for its dative and ablative plural ending? _fīlia, -ae, f._

IV. Grammatica. Read the declension in the shaded box several times.

_____ Nominative _____	**fēles**	**fēlēs**
_____ Genitive _____	**fēlis**	**fēlium**
_____ Dative _____	**fēlī**	**fēlibus**
_____ Accusative _____	**fēlem**	**fēlīs**
_____ Ablative _____	**fēle**	**fēlibus**

Some 3rd declension nouns follow a _slightly_ different pattern from the usual 3rd declension. These nouns are called 3rd declension i-stem nouns. What two differences can you see in the declension of **fēles** above?

These i-stem nouns are not very different from regular 3rd declension nouns and it will not be hard to learn their endings. The real challenge is knowing which 3rd declension nouns are i-stems and which are not! How can you tell them apart? A 3rd declension noun is an i-stem if it fits into one of the two following groups:

1. 3rd declension masculine or feminine nouns whose nominative and genitive singular have two syllables, _and_ whose nominatives end in -_is, -es,_ or -_ēs_, e.g., **avis, avis, f.; fēles, fēlis, f.** There is one big exception: according to the rules, **canis, canis, m./f.** should be an i-stem, but it isn't.

2. 3rd declension masculine or feminine nouns whose stem ends with two consonants, e.g.: **serpēns, serpentis, m./f.; mors, mortis, f.** Although they seem to fit in this group, the nouns **māter, matris, f.; frater, frātris, m.;** and **pater, patris, m.** are not i-stems.

Some 3rd declension neuter nouns are i-stems as well, but we'll learn about them later. Latin is weird sometimes, isn't it?

V. Historia (_Famous Men of Rome_, Chapter XIII, Part III)

Pyrrhus sends the sweet-talking Cineas to Rome to propose peace. Appius Claudius is an old, beloved former senator who is called _Caecus_ because he has become blind. When he hears that the Senate is about to accept Cineas' offer of peace, he goes to the Senate and says, "Better to lose all that we have than to disgrace ourselves by submitting!" Consul Curius Dentatus defeats Pyrrhus at Beneventum.

VI. Dēlēgāta

A. *Scrībe* the new Latin *verba* and their meanings.

	Latīnē		*Anglicē*
1.	avis, avis, f.	1.	bird
2.	canis, canis, m./f.	2.	dog
3.	collis, collis, m.	3.	hill
4.	fēles, fēlis, f.	4.	cat
5.	hostis, hostis, m./f.	5.	enemy
6.	ignis, ignis, m.	6.	fire
7.	mors, mortis, f.	7.	death
8.	nāvis, nāvis, f.	8.	ship
9.	serpēns, serpentis, m./f.	9.	snake

B. *Scrībe* the declension of <u>fēles, fēlis, f.</u> two times.

1.			2.		
fēles	fēlēs		fēles	fēlēs
fēlis	fēlium		fēlis	fēlium
fēlī	fēlibus		fēlī	fēlibus
fēlem	fēlīs		fēlem	fēlīs
fēle	fēlibus		fēle	fēlibus

C. *Scrībe* the *dictum* and its translation.

Latīnē: Cavē cānem.   *Anglicē*:   Beware of the dog.

D. Translate these *verba* and phrases.

1. fifteen   quīndecim   3. vīgintī trēs   twenty-three

2. Loquor Latīnē.   I speak in Latin   4. twenty-two   vīgintī duo

5. "Glōria in excelsīs Deō!" _____ *"Glory to God in the highest!"*

6. "Ego sum via et vēritās et vīta." _____ *"I am the way and the truth and the life."*

7. "Ego sum pāstor bonus." _____ *"I am the good shepherd."*

E. *Scrībe* **the meaning of these** *verba* **in the space provided. Then conjugate them in the tense indicated. (P = present; F = future)**

1. doceō, docēre (P) *to teach*

doceō	*docēmus*
docēs	*docētis*
docet	*docent*

2. sum, esse (P) *to be*

sum	*sumus*
es	*estis*
est	*sunt*

3. cēnō, cēnāre (F) *to dine*

cēnābō	*cēnābimus*
cēnābis	*cēnābitis*
cēnābit	*cēnabunt*

4. possum, posse (P) *to be able*

possum	*possumus*
potes	*potestis*
potest	*possunt*

5. recitō, recitāre (P) *to recite*

recitō	*recitāmus*
recitās	*recitātis*
recitat	*recitant*

6. rīdeō, rīdēre (F) *to laugh*

rīdēbō	*rīdēbimus*
rīdēbis	*rīdēbitis*
rīdēbit	*rīdēbunt*

F. *Scrībe* **the correct Latin form of these** *verba* **in the space provided. Then decline them.**

1. victory *victōria, -ae, f.*

victōria	*victōriae*
victōriae	*victōriārum*
victōriae	*victōriīs*
victōriam	*victōriās*
victōriā	*victōriīs*

2. son *fīlius, -ī, m.*

fīlius	*fīliī*
fīliī	*fīliōrum*
fīliō	*fīliīs*
fīlium	*fīliōs*
fīliō	*fīliīs*

G. Translate these sentences (from Latin to English or from English to Latin).

1. Avis volat.   *The bird flies.*

2. Avēs multum volant.   *Birds fly a lot.*

3. Avēs nunc volābunt.   *The birds will fly now.*

4. Canis ambulat.   *The dog does walk.*

5. Canēs ambulant.   *The dogs are walking.*

6. Magnus ignis lūcet.   *A large fire shines.*

7. Est altus collis.   *There is a high hill.*

8. Fēles saepe pugnat.   *The cat often fights.*

9. Fēlēs ibi pugnant.   *The cats are fighting there.*

10. The new ship is sailing.   *Nāvis nova nāvigat.*

11. It is able to sail well.   *Potest bene nāvigāre.*

12. Old ships cannot sail.   *Nāvēs antīquae nōn possunt nāvigāre.*

13. The cat is singing.   *Fēles cantat.*

14. It can sing.   *Potest cantāre.*

15. The cat will sing badly.   *Fēles male cantābit.*

16. The bird will fly.   *Avis volābit.*

17. The bird can fly.   *Avis volāre potest.*

18. A cow cannot fly.   *Bōs volāre nōn potest.*

19. The dogs never fight.   *Canēs numquam pugnant.*

20. The enemies will fight here.   *Hostēs hīc pugnābunt.*

21. Serpēns et aquila sunt hostēs.   *The serpent and the eagle are enemies.*

22. Homō et canis nōn sunt hostēs.   *The man and dog are not enemies.*

H. *Scrībe* the names of the animals in these pictures.

_____ *porcus* _____

_____ *serpēns* _____

_____ *ursa* _____

_____ *canis* _____

_____ *gallīna* _____

_____ *agnus* _____

_____ *avis* _____

_____ *taurus* _____

_____ *fēles* _____

_____ *bōs* _____

_____ *aquila* _____

_____ *equus* _____

I. Dērīvātī. Complete each sentence with an English *verbum* chosen from the following *verba*. The italicized *verbum* in the sentence should help you think of the Latin root.

canine   hostile   ignite   mortician   aviary

1. My *enemy* is _____ *hostile* _____ to me. Latin root: _____ *hostis, hostis, m./f.* _____

2. To _____ *ignite* _____ something is to set it on *fire*. Latin root: _____ *ignis, ignis, m.* _____

3. An _____ *aviary* _____ is a place where *birds* are kept. Latin root: _____ *avis, avis, f.* _____

4. A _____ *mortician* _____ cares for bodies after *death*. Latin root: _____ *mors, mortis, f.* _____

5. The _____ *canine* _____ division of the police force uses *dogs*. Latin root: _____ *canis, canis, m.* _____

J. Historia. Review the history story and fill in the blanks.

What does Appius Claudius Caecus tell the Senate when Cineas proposes peace?

_____ *It is better to be defeated in war than disgraced by submitting to the treaty.* _____

Disciplīna XXIV – vīgintī quattuor   RĒS IN DOMŌ

I. Dictum

Glōria Patrī et Fīliō	*Glory be to the Father and to the Son*
et Spīrituī Sanctō	*and to the Holy Spirit*

II. Colloquium

	Latīnē	*Anglicē*
Aemīlia:	Hoc nōn mihi placet.	This is no fun. (Lit., This is not pleasing to me.)
Claudius:	Eāmus domum.	Let's go home.

III. Verba

Latīnē	*Anglicē*	*Scrībe tōtum verbum Latīnum.*	*Dērīvātī*
cochleāre, cochleāris, n.	spoon	*cochleāre, cochleāris, n.*	*cochlea*
cubīle, cubīlis, n.	bed	*cubīle, cubīlis, n.*	
lacūnar, lacūnāris, n.	ceiling	*lacūnar, lacūnār, n.*	
mōns, montis, m.	mountain	*mōns, montis, m.*	*mountainous*
nox, noctis, f.	night	*nox, noctis, f.*	*nocturnal*
urbs, urbis, f.	city	*urbs, urbis, f.*	*urban*
speculum, -ī, n.	mirror	*speculum, -ī, n.*	*mirror*
domus, domūs, f.	house, home	*domus, domūs, f.*	*domestic*
spīritus, spīritūs, m.	spirit, breath	*spīritus, spīritūs, m.*	*spirit*

1. **Speculum, -ī, n.** is from ___*2nd*___ declension.

2. What two *verba* are from 4th declension? *Spīritus and domus are from the 4th declension.*

3. The remaining *verba* are from _____*3rd*_____ declension.

4. The ___*gen.*___ ___*sing.*___ case ending identifies the declension of a noun.

IV. Grammatica. Read the paradigm in the shaded box and <u>memorize it</u>.

Case		
Nominative	(varies)	-ēs
Genitive	-is	-ium
Dative	-ī	-ibus
Accusative	-em	-īs
Ablative	-e	-ibus

This chart shows the case endings for masculine and feminine 3rd declension i-stem nouns. They are slightly different from regular 3rd declension nouns. They are called i-stem nouns of 3rd declension because the letter **i** is added in some cases.

The two case endings that are different are the ___*genitive*___ and ___*accusative*___ plural

which end in ___-ium___ and ___-īs___, respectively.

We know that a 3rd declension masculine or feminine noun is an i-stem if:

1. EITHER the nominative and genitive singular have ___2___ syllables <u>and</u> the nominative

   singular also ends with ___-is___, ___-es___, or ___-ēs___;

2. OR the stem of the noun ends with two ___consonants___.

Here is a list of the <u>masculine and feminine i-stem nouns of 3rd declension</u> in this book:

auris, auris, f.   mōns, montis, m.
avis, avis, f.   mors, mortis, f.
collis, collis, m.   nāvis, nāvis, f.
dēns, dentis, m.   nox, noctis, f.
fēles, fēlis, f.   pars, partis, f.
hostis, hostis, m./f.   serpēns, serpentis, m./f.
ignis, ignis, m.   urbs, urbis, f.

V. Historia   There is no new history lesson this week.

VI. Dēlēgāta

A. *Scrībe* the new Latin *verba* and their meanings.

	Latīnē		*Anglicē*
1.	cochleāre, cochleāris, n.	1.	spoon
2.	cubīle, cubīlis, n.	2.	bed
3.	lacūnar, lacūnāris, n.	3.	ceiling
4.	mōns, montis, m.	4.	mountain
5.	nox, noctis, f.	5.	night
6.	urbs, urbis, f.	6.	city
7.	speculum, -ī, n.	7.	mirror
8.	domus, domūs, f.	8.	house, home
9.	spīritus, spīritūs, m.	9.	spirit, breath

B. *Scrībe* the case endings for i-stem nouns of 3rd declension three times.

1. varies	-ēs	2. varies	-ēs	3. varies	-ēs
-is	-ium	-is	-ium	-is	-ium
-ī	-ibus	-ī	-ibus	-ī	-ibus
-em	-īs	-em	-īs	-em	-īs
-e	-ibus	-e	-ibus	-e	-ibus

C. *Scrībe* the *dictum* and its translation.

Latīnē: Glōria Patrī et Fīliō et Spīrituī Sanctō

Anglicē: Glory be to the Father and to the Son and to the Holy Spirit

D. Translate these *verba* and phrases.

1. vīgintī quattuor   *twenty-four*   2. Eāmus domum.   *Let's go home.*

3. Agnus Deī _____*Lamb of God*_____   4. Ōrēmus. _____*Let's pray.*_____

5. ex librīs _____*from the books of*_____   6. antebellum _____*before the war*_____

7. "Ego sum pāstor bonus." _____*I am the good shepherd.*_____

8. "In principiō erat Verbum." _____*In the beginning was the Word.*_____

E. *Scrībe* **the meaning of these** *verba* **in the space provided. Then decline them.**

1. dēns, dentis, m. _____*tooth*_____   2. nox, noctis, f. _____*night*_____

dēns	*dentēs*	*nox*	*noctēs*
dentis	*dentium*	*noctis*	*noctium*
dentī	*dentibus*	*noctī*	*noctibus*
dentem	*dentīs*	*noctem*	*noctīs*
dente	*dentibus*	*nocte*	*noctibus*

3. mors, mortis, f. _____*death*_____   4. avis, avis, f. _____*bird*_____

mors	*mortēs*	*avis*	*avēs*
mortis	*mortium*	*avis*	*avium*
mortī	*mortibus*	*avī*	*avibus*
mortem	*mortīs*	*avem*	*avīs*
morte	*mortibus*	*ave*	*avibus*

5. auris, auris, f. _____*ear*_____   6. urbs, urbis, f. _____*city*_____

auris	*aurēs*	*urbs*	*urbēs*
auris	*aurium*	*urbis*	*urbium*
aurī	*auribus*	*urbī*	*urbibus*
aurem	*aurīs*	*urbem*	*urbīs*
aure	*auribus*	*urbe*	*urbibus*

F. Translate these sentences (from Latin to English or from English to Latin).

1. Cochleāre est magnum.   *The spoon is large.*

2. Mōns est magnus.   *The mountain is large.*

3. Lacūnar est altum.   *The ceiling is high.*

4. Rōma est urbs optima.   *Rome is the best city.*

5. Urbs est tūta.   *The city is safe.*

6. Urbēs sunt tūtae.   *The cities are safe.*

7. Tōta urbs gaudet.   *The whole city rejoices.*

8. Nox tardat.   *The night is slow.*

9. Hominēs saepe tardant.   *People are often slow.*

10. Ursae nōn tardābunt.   *The bears will not be slow.*

11. My mirror is old.   *Speculum meum est antīquum.*

12. Your mirror is new.   *Speculum tuum est novum.*

13. Domus est magna.   *The house is large.*

14. Cubicula nōn sunt lāta.   *The bedrooms are not wide.*

15. The bed is narrow.   *Cubīle est angustum.*

16. The mountain is not small.   *Mōns nōn parvus est.*

17. The mountains are high.   *Montēs sunt altī.*

18. My spirit sings.   *Spīritus meus cantat.*

19. Your spirit will sing.   *Spīritus tuus cantābit.*

20. Now we can sing.   *Nunc possumus cantāre.*

21. Spīritus Sanctus amat et ōrat.   *The Holy Spirit loves and speaks.*

22. Spīritus Sanctus nōn errat.   *The Holy Spirit is not mistaken.*

G. *Scrībe* the names of the household items in these pictures.

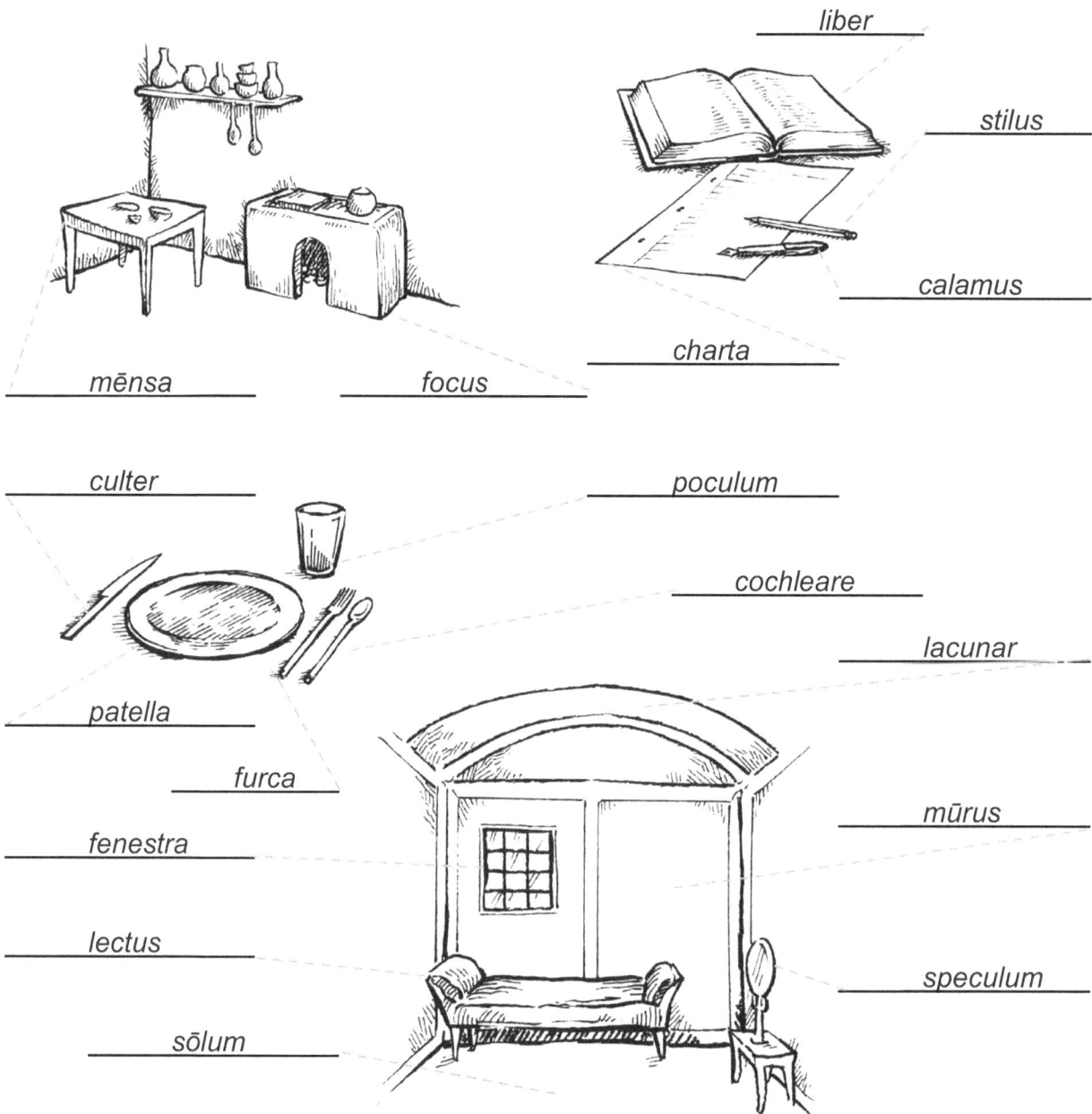

liber

stilus

calamus

charta

mēnsa   _focus_

culter   _poculum_

cochleare

lacunar

patella

furca

mūrus

fenestra

lectus

speculum

sōlum

H. **Dērīvātī.** Complete each sentence with an English *verbum* chosen from the following *verba*. The italicized *verbum* in the sentence should help you think of the Latin root.

domestic   nocturnal   urban

1. _____Nocturnal_____ animals are active at *night*. Latin root:_____nox, noctis, f._____

2. _____Urban_____ transportation includes *city* buses. Latin root:_____urbs, urbis, f._____

3. Peace at *home* can be called _____domestic_____ tranquility. Latin root:_____domus, -ūs, f._____

Glossary – Latin to English
Roman numeral indicates lesson number.

Nōtā bene: Noun dictionary entries are often shortened by listing only the genitive singular *ending* rather than the full genitive singular *form*. So **lectus, lectī, m.** would become **lectus, -ī, m.** and **vallum, vallī, n.** would become **vallum, -ī, n.** This seems confusing at first, but you can still see the stem of these nouns in the nominative singular forms **lectus** and **vallum**.

However, nouns like **culter, cultrī, m.** and **māter, mātris, f.** will *not* be abbreviated, because their stems are not visible in the nominative singular form.

A

aeternus, -a, -um	eternal (XIII)
agnus, -ī, m.	lamb (IX)
agricola, -ae, m.	farmer (XII)
altus, -a, -um	high, deep (XIV)
ambulō, ambulāre	to walk (I)
amō, amāre	to love, to like (I)
amīcus, -ī, m.	friend (XVI)
angustus, -a, -um	narrow (XIII)
annus, -ī, m.	year (XII)
antīquus, -a, -um	old, ancient (XIII)
aqua, -ae, f.	water (III)
aquila, -ae, f.	eagle (V)
arō, arāre	to plow (XII)
auris, auris, f.	ear (XXII)
avis, avis, f.	bird (XXIII)

B

bellus, -a, -um	pretty (XIV)
bellum, -ī, n.	war (XVI)
bene	well (XV)
bonus, -a, -um	good (XIII)
bōs, bovis, m./f.	ox, cow (XXI)
bracchium, -ī, n.	arm (XI)

C

caelum, -ī, n.	sky, heaven (XI)
Caesar, Caesaris, m.	Caesar (XX)
calamus, -ī, m.	pen (X)
canis, canis, m./f.	dog (XXIII)
cantō, cantāre	to sing (I)
capillus, -ī, m.	(a) hair (XVII)
caput, capitis, n.	head (XXII)
cēnō, cēnāre	to dine, to eat (II)
charta, -ae, f.	paper (V)

Christus, -ī, m.	Christ (IX)
cochleāre, cochleāris, n.	spoon (XXIV)
cōgitō, cōgitāre	to think (III)
collis, collis, m.	hill (XXIII)
corōna, -ae, f.	crown (V)
corpus, corporis, n.	body (XXI)
crūs, crūris, n.	leg (XXII)
crux, crūcis, f.	cross (XXI)
cubiculum, -ī, n.	bedroom (XII)
cubīle, cubīlis, n.	bed (XXIV)
culīna, -ae, f.	kitchen (III)
culpa, -ae, f.	fault (VI)
culter, cultrī, m.	knife (XVIII)

D

dēns, dentis, m.	tooth (XXII)
Deus, -ī, m.	God (IX)
digitus, -ī, m.	finger, toe (X)
discipula, -ae, f.	student (XVII)
discipulus, -ī, m.	student (XVII)
doceō, docēre	to teach (VIII)
doleō, dolēre	to ache (VII)
dominus, -ī, m.	lord, master (XII)
domus, domūs, f.	house (XXIV)
dōnum, -ī, n.	gift (XI)
dubitō, dubitāre	to doubt, to be uncertain (IV)
dūrō, dūrāre	to endure (IV)

E

ecclēsia, -ae, f.	church (VI)
equus, -ī, m.	horse (X)
errō, errāre	to err, to wander, to be mistaken (II)

et	and (XVIII)
exedrium, -ī, n.	living room (XVII)

F

fēles, fēlis, f.	cat (XXIII)
fēmina, -ae, f.	woman (III)
fenestra, -ae, f.	window (IV)
festīnō, festīnāre	to hurry (II)
fīlia, -ae, f.	daughter (VI)
fīlius, -ī, m.	son (IX)
fleō, flēre	to weep, to cry (VII)
flūmen, flūminis, n.	river (XXI)
focus, -ī, m.	fireplace, family (XVI)
frāter, frātris, m.	brother (XIX)
furca, -ae, f.	fork (III)

G

Gallia, -ae, f.	Gaul (France) (V)
gallīna, -ae, f.	chicken (VI)
gaudeō, gaudēre	to rejoice (VII)
gaudium, -ī, n.	joy (XI)
gladius, -ī, m.	sword (IX)
glōria, -ae, f.	glory (X)

H

herba, -ae, f.	plant, herb (XVII)
hīc	here (XV)
Hispania, -ae, f.	Spain (VI)
homō, hominis, m.	person, man, human (XX)
hōra, -ae, f.	hour (XVI)
hostis, hostis, m./f.	enemy (XXIII)

I

iānua, -ae, f.	door (VIII)
ibi	there (XV)
ignis, ignis, m.	fire (XXIII)
imperātor, imperātōris, m.	commander, general (XX)
imperō, imperāre	to rule, to order (V)
īnsula, -ae, f.	island (XVI)
intrō, intrāre	to enter (III)

Ītalia, -ae, f.	Italy (IV)
iūdicō, iūdicāre	to judge (II)

L

labōrō, labōrāre	to work (II)
lacūnar, lacūnāris, n.	ceiling (XXIV)
lātus, -a, -um	wide (XIII)
lectus, -ī, m.	couch, bed (XIX)
legiō, legiōnis, f.	legion (XX)
lēx, lēgis, f.	law (XX)
liber, librī, m.	book (XVIII)
lingua, -ae, f.	language, tongue (IV)
lūceō, lūcēre	to shine (VIII)
lūna, -ae, f.	moon (VI)
lūx, lūcis, f.	light (XXI)

M

magister, magistrī, m.	teacher (XVIII)
magistra, -ae, f.	teacher (XVIII)
magnus, -a, -um	large, great (XIII)
male	badly (XV)
malus, -a, -um	bad, wicked (XIII)
maneō, manēre	to remain, to stay (VII)
manus, manūs, f.	hand (XXII)
Maria, -ae, f.	Mary (X)
māter, mātris, f.	mother (XIX)
mendācium, -ī, n.	lie, falsehood (XIX)
mēnsa, -ae, f.	table (VI)
meus, -a, -um	my (XIV)
mīles, mīlitis, m.	soldier (XX)
misereō, miserēre	to be sorry (VII)
mōns, montis, m.	mountain (XXIV)
mors, mortis, f.	death (XXIII)
moveō, movēre	to move (VII)
multum	a lot (XV)
multus, -a, -um	much, many (XIV)
mundus, -ī, m.	world (IX)
mūrus, -ī, m.	wall (XVII)

N

nāsus, -ī, m.	nose (XXII)
nauta, -ae, m.	sailor (XII)
nāvigō, nāvigāre	to sail (II)

nāvis, nāvis, f.	ship (XXIII)
nimbus, -ī, m.	cloud (IX)
nōmen, nōminis, n.	name (XXI)
nōn	not (XVI)
novus, -a, -um	new (XIII)
nox, noctis, f.	night (XXIV)
numquam	never (XV)
nunc	now (XV)
nūntius, -ī, m.	messenger, message (XIX)

O

oculus, -ī, m.	eye (IX)
oppidum, -ī, n.	town (XI)
optimus, -a, -um	best (XIV)
ōrō, ōrāre	to pray, to speak (II)
ōs, ōris, n.	mouth (XXII)

P

pars, partis, f.	part (XXII)
parum	a little (XV)
parvus, -a, -um	small (XIII)
pāstor, pāstōris, m.	shepherd (XX)
patella, -ae, f.	plate (XII)
pater, patris, m.	father (XIX)
pateō, patēre	to be open (VIII)
patria, -ae, f.	country, native land (XVI)
pax, pācis, f.	peace (XXII)
peccātum, -ī, n.	sin (XI)
peccō, peccāre	to sin (II)
pecūnia, -ae, f.	money (V)
pēs, pedis, m.	foot (XXI)
placeō, placēre	to please (VIII)
pōculum, -ī, n.	cup (XVII)
porcus, -ī, m.	pig (IX)
possum, posse	to be able, can (XVII)
praemium, -ī, n.	reward (XVI)
prīmus, -a, -um	first (XIV)
puella, -ae, f.	girl (IV)
puer, puerī, m.	boy (XVIII)
pugnō, pugnāre	to fight (I)
puteus, -ī, m.	a well (X)

R

recitō, recitāre	to recite, to read aloud (III)
rēgīna, -ae, f.	queen (V)
regnō, regnāre	to reign (XII)
rēgnum, -ī, n.	kingdom (XI)
rēx, rēgis, m.	king (XX)
rīdeō, rīdēre	to laugh (VII)
Rōma, -ae, f.	Rome (III)

S

saepe	often (XV)
salveō, salvēre	to be well (VII)
sanctus, -a, -um	holy (XIII)
secundus, -a, -um	second (XIV)
sedeō, sedēre	to sit (VII)
sella, -ae, f.	chair (X)
semper	always (XV)
serpēns, serpentis, m./f.	snake (XXIII)
servus, -ī, m.	slave, servant (X)
signum, -ī, n.	sign (XVII)
sileō, silēre	to be silent (VIII)
silva, -ae, f.	forest (VI)
solum, -ī, n.	floor (XI)
soror, sorōris, f.	sister (XX)
speculum, -ī, n.	mirror (XXIV)
spīritus, spīritūs, m.	spirit (XXIV)
stō, stāre	to stand (V)
stella, -ae, f.	star (VIII)
stilus, -ī, m.	pencil (X)
stomachus, -ī, m.	stomach (XVIII)
sum, esse	to be (VI)
superō, superāre	to overcome, to conquer (III)

T

tardō, tardāre	to be slow (II)
taurus, -ī, m.	bull (XVII)
tēlum, -ī, n.	weapon (XVI)
tempus, temporis, n.	time (XXI)
terra, -ae, f.	land, earth (VI)
timeō, timēre	to fear, be afraid (VIII)
tōtus, -a, -um	whole (XIV)

tūtus, -a, -um	safe (XIV)
tuus, -a, -um	your (sing.) (XIV)

U

urbs, urbis, f.	city (XXIV)
ursa, -ae, f.	bear (IV)

V

valeō, valēre	to be strong, to have power (VIII)
vallum, -ī, n.	wall, rampart (XXIX)
verbum, -ī, n.	word (XI)
vēritās, vēritātis, f.	truth (XIX)
via, -ae, f.	road, way (XVII)
victōria, -ae, f.	victory (V)
vīnum, -ī, n.	wine (XII)
virtūs, virtūtis, f.	courage, virtue, manliness (XIX)
vīta, -ae, f.	life (IV)
volō, volāre	to fly (IV)
vox, vōcis, f.	voice (XXI)

Glossary – English to Latin
Roman numeral indicates lesson number.

<u>Nōtā bene</u>: Noun dictionary entries are often shortened by listing only the genitive singular *ending* rather than the full genitive singular *form*. So **lectus, lectī, m.** would become **lectus, -ī, m.** and **vallum, vallī, n.** would become **vallum, -ī, n.** This seems confusing at first, but you can still see the stem of these nouns in the nominative singular forms **lectus** and **vallum**.

However, nouns like **culter, cultrī, m.** and **māter, mātris, f.** will *not* be abbreviated, because their stems are not visible in the nominative singular form.

A
able, to be	possum, posse (XVII)
ache, to	doleō, dolēre (VII)
afraid, to be	timeō, timēre (VIII)
always	semper (XV)
ancient	antīquus, -a, -um (XIII)
and	et (XVIII)
arm	bracchium, -ī, n.(XI)

B
bad	malus, -a, -um (XIII)
badly	male (XV)
be, to	sum, esse (VI)
bear	ursa, -ae, f. (IV)
bed	lectus, -ī, m. (XIX); cubīle, cubīlis, n. (XXIV)
bedroom	cubiculum, -ī, n. (XII)
best	optimus, -a, -um (XIV)
bird	avis, avis, f. (XXIII)
blame	culpa, -ae, f. (VI)
body	corpus, corporis, n. (XXI)
book	liber, librī, m. (XVIII)
boy	puer, pueri, m. (XVIII)
breath	spīritus, spīritūs, m. (XXIV)
brother	frāter, frātris, m. (XIX)
bull	taurus, -ī, m. (XVII)

C
Caesar	Caesar, Caesaris, m. (XX)
can	possum, posse (XVII)
cat	fēles, fēlis, f. (XXIII)
ceiling	lacūnar, lacūnāris, n. (XXIV)
chair	sella, -ae, f. (X)
chicken	gallīna, -ae, f. (VI)
Christ	Christus, -ī, m. (IX)
church	ecclēsia, -ae, f. (VI)
city	urbs, urbis, f. (XXIV)
cloud	nimbus, -ī, m. (IX)
commander	imperātor, imperātōris, m. (XX)
conquer, to	superō, superāre (III)
couch	lectus, -ī, m. (XIX)
country	patria, -ae, f. (XVI)
courage	virtūs, virtūtis, f. (XIX)
cow	bōs, bovis, m./f. (XXI)
cross	crux, crucis, f. (XXI)
crown	corōna, -ae, f. (V)
cup	pōculum, -ī, n. (XVII)
cry, to	fleō, flēre (VII)

D
daughter	fīlia, -ae, f. (VI)
death	mors, mortis, f. (XXIII)
deep	altus, -a, -um (XIV)
dine, to	cēnō, cēnāre (II)
dog	canis, canis, m./f. (XXIII)
door	iānua, -ae, f. (VIII)
doubt, to	dubitō, dubitāre (IV)

E
eagle	aquila, -ae, f. (V)
ear	auris, auris, f. (XXII)
earth	terra, -ae, f. (VI)
eat, to	cēnō, cēnāre (II)
endure, to	dūrō, dūrāre (IV)
enemy	hostis, hostis, m./f. (XXIII)
enter, to	intrō, intrāre (III)

err, to	errō, errāre (II)
eternal	aeternus, -a, -um (XIII)
eye	oculus, -ī, m. (IX)

F

falsehood	mendācium, -ī, n. (XIX)
family	focus, -ī, m. (XVI)
farmer	agricola, -ae, m. (XII)
father	pater, patris, m. (XIX)
fatherland	patria, -ae, f. (XVI)
fault	culpa, -ae, f. (VI)
fear, to	timeō, timēre (VIII)
fight, to	pugnō, pugnāre (I)
finger	digitus, -ī , m. (X)
fire	ignis, ignis, m. (XXIII)
fireplace	focus, -ī, m. (XVI)
first	prīmus, -a, -um (XIV)
floor	solum, -ī, n. (XI)
fly, to	volō, volāre (IV)
foot	pēs, pedis, m. (XXI)
forest	silva, -ae, f. (VI)
fork	furca, -ae, f. (III)
France	Gallia, -ae, f. (V)
friend	amīcus, -ī, m. (XVI)

G

Gaul	Gallia, -ae, f. (V)
general	imperātor, imperātōris (XX)
gift	dōnum, -ī, n. (XI)
girl	puella, -ae, f. (IV)
glory	glōria, -ae, f. (X)
God	Deus, -ī, m. (IX)
good	bonus, -a, -um (XIII)
great	magnus, -a, -um (XIII)

H

hair (a)	capillus, -ī, m. (XVII)
hand	manus, manūs, f. (XXII)
have power, to	valeō, valēre (VIII)
head	caput, capitis, n. (XXII)
heaven	caelum, -ī, n. (XI)
herb	herba, -ae, f. (XVII)
here	hīc (XV)

high	altus, -a, -um (XIV)
hill	collis, collis, m. (XXIII)
holy	sanctus, -a, -um (XIII)
home	domus, domūs, f. (XXIV)
horse	equus, -ī, m. (X)
hour	hōra, -ae, f. (XVI)
house	domus, domūs, f. (XXIV)
human being	homō, hominis, m. (XX)
hurry, to	festīnō, festīnāre (II)

I

island	īnsula, -ae, f. (XVI)
Italy	Ītalia, -ae, f. (IV)

J

joy	gaudium, -ī, n. (XI)
judge, to	iūdicō, iūdicāre (II)

K

king	rēx, rēgis, m. (XX)
kingdom	rēgnum, -ī, n. (XI)
kitchen	culīna, -ae, f. (III)
knife	culter, cultrī, m. (XVIII)

L

lamb	agnus, -ī, m. (IX)
land	terra, -ae, f. (VI)
language	lingua, -ae, f. (IV)
large	magnus, -a, -um (XIII)
laugh, to	rīdeō, rīdēre (VII)
law	lēx, lēgis, f. (XX)
leg	crūs, crūris, n. (XXII)
legion	legiō, legiōnis, f. (XX)
lie	mendācium, -ī, n. (XIX)
life	vīta, -ae, f. (IV)
light	lūx, lūcis, f. (XXI)
like, to	amō, amāre (I)
little, a	parum (XV)
living room	exedrium, -ī, n. (XVII)
lord	dominus, -ī, m. (XII)
lot, a	multum (XV)
love, to	amō, amāre (I)

M

man	homō, hominis, m. (XX)
manliness	virtus, virtūtis, f. (XIX)
many	multus, -a, -um (XIV)
Mary	Maria, -ae, f. (X)
master	dominus, -ī, m. (XII)
message	nuntius, -ī, m. (XIX)
messenger	nūntius, -ī , m. (XIX)
mirror	speculum, -ī, n. (XXIV)
mistaken, to be	errō, errāre (II)
money	pecūnia, -ae, f. (V)
moon	lūna, -ae, f. (VI)
mother	māter, mātris, f. (XIX)
mountain	mons, montis, m. (XXIV)
mouth	ōs, ōris, n. (XXII)
move, to	moveō, movēre (VII)
much	multus, -a, -um (XIV)
my	meus, -a, -um (XIV)

N

name	nōmen, nōminis, n. (XXI)
narrow	angustus, -a, -um (XIII)
never	numquam (XV)
new	novus, -a, -um (XIII)
night	nox, noctis, f. (XXIV)
nose	nāsus, -ī, m. (XXII)
not	nōn (XVI)
now	nunc (XV)

O

often	saepe (XV)
old	antīquus, -a, -um (XIII)
open, to be	pateō, patēre (VIII)
order, to	imperō, imperāre (V)
overcome, to	superō, superāre (III)
ox	bōs, bovis, m./f. (XXI)

P

paper	charta, -ae, f. (V)
part	pars, partis, f. (XXII)
peace	pax, pācis, f. (XXII)
pen	calamus, -ī, m. (X)
pencil	stilus, -ī, m. (X)
person	homō, hominis, m. (XX)
pig	porcus, -ī, m. (IX)

plant	herba, -ae, f. (XVII)
plate	patella, -ae, f. (XII)
please, to	placeō, placēre (VIII)
plow, to	arō, arāre (XII)
power, to have	valeō, valēre (VIII)
pray, to	ōrō, ōrāre (II)
pretty	bellus, -a, -um (XIV)

Q

queen	rēgīna, -ae, f. (V)

R

rampart	vallum, -ī, n. (XIX)
read aloud, to	recitō, recitāre (III)
recite, to	recitō, recitāre (III)
reign, to	rēgnō, rēgnāre (XII)
rejoice, to	gaudeō, gaudēre (VII)
remain, to	maneō, manēre (VII)
reward	praemium, -ī, n. (XVI)
river	flūmen, flūminis, n. (XXI)
road	via, -ae, f. (XVII)
Rome	Rōma, -ae, f. (III)
rule, to	imperō, imperāre (V)

S

safe	tūtus, -a, -um (XIV)
sail, to	nāvigō, nāvigāre (II)
sailor	nauta, -ae, m. (XII)
second	secundus, -a, -um (XIV)
serpent	serpēns, serpentis, m./f. (XXIII)
servant	servus, -ī, m. (X)
shepherd	pāstor, pāstōris, m. (XX)
shine, to	lūceō, lūcēre (VIII)
ship	nāvis, nāvis, f. (XXIII)
sign	signum, -ī, n. (XVII)
silent, to be	sileō, silēre (VIII)
sin	peccātum, -ī, n. (II)
sin, to	peccō, peccāre (II)
sing, to	cantō, cantāre (I)
sister	soror, sorōris, f. (XX)
sit, to	sedeō, sedēre (VII
sky	caelum, -ī, n. (XI)
slave	servus -ī, m. (X)
slow, to be	tardō, tardāre (II)

small	parvus, -a, -um (XIII)	**W**	
snake	serpēns, serpentis, m./f. (XXIII)	walk, to	ambulō, ambulāre (I)
		wall	vallum, -ī, n. (XIX) (of a fortress)
soldier	mīles, mīlitis, m. (XX)		
son	fīlius, -ī, m. (IX)	wall	mūrus, -ī, m. (XVII) (of a room)
sorry, to be	misereō, miserēre (VII)		
Spain	Hispania, -ae, f. (VI)	wander, to	errō, errāre (II)
speak, to	ōrō, ōrāre (II)	war	bellum, -ī, n. (XVI)
spirit	spīritus, spīritūs, m. (XXIV)	water	aqua, -ae, f. (III)
		way	via, -ae, f. (XVII)
spoon	cochleāre, cochleāris, n. (XXIV)	weapon	tēlum, -ī, n. (XVI)
		weep, to	fleō, flēre (VII)
stand, to	stō, stāre (V)	well, to be	salveō, salvēre (VII)
star	stella, -ae, f. (VIII)	well	puteus, -ī, m. (X)
stay, to	maneō, manēre (VII)	well	bene (XV)
stomach	stomachus, -ī, m. (XVIII)	whole	tōtus, -a, -um (XIV)
strong, to be	valeō, valēre (VIII)	wicked	malus, -a, -um (XIII)
student	discipulus, -ī, m. discipula, -ae, f. (XVII)	wickedly	male (XV)
		wide	lātus, -a, -um (XIII)
sword	gladius, -ī, m. (IX)	window	fenestra, -ae, f. (IV)
		wine	vīnum, -ī, n. (XII)
T		woman	fēmina, -ae, f. (III)
table	mēnsa, -ae, f. (VI)	word	verbum, -ī, n. (XI)
teach, to	doceō, docēre (VIII)	work, to	labōrō, labōrāre (II)
teacher	magister, magistrī, m. magistra, -ae, f. (XVIII)	world	mundus, -ī, m. (IX)
		Y	
there	ibi (XV)	year	annus, -ī, m. (XII)
think, to	cōgitō, cōgitāre (III)	your (sing.)	tuus, -a, -um (XIV)
time	tempus, temporis, n. (XXI)		
toe	digitus, -ī, m. (X)		
tongue	lingua, -ae, f. (IV)		
tooth	dēns, dentis, m. (XXII)		
town	oppidum, -ī, n. (XI)		
truth	vēritās, vēritātis, f. (XIX)		
U			
uncertain, to be	dubitō, dubitāre (IV)		
V			
victory	victōria, -ae, f. (V)		
virtue	virtūs, virtūtis, f. (XIX)		
voice	vox, vōcis, f. (XXI)		

Glossary – Numbers
Below are the cardinal (counting) numbers.

Numbers

0		nihil
1	I	ūnus
2	II	duo
3	III	trēs
4	IV	quattuor
5	V	quīnque
6	VI	sex
7	VII	septem
8	VIII	octō
9	IX	novem
10	X	decem
11	XI	ūndecim
12	XII	duodecim
13	XIII	tredecim
14	XIV	quattuordecim
15	XV	quīndecim
16	XVI	sēdecim
17	XVII	septendecim
18	XVIII	duodēvīgintī
19	XIX	ūndēvīgintī
20	XX	vīgintī
21	XXI	vīgintī ūnus
22	XXII	vīgintī duo
23	XXIII	vīgintī trēs
24	XXIV	vīgintī quattuor
25	XXV	vīgintī quīnque
26	XXVI	vīgintī sex
27	XVII	vīgintī septem
28	XVIII	duodētrīgintā
29	XXIX	ūndētrīgintā
30	XXX	trīgintā
40	XL	quādrāgintā
50	L	quīnquāgintā
60	LX	sexāgintā
70	LXX	septuāgintā
80	LXXX	octōgintā
90	XC	nōnāgintā
100	C	centum
500	D	quīngentī, -ae, -a
1000	M	mīlle

151

Vocabulary by Disciplīna

Nōtā bene: Noun dictionary entries are often shortened by listing only the genitive singular *ending* rather than the full genitive singular *form*. So **lectus, lectī, m.** would become **lectus, -ī, m.** and **vallum, vallī, n.** would become **vallum, -ī, n.** This seems confusing at first, but you can still see the stem of these nouns in the nominative singular forms **lectus** and **vallum**.

However, nouns like **culter, cultrī, m.** and **māter, mātris, f.** will *not* be abbreviated, because their stems are not visible in the nominative singular form.

I – Disciplīna ūnus

ambulō, ambulāre	to walk
amō, amāre	to love, to like
cantō, cantāre	to sing
pugnō, pugnāre	to fight

II – Disciplīna duo

cēnō, cēnāre	to dine, to eat
errō, errāre	to err, wander, be mistaken
festīnō, festīnāre	to hurry
iūdicō, iūdicāre	to judge
labōrō, labōrāre	to work
nāvigō, nāvigāre	to sail, to navigate
ōrō, ōrāre	to pray, to speak
peccō, peccāre	to sin
tardō, tardāre	to be slow

III – Disciplīna trēs

cōgitō, cōgitāre	to think
intrō, intrāre	to enter
recitō, recitāre	to recite, to read aloud
superō, superāre	to overcome, to conquer
aqua, -ae, f.	water
culīna, -ae, f.	kitchen
fēmina, -ae, f.	woman
furca, -ae, f.	fork
Rōma, -ae, f.	Rome

IV – Disciplīna quattuor

dubitō, dubitāre	to doubt, be uncertain
dūrō, dūrāre	to endure
fenestra, -ae, f.	window
Italia, -ae, f.	Italy
lingua, -ae, f.	language, tongue
puella, -ae, f.	girl
ursa, -ae, f.	bear
vīta, -ae, f.	life
volō, volāre	to fly

V – Diciplīna quīnque

aquila, -ae, f.	eagle
charta, -ae, f.	paper
corōna, -ae, f.	crown
Gallia, -ae, f.	Gaul (France)
imperō, imperāre	to rule, to order
pecūnia, -ae, f.	money
rēgīna, -ae, f.	queen
stō, stāre	to stand
victōria, -ae, f.	victory

VI – Disciplīna sex

culpa, -ae, f.	fault, blame
ecclēsia, -ae, f.	church
fīlia, -ae, f.	daughter
gallīna, -ae, f.	chicken
Hispania, -ae, f.	Spain
lūna, -ae, f.	moon
mēnsa, -ae, f.	table
silva, -ae, f.	forest
terra, -ae, f.	land, earth
sum, esse	to be

VII – Disciplīna septem

doleō, dolēre	to ache
fleō, flēre	to weep, to cry
gaudeō, gaudēre	to rejoice
maneō, manēre	to stay, to remain
misereō, miserēre	to be sorry
moveō, movēre	to move
rīdeō, rīdēre	to laugh
salveō, salvēre	to be well
sedeō, sedēre	to sit

VIII – Disciplīna octō

doceō, docēre	to teach
iānua, -ae, f.	door
lūceō, lūcēre	to shine
pateō, patēre	to be open
placeō, placēre	to please
sileō, silēre	to be silent
stella, -ae, f.	star
timeō, timēre	to fear
valeō, valēre	to be strong, to have power

IX – Disciplīna novem

agnus, -ī, m.	lamb
Christus, -ī, m.	Christ
Deus, -ī, m.	God
fīlius, -ī, m.	son
gladius, -ī, m.	sword
mundus, -ī, m.	world
nimbus, -ī, m.	cloud
oculus, -ī, m.	eye
porcus, -ī, m.	pig

X – Disciplīna decem

calamus, -ī, m.	pen
digitus, -ī, m.	finger, toe
equus, -ī, m.	horse
glōria, -ae, f.	glory
Maria, -ae, f.	Mary

puteus, -ī, m.	well
sella, -ae, f.	chair
servus, -ī, m.	slave, servant
stilus, -ī, m.	pencil

XI – Disciplīna ūndecim

brācchium, -ī, n.	arm
caelum, -ī, n.	sky, heaven
dōnum, -ī, n.	gift
gaudium, -ī, n.	joy
oppidum, -ī, n.	town
peccātum, -ī, n.	sin
rēgnum, -ī, n.	kingdom
solum, -ī, n.	floor
verbum, -ī, n.	word

XII – Disciplīna duodecim

agricola, -ae, m.	farmer
annus, -ī, m.	year
arō, arāre	to plow
cubiculum, -ī, n.	bedroom
dominus, -ī, m.	lord, master
nauta, -ae, m.	sailor
patella, -ae, f.	plate
rēgnō, rēgnāre	to reign
vīnum, -ī, n.	wine

XIII – Disciplīna tredecim

aeternus, -a, -um	eternal
angustus, -a, -um	narrow
antīquus, -a, -um	ancient, old
bonus, -a, -um	good
lātus, -a, -um	wide
magnus, -a, -um	great, large
malus, -a, -um	bad, wicked
novus, -a, -um	new
parvus, -a, -um	small
sanctus, -a, -um	holy

XIV – Disciplīna quattuordecim

altus, -a, -um	high, deep
bellus, -a, -um	pretty
meus, -a, -um	my
multus, -a, -um	much, many
optimus, -a, -um	best
prīmus, -a, -um	first
secundus, -a, -um	second
tōtus, -a, -um	whole
tūtus, -a, -um	safe
tuus, -a, -um	your (singular)

XV – Disciplīna quīndecim

bene	well
hīc	here
ibi	there
male	badly, wickedly
multum	a lot
numquam	never
nunc	now
parum	a little
saepe	often
semper	always

XVI – Disciplīna sēdecim

amīcus, -ī, m.	friend
bellum, -ī, n.	war
focus, -ī, m.	fireplace, family
hōra, -ae, f.	hour
īnsula, -ae, f.	island
nōn	not
patria, -ae, f.	country, fatherland
praemium, -ī, n.	reward
tēlum, -ī, n.	weapon

XVII – Disciplīna septendecim

capillus, -ī, m.	(a) hair
discipula, -ae, f.	student (female)
discipulus, -ī, m.	student (male)
exedrium, -ī, n.	living room
herba, -ae, f.	plant, herb
mūrus, -ī, n.	wall
pōculum, -ī, n.	cup
signum, -ī, n.	sign, standard
taurus, -ī, m.	bull
via, -ae, f.	way, road
possum, posse	to be able

XVIII – Disciplīna duodēvīgintī

culter, cultrī, m.	knife
et	and
liber, librī, m.	book
magister, magistrī, m.	teacher (male)
puer, puerī, m.	boy
stomachus, -ī, m.	stomach

XIX – Disciplīna ūndēvīgintī

frāter, frātris, m.	brother
māter, mātris, f.	mother
pater, patris, m.	father
vēritās, vēritātis, f.	truth
virtūs, virtūtis, f.	courage, manliness, virtue
lectus, -ī, m.	bed, couch
mendācium, -ī, n.	lie
nūntius, -ī, m.	messenger, message
vallum, -ī, n.	rampart, wall

XX – Disciplīna vīgintī

Caesar, Caesaris, m.	Caesar
homō, hominis, m.	person, man, human being
imperātor, imperātōris, m.	commander, general
legiō, legiōnis, f.	legion
lēx, lēgis, f.	law
mīlēs, mīlitis, m.	soldier
pāstor, pāstōris, m.	shepherd
rēx, rēgis, m.	king
soror, sorōris, f.	sister

XXI – Disciplīna vīgintī ūna

bōs, bovis, m./f.	ox, cow
crux, crūcis, f.	cross
lūx, lūcis, f.	light
pēs, pedis, m.	foot
vox, vōcis, f.	voice
corpus, corporis, n.	body
flūmen, flūminis, n.	river
nōmen, nōminis, n.	name
tempus, temporis, n.	time

XXII – Disciplīna vīgintī duo

auris, auris, f.	ear
caput, capitis, n.	head
crūs, crūris, n.	leg
dēns, dentis, m.	tooth
ōs, ōris, n.	mouth
pars, partis, f.	part
pax, pācis, f.	peace
manus, manūs, f.	hand
nāsus, -ī, m.	nose

XXIII – Disciplīna vīgintī trēs

avis, avis, f.	bird
canis, canis, m./f.	dog
collis, collis, m.	hill
fēles, fēlis, f.	cat
hostis, hostis, m./f.	enemy
ignis, ignis, m.	fire
mors, mortis, f.	death
nāvis, nāvis, f.	ship
serpēns, serpentis, m./f.	snake

XXIV – Disciplīna vīgintī quattuor

cochleāre, cochleāris, n.	spoon
cubīle, cubīlis, n.	bed
lacūnar, lacūnāris, n.	ceiling
mōns, montis, m.	mountain
nox, noctis, f.	night
urbs, urbis, f.	city
speculum, -ī, n.	mirror
domus, domūs, f.	house
spīritus, spīritūs, m.	spirit

Paradigms

II: cēnō, cēnāre – 1st conjugation present tense personal endings

	SINGULAR	PLURAL
1st PERSON	-ō	-mus
2nd PERSON	-s	-tis
3rd PERSON	-t	-nt

cēnō, cēnāre – present tense

1st PERSON	cēnō	cēnāmus
2nd PERSON	cēnās	cēnātis
3rd PERSON	cēnat	cēnant

IV: ursa, -ae, f. – 1st declension m./f.

NOM.	ursa	ursae
GEN.	ursae	ursārum
DAT.	ursae	ursīs
ACC.	ursam	ursās
ABL.	ursā	ursīs

V: 1st declension m./f. case endings

NOM.	-a	-ae
GEN.	-ae	-ārum
DAT.	-ae	-īs
ACC.	-am	-ās
ABL.	-ā	-īs

VI: sum, esse – present tense

1st PERSON	sum	sumus
2nd PERSON	es	estis
3rd PERSON	est	sunt

VII: maneō, manēre – 2nd conjugation present tense

1st PERSON	maneō	manēmus
2nd PERSON	manēs	manētis
3rd PERSON	manet	manent

IX: nimbus, -ī, m. – 2nd declension m./f.

	SINGULAR	PLURAL
NOM.	nimbus	nimbī
GEN.	nimbī	nimbōrum
DAT.	nimbō	nimbīs
ACC.	nimbus	nimbōs
ABL.	nimbō	nimbīs

X: 2nd declension m./f. case endings

NOM.	-us	-ī
GEN.	-ī	-ōrum
DAT.	-ō	-īs
ACC.	-um	-ōs
ABL.	-ō	-īs

XI: dōnum, -ī, n. – 2nd declension N

NOM.	dōnum	dōna
GEN.	dōnī	dōnōrum
DAT.	dōnō	dōnīs
ACC.	dōnum	dōna
ABL.	dōnō	dōnīs

XII: 2nd declension n. case endings

NOM.	-um	-a
GEN.	-ī	-ōrum
DAT.	-ō	-īs
ACC.	-um	-a
ABL.	-ō	-īs

XIII: 1st and 2nd declension adjectives

SINGULAR

	M.	F.	N.
NOM.	bonus	bona	bonum
GEN.	bonī	bonae	bonī
DAT.	bonō	bonae	bonō
ACC.	bonum	bonam	bonum
ABL.	bonō	bonā	bonō

PLURAL

	M.	F.	N.
NOM.	bonī	bonae	bona
GEN.	bonōrum	bonārum	bonōrum
DAT.	bonīs	bonīs	bonīs
ACC.	bonōs	bonās	bona
ABL.	bonīs	bonīs	bonīs

XIV: future tense personal endings

	SINGULAR	PLURAL
1st PERSON	-bō	-bimus
2nd PERSON	-bis	-bitis
3rd PERSON	-bit	-bunt

XV: amō, amāre – 1st conjugation
future tense

1st PERSON	amābō	amābimus
2nd PERSON	amābis	amābitis
3rd PERSON	amābit	amābunt

XVI: maneō, manēre – 2nd conjugation
future tense

1st PERSON	manēbō.	manēbimus
2nd PERSON	manēbis	manēbitis
3rd PERSON	manēbit	manēbunt

XVII: possum, posse – present tense

1st PERSON	possum	possumus
2nd PERSON	potes	potestis
3rd PERSON	potest	possunt

XVIII: 2nd declension m. in *-er*

NOM.	liber	librī
GEN.	librī	librōrum
DAT.	librō	librīs
ACC.	librum	librōs
ABL.	librō	librīs

XIX: pater, patris, m. – 3rd decl. M/F

NOM.	pater	patrēs
GEN.	patris	patrum
DAT.	patrī	patribus
ACC.	patrem	patrēs
ABL.	patre	patribus

XX: 3rd declension m./f. case endings

NOM.	(varies)	-ēs
GEN.	-is	-um
DAT.	-ī	-ibus
ACC.	-em	-ēs
ABL.	-e	-ibus

XXI: flumen, fluminis, n. – 3rd decl. N

	SINGULAR	PLURAL
NOM.	flūmen	flūmina
GEN.	flūminis	flūminum
DAT.	flūminī	flūminibus
ACC.	flūmen	flūmina
ABL.	flūmine	flūminibus

XXII: 3rd declension n. case endings

NOM.	(varies)	-a
GEN.	-is	-um
DAT.	-ī	-ibus
ACC.	(varies)	-a
ABL.	-e	-ibus

XXIII: feles, felis, f. 3rd decl. M/F i-stem

NOM.	fēles	fēlēs
GEN.	fēlis	fēlium
DAT.	fēlī	fēlibus
ACC.	fēlem	fēlīs
ABL.	fēle	fēlibus

XXIV: 3rd decl. m./f. i-stem case endings

NOM.	(varies)	-ēs
GEN.	-is	-ium
DAT.	-ī	-ibus
ACC.	-em	-īs
ABL.	-e	-ibus

Dicta
Roman numeral indicates lesson number.

I	Crēdō in ūnum Deum.	I believe in one God.
II	Ōrā et labōrā.	Pray and work.
III	Cōgitō ergō sum. (Descartes)	I think; therefore, I am.
IV	Ars longa; vīta brevis.	The art is long; life is short.
V	et cētera	and the rest
VI	terra incognita	unknown land
VII	Rīdent stolidī verba Latīna. (Ovid)	Fools laugh at the Latin language.
VIII	Hominēs, dum docent, discunt. (Seneca)	People learn while they teach.
IX	Agnus Deī quī tollis peccāta mundī	Lamb of God who takes away the sins of the world
X	Glōria in excelsīs Deō (from Luke 2:14)	Glory to God in the highest
XI	In principiō erat Verbum . . . (Secumdum Ioannem 1:1a)	In the beginning was the Word . . . (John 1:1a)
XII	Annō Dominī (AD)	In the year of our Lord
XIII	Nihil sub sōle novum est. (Liber Ecclesiastes 1:10a)	Nothing is new under the sun. (Ecclesiastes 1:10a)
XIV	Ūsus est magister optimus.	Practice is the best teacher.
XV	semper fidēlis	always faithful
XVI	ante bellum	before the war
XVII	Errāre hūmānum est. (Terence)	To err is human.
XVIII	ex librīs	from the books of
XIX	Ego sum via et vēritās et vīta. (Secundum Ioānnem 14:6a)	I am the way and the truth and the life. (John 14:6a)
XX	Ego sum pāstor bonus. (Secundum Ioānnem 10:11a)	I am the good shepherd. (John 10:11a)

XXI	"Fīat lūx." (from Liber Genesis 1:3)	"Let there be light." (from Genesis 1:3)
XXII	Requiescat in pāce. (R.I.P.)	May he (she, it) rest in peace.
XXIII	Cavē canem.	Beware the dog.
XXIV	Glōria Patrī et Fīliō et Spīrituī Sanctō	Glory to the Father and to the Son and to the Holy Spirit

Colloquia
Roman numeral indicates lesson number.

I   Salvēte / Valēte discipulī!   Hello / Good-bye, students!

       Salvē / Valē magistra!   Hello / Good-bye, teacher!

II   Quod praenōmen tibi est?   What is your (first) name?

       Nōmen mihi _____ est.   My name is _____.

Most Roman names had both a 2nd declension masculine form for men, and a 1st declension feminine form for women. Both are listed below. *Iēsus* and *Monica* are exceptions.

Aemilius / Aemilia	Gāius / Gāia	Publius / Publia
Antōnius / Antōnia	Iūlius / Iūlia	Quīntus / Quīnta
Cassius / Cassia	Līvius / Līvia	Sextus / Sexta
Claudius / Claudia	Lūcius / Lūcia	Tiberius / Tiberia
Cornēlius /Cornēlia	Marcus / Marcia	Valerius / Valeria
Fābius / Fābia	Marius / Maria	Iēsus, Iēsū, m.
Flāvius / Flāvia	Porcius / Porcia	Monica, -ae, f.

III   Grātiās tibi agō.   Thank you.

       Libenter!   You're welcome!

IV   Repetite.   Repeat.

V   Quomodō tē habēs hodiē?   How are you today?

       Bene, grātiās tibi agō. Et tū?   Well, thank you. And you?

       Here are some other responses:

       Optimē mē habeō!   I feel great!

       Satis bene mē habeō.   I feel well enough.

       Nōn ita bene mē habeō.   I don't feel so good.

       Male mē habeō.   I feel poorly.

       Pessimē mē habeō!   I feel terrible!

VI   Quid est hoc?   What is this?

       Hoc est mēnsa.   This is a table.

VII   Caput mihi dolet.   My head aches.

       Mē paenitet!   I'm sorry!

VIII   Quot annōs nātus(a) es?   How old are you?

       _____ annōs nātus(a) sum.   I am _____ years old.

IX	Loquerisne Latīnē?	Do you speak Latin?
	Ita. Loquor Latīnē.	Yes. I speak Latin.
X	Fēlīcem nātālem tibi.	Happy birthday to you.
XI	Quaenam est tempestās hodiē?	What is the weather today?
	Sōl (nōn) lūcet.	The sun is (not) shining.
	Pluit.	It's raining.
	Frīgidum (calidum) est.	It's cold (warm).
	Quōmodō hoc Latīnē dīcitur?	How do you say this in Latin?
XII	Fēlīcem nātālem Christī!	Merry Christmas!
	Fēlīcem annum novum!	Happy new year!
XIII	Nūbilum / Ventōsum / Nebulōsum est.	It's cloudy / windy / foggy.
XIV	Ignōsce mihi, quaesō.	Please, excuse me.
	Mea culpa! Mē paenitet!	My fault! I'm sorry!
XV	Loquerisne Latīnē?	Do you speak Latin?
	Latīnē parum loquor.	I speak Latin a little.
XVI	Hic est meus amīcus _____.	This is my friend _____. (male)
XVII	Haec est mea amīca _____.	This is my friend _____. (female)
XVIII	Repetitiō māter memoriae.	Repetition is the mother of memory.
	Est dictum bonum.	This is a good saying.
XIX	Nōnne sūdum est?	Isn't the weather nice?
	Ita. Sūdum est.	Yes. It's nice.
XX	Fulgurat!	It's lightning!
	Tōnat!	It's thundering!
XXI	Lūdō lūdāmus.	Let's play a game.
	Bene. Quī lūdus?	Okay. Which game?
	Tabula aut Mendāx	Tabula or Mendax
XXII	Eāmus ad scholam.	Let's go to school.
XXIII	Īmus ad scholam.	We're going to school.
	Bene sit vōbīs!	Have fun!
XXIV	Hoc nōn mihi placet.	This is no fun.
	Eāmus domum.	Let's go home.

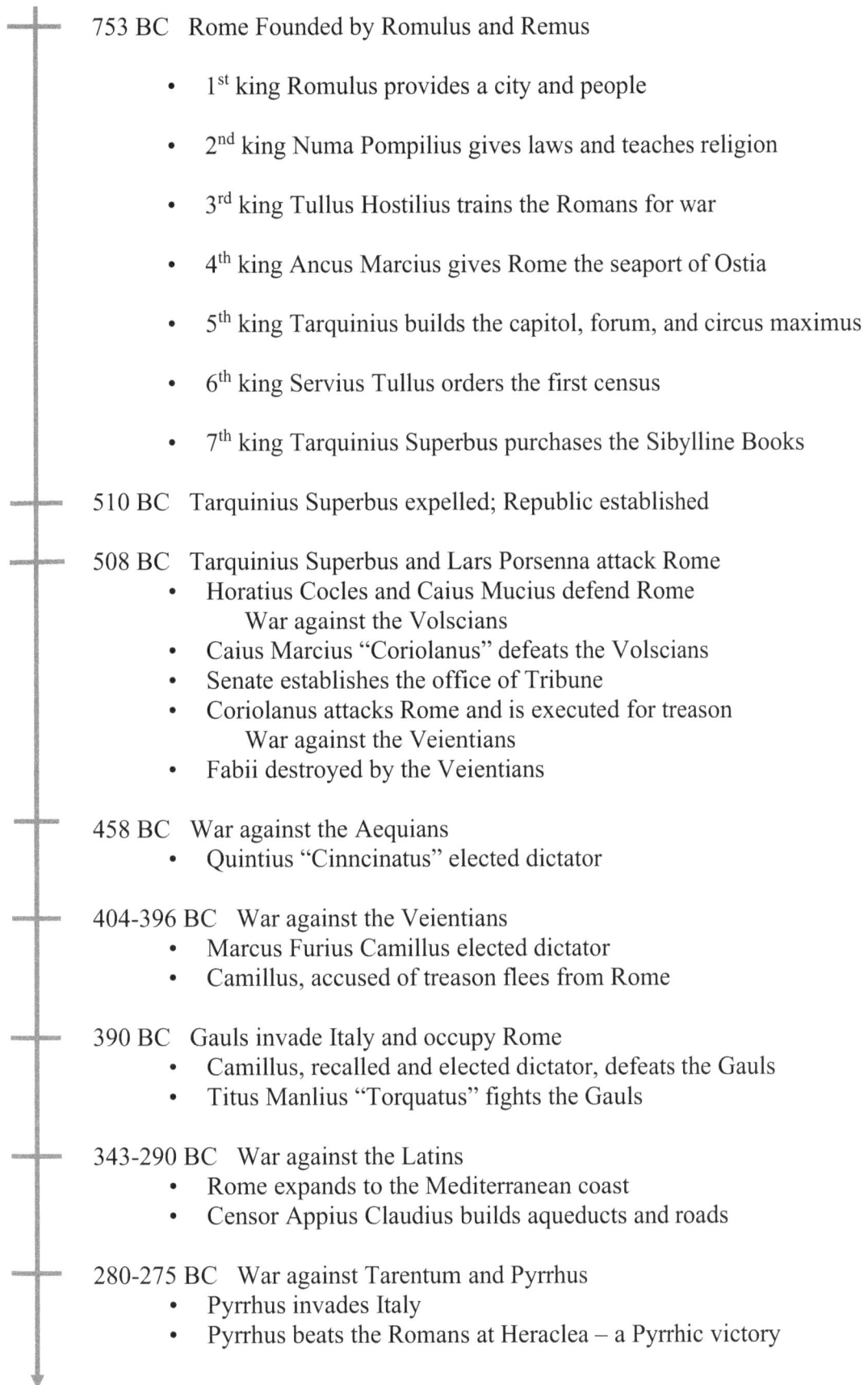

753 BC   Rome Founded by Romulus and Remus

- 1st king Romulus provides a city and people

- 2nd king Numa Pompilius gives laws and teaches religion

- 3rd king Tullus Hostilius trains the Romans for war

- 4th king Ancus Marcius gives Rome the seaport of Ostia

- 5th king Tarquinius builds the capitol, forum, and circus maximus

- 6th king Servius Tullus orders the first census

- 7th king Tarquinius Superbus purchases the Sibylline Books

510 BC   Tarquinius Superbus expelled; Republic established

508 BC   Tarquinius Superbus and Lars Porsenna attack Rome
- Horatius Cocles and Caius Mucius defend Rome
        War against the Volscians
- Caius Marcius "Coriolanus" defeats the Volscians
- Senate establishes the office of Tribune
- Coriolanus attacks Rome and is executed for treason
        War against the Veientians
- Fabii destroyed by the Veientians

458 BC   War against the Aequians
- Quintius "Cinncinatus" elected dictator

404-396 BC   War against the Veientians
- Marcus Furius Camillus elected dictator
- Camillus, accused of treason flees from Rome

390 BC   Gauls invade Italy and occupy Rome
- Camillus, recalled and elected dictator, defeats the Gauls
- Titus Manlius "Torquatus" fights the Gauls

343-290 BC   War against the Latins
- Rome expands to the Mediterranean coast
- Censor Appius Claudius builds aqueducts and roads

280-275 BC   War against Tarentum and Pyrrhus
- Pyrrhus invades Italy
- Pyrrhus beats the Romans at Heraclea – a Pyrrhic victory

ALPES MONTES

NORICUM

Aquincum

Dravus

PANNONIA

Augusta Praetoria

Comum

Aquileia

Savus

Verona

Mediolan(i)um

Padus

Mantua

DALMATIA

AEMILIA

LIGURIA

APPENNINUS

Luna

(H)ADRIATICUM MARE

Arnus

Forum Iulii

Pisae

UMBRIA

Tiberis

SABINI

PICENUM

Corsica

ETRURIA

MONS

Aleria

Tarquinii

Reate

MARSI

Nomentum

Roma

Tusculum

APULIA

Lavinium

LATIUM

Cannae

Formiae

CAMPANIA

Caieta

Venusia

Brundisium

VESUVIUS MONS

Pompeii

Tarentum

CALABRIA

LUCANIA

Sardinia

TYRRHENUM

MARE

Carales

Bruttii

Sicilia

AETNA MONS

AFRICUM MARE

Himeras

Hippo Regius

Agrigentum

SICULUM / AUSONIUM

Carthago

Syracusae

MARE

INTERNUM MARE

Hadrumetum

Used by permission of
the Ancient World Mapping Center

AFRICA

N

W   E

S

| 0 | 50 | 100 | 150 | 200 Miles |

| 0 | 50 | 100 | 150 | 200 | 250 | 300 Kilometers |

Famous Men of Rome
by John H. Haaren and A. B. Poland
Revised by Thomas Caucutt and Ruth Baldwin

I – Disciplīna Ūnus (*Famous Men of Rome* I.1-2)

Many, many years ago, in the pleasant land of Italy, there was a little city called Alba. It stood on the sunny side of a mountain, near the river Tiber and not far from the Mediterranean Sea. In this city and around the mountain lived a brave, intelligent people known as Latins. Several other tribes inhabited the adjacent mountains and plains.

According to ancient stories, Troy was destroyed by the Greeks after a long war. Its ruins can still be seen.

The Latins were ruled by kings, and one of their kings in very early times was named Ae-ne´as. He was a famous Trojan chief who had come over the seas to Italy and settled there with his family and friends after Troy was destroyed by the Greeks.

A great many years after the death of Aeneas, one of his descendants, named Pro´cas, was king of Alba. He ruled wisely and well for a long time, and his rather small kingdom on the mountain side, with its wheat fields and vineyards, was very prosperous. He had two sons, one named Nu´mi-tor, and the other A-mu´li-us. As Numitor was the elder, he was heir to his father's throne, but when King Procas died, Amulius seized the kingdom by force and made himself king.

Procas, King of Alba

Amulius and Numitor

Then Numitor, with his two children, a boy and a girl, left the king's palace at Alba and went to reside on a farm a short distance away.

Amulius was now king, but he did not feel quite happy. He was much troubled about Numitor's son and daughter. The son, he thought, might someday claim the right to be king as heir of his father, or the daughter might marry and have a son who could become king as grandchild of Numitor.

Amulius usurps the throne of his brother.

To prevent either of these things from happening, Amulius had Numitor's son secretly put to death, and he appointed the daughter, Syl´vi-a, to be a priestess, or an attendant, in the temple of the goddess Ves´ta. Only young girls were appointed attendants in this temple, and they had to take a vow that they would not marry for 30 years. They were called Vestal Virgins. It was their duty to keep a fire burning continually on the altar of the goddess. This was called the Sacred Fire, and it was believed that if it went out, some great disaster would happen to the city.

Vesta was worshipped as the goddess of home and family. Vestals spent ten years learning their duties, ten years serving as priestesses, and ten years teaching the new priestesses their duties.

Amulius now thought there was nothing to hinder him from being king of Alba all his life. But one day the god Mars came down to the city from his palace on a high mountaintop and saw Sylvia as she went out of the temple to get water at a well. He fell deeply in love with her. She also fell in love with the god, for he had the appearance of a handsome young man. They were married secretly, and in course of time, Sylvia had beautiful twin boys. When Amulius heard of this, he gave orders that

Sylvia's twin sons

Sylvia should be put to death for breaking her vow and that the two infants should be thrown into the Tiber. These wicked orders were carried out, for no one dared to disobey the king.

Fortunately, however, the babies had been placed in a stout basket, which floated along the Tiber until it was carried by the waters to the foot of a hill called Pal´a-tine Hill. Here the huge roots of a wild fig tree upset the basket, and the little ones were thrown out upon the riverbank.

A wolf saves the boys.

At this moment a great she-wolf came strolling down the hill to drink at the river's edge. She heard the feeble cries of the infants and went to the place where they lay helpless on the wet sands. She touched them gently with her rough paws, turned them over, and licked their faces and plump bodies. Perhaps she thought they were some of her own cubs. At any rate, she carried the babies up the hill to her cave under a large rock. There she fed them as she fed her own cubs and seemed pleased to have them near her. It is said that a woodpecker flew in and out of the cave many times a day, bringing berries for the boys to eat.

Faustulus

One morning as Faust´u-lus, the herdsman of King Amulius, was going over the Palatine Hill looking for cattle that had gone astray, he saw the boys playing with the wolf at the mouth of her cave. He frightened the wolf away and took the boys to his home. His wife pitied the little foundlings and cared for them as though they were her own children.

Romulus and Remus

The herdsman named them Rom´u-lus and Re´mus. They grew up to be strong, handsome youths, brave and kind. Until they were 20 years old, they lived with the herdsman and helped him in his work and roamed over the hills light-hearted and free.

II - DISCIPLĪNA DUO (*Famous Men of Rome* I.2)

During all these years Numitor lived on his farm, and his brother, Amulius, remained king of Alba. Numitor did not know that his two grandsons had been saved from a watery grave and were living so near to him.

But one day Remus had a quarrel with some of the herdsmen of Numitor, and they took him prisoner. They then brought him before Numitor, who was much impressed with the noble appearance of the youth and asked him who he was.

Romulus and Remus are reunited with their grandfather, Numitor.

Remus told all he knew about himself and Romulus, how they had been found at the cave of the she-wolf and had been reared by the king's herdsman. Just then Faustulus and Romulus came searching for Remus and were full of joy when they found that no harm had come to him. Numitor questioned the herdsman about the finding of the twins, and after hearing his story, was convinced that Romulus and Remus were Sylvia's boys, who had been strangely saved from the wrath of their cruel uncle. He was very happy at finding his grandsons, and he thanked the herdsman for his good care of them.

Romulus and Remus were also very happy at finding a grandfather and at the sudden change of their fortune. When they were told about Amulius and his wicked deeds, they resolved to punish him for the murder of their mother. So with a few followers, they rushed to the palace at Alba and entered the king's chamber.

"Behold! We are Sylvia's sons whom you thought you had killed," they shouted to Amulius, as he started up in alarm at their entrance. "You killed our mother, and you shall die for it."

Amulius the usurper killed

Before he could utter a word, they sprang on him with drawn swords and cut his head off. Then they brought Numitor to the palace, and the people welcomed him as the rightful king of Alba.

III - Disciplīna Trēs (*Famous Men of Rome* I.3)

After a little time the two brothers thought they would build a city on Palatine Hill, where the she-wolf had nursed them. So they began to talk of a name for their city.

The founding of Rome

"I will be king and give the new city my name," said Romulus.

"No," cried Remus. "I will be the king and name the city after myself. I have just as much right as you have."

So the brothers argued for a while, but at last they agreed to settle the matter in this way:

At midnight Romulus was to stand on Palatine Hill, and Remus was to stand on another hill a short distance off. Then they were to ask the gods to show a sign of favor in the sky, and the first one who should see anything very remarkable was to name the new city and be its king.

So they went to watch, but nothing happened until sunrise of the second day, when Remus saw six great vultures flying across the sky from north to south. He ran swiftly to Palatine Hill and told Romulus what he had seen. But just then twelve vultures, one after another, flew high over the head of Romulus in an almost unbroken line and were soon lost to view.

Then Romulus claimed that he had the favor of the gods, as more birds appeared to him first. Romulus asked the opinion of some of his friends, and as they all agreed that he was right in his claim, he paid no further attention to Remus but began to lay out the new city. He gave it the name of Ro´ma, after himself. With a plow he marked out the space on Palatine Hill and along the banks of the Tiber. Then he built a low wall round about to protect the city from invaders.

Romulus, founder of Rome and its first king. Each of Rome's seven kings built up the city and strengthened the Roman people.

One day while the work was going on, Remus came by in a very bitter mood. He was still angry with Romulus. He laughed scornfully at the little wall and said to his brother, "Shall such a defense as this keep your city? It may prevent children from getting in, but not men, for they can jump over it."

Remus scoffs at Romulus' wall and is killed.

So saying, Remus put his hands on the wall and sprang over it to show that his words were true. Romulus, in a sudden outburst of rage, struck

Archaeologists have discovered the remains of a little timber hut on the Palatine Hill. It may be the remains of the *Casa Romulī,* or "hut of Romulus," a copy of one of the early huts which the ancient Romans kept and maintained much like a museum of earlier times.

The Romans believed that their city was established on April 21, 753 BC.

We often think of the entire Italian peninsula as belonging to the Romans, but it did not at first. There were many other Italian peoples such as the Latins, Sabines, Etruscans, Aequians, Umbrians, Oscans, and Samnites. These peoples all had their own religions, customs, laws, and languages.

The Sabine women

War with the Sabines

him on the head with a spade and instantly killed him, at the same time crying out, "So perish anyone who shall hereafter attempt to leap over my wall."

Then Romulus continued his work. While he was building his wall, he also built some wooden houses. The first houses were nothing more than wood huts covered with mud and straw. But in course of time the Romans had houses of stone, and they built fine temples and theatres and streets and squares, and at last Rome became the greatest and grandest city in the whole world.

IV – Disciplīna Quattuor (*Famous Men of Rome* I.4)

Romulus founded Rome in the year 753 BC, but after he had built his city, he had some difficulty getting people to live in it. He only had a few followers and was not able to obtain any more. He decided, therefore, to make Rome a place of refuge, to which people who had gotten into trouble in other countries might come for safety.

And so when those who had committed crime in other places and had to flee from their homes to escape punishment found out that Romulus would give them refuge, they came in large numbers to his city. People also came who had been driven from home by enemies or had run away for one reason or another. It was not long, therefore, until Rome was full of men. There were men from many different tribes and countries. Thus the Roman nation began, and for years it steadily grew and prospered.

But the Romans were much troubled about one thing. A great many of them had no wives, and they could not get any, because the women of the neighboring tribes would not marry them; the Romans had a bad name. Romulus was very anxious that his people should have good wives, but how they should get them greatly puzzled him for a long time. At last he hit upon a plan and began at once to carry it out.

He sent messengers to the cities all around to announce that on a certain day a great festival in honor of the god Ju´pi-ter would be held on the plain in front of Rome. There were to be games, combats, horse-racing, and other sports. The people were invited to attend the festival and also to take part in the contests for the prizes.

When the festival day came, a multitude of men and women from far and near assembled before the walls of Rome. Hundreds of pretty girls were there in fine dresses. A great many came from the Sa´bine tribe. This was a tribe of warriors that lived on a mountain near Rome.

Suddenly Romulus blew a loud blast upon a horn. Then, quick as a flash, the Romans seized the girls and bore them off to Rome.

The Sabines were greatly enraged at this, and their king, Ti´tus Ta´ti-us, raised a large army and at once began a war against the Romans. The war went on for three years, but the Sabines were so strong that Romulus could not defeat them in the field. He therefore withdrew his army into the city. King Tatius quickly marched after him, resolved to take Rome or perish in the attempt.

Now Romulus had built a strong fortress on a hill near Palatine Hill to keep invaders from Rome. The hill was called the Sa-tur′ni-an Hill, and the fortress was in the charge of a brave Roman captain, who had a daughter named Tar-pe′ia.

Tarpeia

When the Sabines reached this fortress, they could go no farther. They marched up and down, seeking a spot where they might force an entrance, but they could find none. There was a small, barred gate in the fortress, and through this gate Tarpeia came out to get water. King Tatius saw her. He at once stepped forward and said, "Fair maiden, open the gate and let us in. If you do, you shall have for your reward anything you ask."

Tarpeia was gazing with admiration at the bracelets of gold which the Sabines wore on their arms.

"I will open the gate," said she, "if you will give me some of those things which your soldiers wear upon their arms."

King Tatius agreed, and Tarpeia opened the gate. As the Sabines strode past the silly maiden, each threw at her, not his bracelet, but his shield.

The shield was round or oblong and was made of bronze or of wicker-work or of ox hide covered with metal plates. It had two handles at the back, and the soldier held it up with his left hand and arm so that he could move it up or down to save his head or breast from blows.

Tarpeia stood in amazement as the heavy shields began to pile up around her. One struck her, and then another and another. At last she fell to the ground and was soon crushed to death.

When the soldiers saw that Tarpeia was dead, they took up the shields they had thrown at her. Then they hurled her body from the top of a great rock that was near the gate she had opened. The rock was afterward known as the Tarpeian Rock, and for hundreds of years the punishment for traitors was to be thrown from this rock.

As soon as they passed the fortress, the Sabines ran down the Saturnian Hill to make an attack on Rome. But Romulus and his band of warriors bravely came out of the city to drive back the enemy. The two forces met in the valley, and then a fierce battle began.

While they were fighting, a crowd of excited women came running from the city. They were the Sabine women whom the Romans had carried off. Some of them had their infants in their arms, and they rushed between the lines of soldiers and begged that the fighting stop.

"Do not fight any more for us," they said to their fathers and brothers. "We love the Romans, and we have married them. They have been good to us, and we do not wish to leave them."

Of course, this settled the matter. Romulus had a talk with King Tatius, and they agreed not to fight any more. They also agreed that the two nations should be as one. They joined their governments and their armies, and each of the kings had equal power.

Soon afterward King Tatius died, and Romulus ruled his kingdom alone for nearly 40 years. He was a wise and just king and did a great deal of good for his people. He established a body called the Senate to help him in important affairs of government. It was called the Senate, from *senex*, the Latin world for an *old man*. It was formed of the chiefs, or *old men*, of the earliest settlers in Rome. The descendants of those settlers were called *patricians*, or fathers, from the Latin word *pāter*, meaning *father*. They were the nobles, or upper class, in Rome. The ordinary citizens were called *plebeians*, from *plēbs*, the Latin word for *common people*.

The Senate

The patricians

The plebeians

Romulus took care to train up the young Romans to be good soldiers. Outside the city, along the bank of the Tiber, there was a great plain which in later times was called the Cam´pus Mar´ti-us, or Field of Mars. Here the Roman soldiers were drilled. They were taught how to use the spear and the javelin and the sword and the shield. They were also exercised in running and jumping, wrestling and swimming, and carrying heavy loads. Thus the young men were made fit to bear the hardships of war and to fight and win battles for their country.

It is related that in his old age Romulus suddenly disappeared from the earth. He called his people together on a great field one day, and while he was speaking to them, a violent storm came on. The rain fell in torrents, and the lightning and thunder were so terrible that the people fled to their homes.

When the storm was over, the people went back to the field, but Romulus was nowhere to be found. Then it was said that his father, the god Mars, had taken him up to the clouds in a golden chariot.

Next morning at early dawn, a Roman citizen named Ju´li-us saw a figure descending from the heavens. It had the appearance of Romulus, and it approached Julius and said, "Go and tell my people that it is the will of the gods that Rome shall be the greatest city of the world. Let them be brave and warlike, and no human power shall be able to conquer them."

Afterward the Romans worshiped Romulus as a god. They worshiped him under the name Quir´in-us, which was one of the names of the god Mars, and they built a temple to him on a hill which was called the Quir´in-al Hill.

V – Disciplīna Quīnque (*Famous Men of Rome* II)

For a year after the disappearance of Romulus there was no king of Rome. The city was ruled by the Senate. But the people were not satisfied. They preferred to be ruled by one man, and although they had the right to elect a king themselves, they left the choice to the Senate. The Senate chose Nu´ma Pom-pil´i-us, a very good and wise man who belonged to the nation of the Sabines.

Numa Pompilius, second king of Rome, establishes laws for peace and teaches the Romans to fear the gods.

The first thing that Numa did after learning that he had been chosen king was to consult the augurs to find out if it was the will of the gods that he should be the ruler of Rome.

The augurs were what we would call fortune tellers. A number of them lived in Rome. They were much respected and occupied a large temple at the expense of the public. They pretended that by watching the sky and observing how birds and animals acted they could tell what would happen to people and to nations. Then when they were alone, they would have a great deal of fun over the tricks they played upon the foolish people.

Numa made many important changes at the very beginning of his rule. Before he came to the throne, Roman young men were not brought up to know any business but war. It was considered disgraceful for a Roman citizen, whether rich or poor, to work at any trade or manufacture. The slaves, who were prisoners captured in battle, did all the hard work. They made all the clothing, tools, weapons, and household articles. They cooked and served the meals and were general servants for the Roman families. Roman citizens might, however, without being degraded, work on farms and vineyards, and many of them made their living in this way.

Shortly after King Numa began his reign, he divided some of the public lands into small farms and gave one of these farms to every poor Roman. The public lands were lands that belonged to the nation and not to private persons.

It was rather hard at first for the newly made farmers to be contented on their farms and to do good work. They were mostly soldiers and had very little knowledge of anything except marching and fighting. But it was not long before they began to understand what a blessing it is to be self-supporting and independent. Their little farms were pleasant homes. They began to love their new life, and soon they were able to raise enough for the support of themselves and their families, with something to spare.

King Numa made many good laws. These laws were engraved on tablets of brass and at certain times were read and explained to the people by lawyers.

Numa was very friendly with the people of the countries surrounding Rome. He gave them help in times of trouble and would never listen to any talk of war with them. During the many years he was king, Rome had no enemies and no wars.

Numa reforms the laws of Rome.

In a sacred grove, just outside the walls of Rome, a beautiful woman named E-ger´i-a lived in a handsome grotto, or cavern. She seemed to have a great knowledge of magic and could do wonderful things. Whenever she called to the songbirds, they would come flying around her. They would also perch on her head and shoulders and hands and sing their sweetest songs. Even the fierce animals of the woods were her friends, and great bears and wolves would lie at her feet for hours and purr like cats.

This mysterious woman goddess, or fairy, or whatever she was, greatly loved and honored good King Numa, and at last they were married. Then she taught him many of the magical secrets she possessed. He carefully studied the lessons she gave him, and in time he was able to do wonderful things himself.

The Romans were earnest worshipers of the gods and goddesses. They believed that there were many such beings; they had many grand temples for religious service.

King Numa always paid great attention to religion. He appointed a large number of officials to take care of the temples and to see that all the sacred ceremonies were properly carried out. He was constant and faithful in his own worship and thus, by his example, gradually induced the whole Roman people to become attentive to their religion.

The greatest of the gods that the Romans believed in was the god Jupiter. He was supposed to rule both the sky and the earth. He was so powerful that he could send thunderbolts from the heavens and make the earth tremble by his nod. He had a wife named Ju´no, who had a great deal to do with managing the affairs of the earth. It was at one time believed that Jupiter resided with many other gods on the top of a high mountain in Greece. This mountain was so thickly covered by clouds that the gods could not be seen, but they could see everything that took place on the earth.

Jupiter had two brothers, named Nep´tune and Plu´to. Neptune was the god of the sea. He lived in a grand, golden palace at the bottom of the Mediterranean. He ruled everything under and upon the waters of the world. Now and then he sailed over the ocean in a grand chariot drawn by large fish called dolphins. When he was angry, he caused the sea to rise in huge waves.

Pluto, the other brother of Jupiter, was the god of Ha´des, or the land of the dead. His home was far down in the earth, where all was dark and gloomy. The Romans believed that when people died, they were carried away to the gloomy kingdom of Pluto.

The other principal gods were Mars, Mer´cu-ry, Vul´can, A-pol´lo, and Ja´nus.

Mars was the god of war and was especially honored in Rome because it was believed that he was the father of Romulus. Certain days of the year were made festival days in his honor, and then there were splendid processions, songs of praise, and religious dances.

Mercury, the son of Jupiter, was the god of eloquence and commerce. He was also the messenger of the other gods. He was generally represented as flying swiftly through the air, carrying messages from place to place to place. On his head and feet were small wings, and in his hand he bore a golden staff with serpents twined around it.

Vulcan was a skillful worker in metals. He had a great forge in the heart of a burning mountain, where he made wonderful things of iron, copper, and gold. He looked after the welfare of blacksmiths,

Jupiter and Juno

Neptune

Pluto

Mars

Mercury

Vulcan

coppersmiths, and goldsmiths and was their special god.

Apollo, also called Phoe´bus, which meant *the sun*, was the god of day. He gave light and heat to the world. He was also the god of music, archery, and medicine. His sister, Di-a´na, was the moon goddess or goddess of the night. She was also the goddess of hunting. In pictures she is sometimes represented with a quiver of arrows over her left shoulder and holding a stag by the horns.

Apollo

Diana

The god Janus was very much honored by the Romans. It was believed that this god presided over the beginning of every undertaking, and so when the Romans began any important work or business, they prayed first to Janus. For this reason, the first month or beginning of the year was called the month of Janus, or *January*. Janus was also the god of gates and doors. In statuary and pictures, he is often shown with two faces looking in opposite directions, because every door faces two ways – outward and inward.

Janus

Numa Pompilius built a temple in honor of Janus. The door of this temple was always open in time of war, as a sign that the god had gone out to help the Romans. In time of peace the door was shut.

The Romans also believed in Ve´nus, the goddess of love; Mi-ner´va, the goddess of wisdom; Flora, the goddess of flowers; and many others.

Venus, Minerva, and Flora

The Romans had no special day, such as our Sunday, for religious services, but their temples (except the temple of Janus) were open every day. They had prayers and songs and sometimes what they called sacred dances. They also made offerings such as fruits or vegetables, oxen, lambs, or goats to the gods. The offerings finally went into the hands of the priests of the temples.

Numa Pompilius reigned for nearly half a century, and under him the Romans were a peaceful, prosperous, and happy people.

VI - Disciplīna Sex (*Famous Men of Rome* III)

The third king of Rome was Tul´lus Hos-til´i-us. In his reign a remarkable combat took place between three Roman brothers and three Latin brothers. The combat came about in this way:

Tullus Hostilius, third king of Rome, taught the Romans how to fight bravely.

For years the people of Rome and the people of Alba, also called Latins, as has been already said, were continually quarreling. They would invade and plunder each other's lands. At last, after many petty contests, war was declared between the two nations.

War with the Latins

King Tullus marched the Roman army to the border of Alba, but here his progress was stopped by a great force of Latins, under the command of Met´ti-us, the Alban king.

Tullus looked at the strong lines of Latin soldiers, standing firm and resolute to resist the advance of the Romans, and thought that it might be well to have a meeting with Mettius to see whether they could agree on some way of settling the quarrel without a fight between the two armies. He sent for Mettius and they talked the matter over. Mettius also wished very much to avoid a battle, and he said to Tullus, "Would it not be well to fight in such a way that only a few of our soldiers would be killed instead of many? My plan is this: You shall select three of the best fighting men in the Roman army, and I will select the best three in the army of Alba. The six men shall fight in the presence of the two armies. If the Romans win, Alba will submit to Rome; but if the Latins win, then Rome must submit to Alba. What say you to the plan?"

"It is a good one," said King Tullus, "and I agree to it. May the best men win!"

With these words they separated and went to prepare for the combat on which was to depend the fate of the two nations.

The Horatii

The Romans selected as their champions three brothers belonging to a family known as the Horatius family. The brothers were called the Hora'ti-i because this word is the plural form of *Horatius*. The Horatii brothers were tall, handsome men with wonderful strength, endurance, and courage.

The Curiatii

The Albans also selected three brothers as their champions. They were called the Cu-ri-a'ti-i. They were bold, skillful soldiers, famous for manly beauty and strength, and were champions well worthy to fight for a nation.

When all was ready, the Horatii and the Curiatii advanced to the center of a large field and took their places. They carried short, thick swords and large, round shields made of stout leather and metal. The two armies gathered around the six champions but at a distance, so as to leave them plenty of room to fight.

There was silence for a few moments, and then the shrill notes of a trumpet rang out as a signal for the battle to begin. Clash! Clang! went the swords upon the shields, and the fight began.

Quick, skillful blows were given for a short time, but no one was seriously hurt. Suddenly the Latins shouted in intense excitement. Lo! One of the Horatii, after a fierce struggle with one of the Curiatii, was stricken down dead! The Romans groaned, hung their heads, and looked in anxious doubt at their remaining two champions.

Bravely the Horatii stood – two to three – and fought with all their might. Step by step they drove the Curiatii back across the field. Cheers rang out from the Romans at this heroic effort. The victory might yet be theirs!

But alas! one of the Curiatii, with a swift, sly sword thrust, killed another of the Horatii. The Albans shouted, "We have won! We have won! We have won! Hail to the brave Curiatii!"

The Romans were wild with grief and rage. They now had only one champion left – Horatius, the last of the heroic Horatii – and he was running from the field as if he had given up the fight. He was followed by the Curiatii though they were all wounded. One of them, running ahead of the others, came up to Horatius and was raising his sword when the Roman turned upon him quickly and killed him.

The cries of the two armies were now hushed as if by magic. All eyes were upon the champions, and there was a painful silence.

Another of the Curiatii now came up and began to fight Horatius. But the Roman met the attack with great coolness and skill, and soon he killed the second Latin. Thus, under the pretense of running away, Horatius separated the three Curiatii and killed two of them. Then he advanced in a furious manner on the other Latin and began a desperate fight with him. Soon he struck him down with a deadly blow. Rome was victorious! From the whole Roman army now came the cry, as if from one man, "Hail to the brave Horatius! Hail to the champion and savior of his country!"

Then they seized Horatius in their arms and carried him in triumph to King Tullus, who placed the laurel wreath of victory on his head. This was one of the ways by which the Romans honored their soldiers who had been very brave in battle. They also honored Horatius by erecting a statue of him in one of the temples of the city.

With songs of joy the army marched back to Rome. Horatius walked by the side of the king. A throng of women came forth from the gates of the city, eager to greet the soldiers and to rejoice with them over the great victory. The sister of Horatius was in the throng. She had been secretly engaged to be married to one of the Curiatii, for the Romans and Albans were near neighbors and frequently visited one another in times of peace. When she learned that her brother had slain her lover, she began to weep bitterly. Then pointing at Horatius she cried out, "You have killed my lover! Do not come near me! I hate and curse you!"

Horatius, in a fit of anger, suddenly drew his sword and stabbed her to the heart. As she fell dead at his feet, he cried in a loud voice, "So perish the Roman maiden who weeps for her country's enemy!"

For this shocking murder Horatius was tried and sentenced to death, but the people would not allow the sentence to be carried out. He was made to do a certain penance for the crime and afterward was set free.

VII – DISCIPLĪNA SEPTEM (*Famous Men of Rome* IV.1-3)

The next king of Rome was An´cus Mar´ci-us. He was a grandson of Numa Pompilius and a very good king. He thought that it would be an advantage to Rome to have a sea harbor for ships, so he founded a city at one of the mouths of the Tiber, on the coast of the Mediterranean, about fifteen miles from Rome. The city was called Ostia, which is the Latin word meaning *mouths*. Latin was the language spoken by the Roman people.

During the reign of Ancus Marcius, a rich man named Lu´cu-mo came

Ancus Marcius, fourth king of Rome, built Ostia, Rome's seaport.

Lucumo, or Tarquin, a nobleman from Etruria. Etruria was a rich and powerful region of Italy north of Rome. The people who lived there were called Etruscans. They were sometimes at peace with Rome and at other times were the Romans' bitter enemies.

to live in Rome. He came from Tar-quin´i-i, a town some miles distant from Rome, in the country called E-tru´ri-a, so the Romans called him Tar-quin´i-us, which in English is *Tarquin*.

A very wonderful thing happened to Tarquin while he was on his way to Rome. He drove in a chariot, with his wife Tan´a-quil seated beside him, and their servants following behind. As they were approaching the city, an eagle which appeared in the sky above them came gently down and snatched the cap from Tarquin's head with its beak. After hovering around for a few moments, the eagle replaced the cap, and with loud screams, flew away.

Tarquin was much surprised at this strange event. He did not know what to think of it. But Tanaquil was much pleased. She said to her husband that it was a sign sent by the gods and meant that he was to be a great man – perhaps a king.

Tarquin was not in Rome long before he became a favorite with everybody. The people liked him because he spent a great deal of money in doing good. The king also liked him and often asked his advice in affairs of government, for Tarquin was a man of great knowledge and wisdom. And when King Ancus became old and felt that his death was near, he appointed Tarquin the guardian of his two sons who were then but boys.

Tarquinius, fifth king of Rome, was a great builder.

Soon afterward Ancus died, and the people elected Tarquin king. He reigned for nearly 40 years and did a great deal for the good of the city.

It was King Tarquin who began the building of the famous temple of Jupiter on Saturnian Hill – the same hill on which stood the fortress that Romulus built. While the workmen were digging for the foundations of the temple, they found a man's head so well preserved that it looked as if it had been buried quite recently. This was so strange a thing that the augurs were asked about it, and they said it was a sign that Rome would become the *head* or chief city of the world. So the new building was

The Capitol

called the Capitol, from *caput*, the Latin word for *head*, and the hill was called Cap´it-o-line Hill. This has given our language a word. We call the building in which our congress meets – as well as that in which a state legislature meets – the Capitol.

It took a long time to finish the Capitol, but when finished, it was a great and beautiful building. It covered more than eight acres. Its gates or doors were of solid brass, thickly plated with gold. The walls inside were all marble, ornamented with beautiful figures engraved in silver.

Tarquin also began several other works in Rome which were too great and costly to be finished in a lifetime. One of them was to enlarge the wall around the city. The wall that Romulus had made was only around Palatine Hill, but since then, the city had been much enlarged. In course of time it covered seven hills. This is why Rome is often called the seven-hilled city. The seven hills were the Palatine, the Capitoline, the Cae´li-an, the Quirinal, the Es´qui-line, the Vim´in-al, and the A´ven-tine.

The seven hills of Rome

One of the other things Tarquin did was to establish a kind of police called *lictors*. These were officers who always walked before the king whenever he appeared in public. Each lictor bore upon his shoulder an ax enclosed in a bundle of rods tied with a red strap. This was called the *fas'-ces*. It was a mark of the power of the king. The ax meant that the king might order criminals to be beheaded, and the rods meant that he might punish offenders by flogging.

The lictors

Another work of Tarquin was the Circus, afterwards called the Circus Max'i-mus (*great circus*). This was a place where horse races and games and shows of various kinds were held. The Romans were very fond of such amusements. Great numbers of them always went to the shows, but it was easy for them to go, for they did not have to pay for admission. The cost of the shows was paid often by rich Romans who wanted to gain the favor of the people and often by the government.

The Circus Maximus

The circus had no roof, but there were a great many seats all round, and in the middle was a large open space for the performers. This space was covered with sand and was called the *arena*, a word which is Latin for *sand*.

Because so many people attended the circus, it had to be very large. In the time when Rome was an empire, about which you will read later on in this book, the Circus Maximus was so large that it contained seats for 250,000 people. From the circus and arena of the Romans, these words have come into use in our own language.

Besides building the Circus, King Tarquin also greatly improved the Forum by making covered walks or porticos all around it. The Forum was a large open space at the foot of the Capitoline Hill, where public meetings were held and where people came to hear the news or to talk about politics. It was also used as a marketplace, and merchants showed their goods in shops or stores along the porticos. In course of time, great buildings were erected around the Forum. There were courts of justice and temples and statues and monuments of various kinds. The Senate House, where the Senate held its meetings, was also in the Forum. From the end of the Forum, next to the Capitoline Hill, there was a passage leading up to the Capitol.

The Forum

The Curia, or Senate House

The most useful thing King Tarquin did was the building of a great sewer through the city and into the Tiber. Before his time there were no sewers in Rome, though the places between the hills were swampy and wet. This made many parts of the city very unhealthy. Tarquin's sewer drained the swamps and carried the water into the river. It crossed the entire city. It was so high and wide that men could sail into it in boats, and it was so strongly built that it has lasted to the present time. The great sewer is still in use.

The Cloaca Maxima, or Great Sewer of Rome

Tarquin wanted very much to change one of the laws about the army, but an augur named At'ti-us Na'vi-us told him such a thing could not be done without a sign from the gods. This made the king angry, and he thought he would try to show that the augurs did not have the power or knowledge they were supposed to have, so he said to Attius, "Come now, I will give you a question. I am thinking whether a certain thing I have in my mind can be done or not. Go and find out from your sign if it can be done."

Navius went away, and shortly afterward returned and told the king that the thing could be done. Then Tarquin said, "Well, I was thinking whether or not you could cut this stone in two with this razor. As you say it can be done, do it."

Navius took the razor and immediately cut the stone in two with the greatest ease. The king never again doubted the power of the augurs.

VIII - DISCIPLĪNA OCTŌ (*Famous Men of Rome* IV.4)

Servius Tullius, sixth king of Rome, finished Tarquin's wall.

On the death of Tarquin, his son-in-law, Ser´vi-us Tul´li-us was made king. Tarquin had two young sons, and the sons of Ancus Marcius were also living; but the people preferred to have Servius Tullius for their king.

Servius was a very good king. He made many good laws and, like King Numa Pompilius, he divided some of the public lands among the poor people of the city.

The Servian Wall

One of the important things Servius did was to finish the wall around the city which Tarquin had begun. This wall was very high. It was made of stone and earth, and on the outside there was a ditch 130 feet deep. There were several gates in the wall, but they were all well guarded night and day by soldiers, so that no enemy could enter.

The census

King Servius was the first to have a census taken in Rome. He made a rule or law that once every five years all the people should assemble in the Campus Martius to be counted. The word *census* is a Latin word meaning a *counting* or reckoning, and we use it in our own country for the counting of people, which takes place every ten years.

Tarquinius Superbus, seventh king of Rome

Servius Tullius was killed by King Tarquin's son, who was also called Tarquin but who got the name Su-per´bus, or *Proud*, because he was a very haughty and cruel man. The dead body of Servius was left lying on the street where he had been killed, and Tul´li-a, wife of the wicked Tarquin and daughter of the murdered king, drove her chariot over it.

The Sybiline Books

Tarquin the Proud now became king. It was during his reign that the Sib´y-line Books were brought to Rome. These books were not like our books. They were merely three bundles of loose pieces of parchment, having moral sentences on them written in the Greek language. This is the story of how the books were obtained:

One morning an old woman came to King Tarquin carrying nine books in her hands. She offered to sell them to the king, but when she named a large sum as the price, he laughed at her and ordered her away. The next day the woman came again but with only six books. She had burned the other three. She offered to sell the six, but she asked the same price that she had asked the day before for the whole nine. The king again laughed at her and drove her away.

The same day Tarquin went to visit the augurs in their temple, and he told them about the old woman and her books. The augurs declared that she was certainly a sibyl and that her books doubtless contained important predictions about Rome.

The sibyls were women who pretended to be able to foretell events. There were sibyls in many countries, but the most famous of them all was the Sibyl of Cu´mae, a town in the south of Italy. This was the sibyl who brought the books to Tarquin.

The Sibyl

Tarquin was now sorry he had not taken the books, and he hoped the woman would come again. She did come on the following day, but she had only three books instead of six. She had burned the other three the day before. The king was very glad to see her. He bought the remaining three books, but he had to pay just as much for them as the old woman had asked at first for the nine. Then the sibyl disappeared and was never seen again.

The ordinary books the Romans had were not like the Sibylline Books. They had no printed books, for printing was not known for many centuries after. Their books were written with pens made of reeds. Their paper was made of the pith of a plant called the *papyrus,* and from this name the word *paper* is derived. To make a book, they cut the paper into leaves or pages, and after writing on them, they pasted the pages one to another sidewise until all the pages of one book were put together. This long strip was made into a cylindrical roll and was called a *volume*, from the Latin word *volūmen*, a roll. When the volume was being read, it was held in both hands, the reader unrolling it with one hand and rolling it with the other.

The Sibylline Books were put in the temple of Jupiter on the Capitoline Hill. Two officers were appointed to keep watch over them. Whenever the Romans were going to war or had any serious trouble, they would consult the books. The way they did it was this: one of the officers would open the stone chest where the books were kept and take out the first piece of parchment on which he laid his hand. Then the Greek sentence found on the piece would be translated into Latin. It was sometimes very hard to tell what the sentence really meant. Often they had to guess. When they made sense out of it, they said that it was a prophecy of the Sibyl and would surely come to pass.

IX - DISCIPLĪNA NOVEM (*Famous Men of Rome* V.1-2)

Tarquin the Proud had a nephew named Junius Brutus. He seemed to be a simpleton, but he was really a very wise man. His brother had been murdered by the king, and he feared the same fate himself, so he pretended to be half-witted and went about saying and doing silly things. Tarquin therefore did him no harm but rather pitied him.

Junius Brutus

Two sons of Tarquin once went to a noted fortune teller, taking Brutus with them. The young men asked several questions. One was, "Who shall rule Rome after Tarquin?"

The fortune-teller gave this answer: "Young men, whichever of you shall first kiss your mother shall be the next ruler of Rome."

The king's sons at once started for home, each eager to be the first to kiss his mother. But Brutus thought that something else was really meant by the answer. So after they had left the fortune-teller, he managed to stumble and fall on his face. Then he kissed the ground, saying, "The earth is the true mother of us all." And as we shall see, Brutus became the next ruler of Rome.

Lucretia and the crime of Tarquinius Sextus

The eldest son of Tarquin was named Sex´tus. He was a very bad man. He deeply injured a beautiful woman named Lu-cret´i-a, the wife of Col-la-ti´nus, his cousin. Lucretia told her husband and father and Junius Brutus what Sextus had done and called upon them to punish him for his wicked deed. Then she plunged a dagger into her breast and fell dead. Brutus drew the dagger from her bleeding body and, holding it up before his horrified companions, exclaimed,

"I vow before the gods to avenge the wronged Lucretia. Not one of the Tarquins shall ever again be king in Rome. Rome shall have no more kings."

Junius Brutus' revenge

They all vowed with Brutus that Lucretia should be avenged and that there should be no more kings in Rome. Then they took up her body and carried it to the Forum. There they showed it to the people, who gathered around in horror at the sight. Brutus no longer appeared dull and simple but stood with head erect and flashing eyes and spoke to the crowd in eloquent, stirring words.

"See what has come from the evil deeds of the Tarquins!" He shouted, pointing to the dead woman. "Let us free ourselves from the rule of these wicked men. Down with Tarquin the tyrant! No more kings in Rome!"

The monarchy ended

The people were much excited by his speech, and they made the Forum ring with their cries: "Down with Tarquin! Down with Tarquin! No more kings! No more kings!"

Then the people resolved to take the power of the king away from Tarquin and to banish him and his family from Rome. They also decided to adopt the good laws which had been made years before by King Servius Tullius and to choose two men each year to govern the nation, instead of a king. The men were to be called consuls and were to rule in turn – one for each month, the other for the next, and so on for twelve months. At the end of the year, two new consuls were to be elected.

The consuls

Meanwhile news of the revolt reached King Tarquin, who was at the time in camp with his army some distance from Rome. He instantly mounted his horse and rode in haste to the city. When he reached the gates, he found them shut against him. As he stood impatiently demanding to be admitted, a Roman officer appeared on the wall and told him of the sentence of banishment. Tarquin rode away, and Rome was rid of him forever (510 BC).

X – Disciplīna Decem (*Famous Men of Rome* V.3)

The people elected Junius Brutus and Lu´ci-us Collatinus, the husband of Lucretia, to be their consuls; but after a short time, Collatinus resigned because he was himself a Tarquin. Pu´bli-us Va-le´ri-us was elected in his stead.

The first consuls of the new Roman Republic

Tarquin now sent messengers to collect his household goods and other things belonging to him which were in Rome. While in the city, the messengers had secret meetings with a number of young men of noble families, and a plot was formed to restore Tarquin to the throne.

A plot to restore Tarquin to the throne

The young nobles vowed that they would destroy the new republic and bring back the king, for they did not like government by the common people. But while they were making their plans, an intelligent slave overheard what they were saying. This slave went to Brutus and told him of the plot. All engaged in it were at once arrested and put in prison. Two sons of Brutus himself, Ti´tus and Ti-be´ri-us, were found among the plotters.

When Brutus learned that his own children were traitors, he was overcome with sorrow. For several days he shut himself up in his house and would see no one. But when the day for the trial came, he did his duty sternly as a judge – the consuls were judges as well as rulers. Titus and Tiberius were proved guilty of treason, together with the others, and Brutus sentenced them to be whipped with rods and then beheaded. He even witnessed the execution of the sentence, and we are told that he sat unmoved in his chair and did not turn away his eyes while his two sons were put to death. It was his duty to punish traitors, and he did so without sparing his own flesh and blood.

After the loss of his sons, Brutus became dull and melancholy and appeared to care very little for life. Tarquin made an attempt to take Rome with the aid of the people of two cities of Etruria. Brutus led the Romans to the field to fight against their former king. During the first part of the battle, a son of Tarquin rode furiously at Brutus to kill him. Brutus saw him and advanced rapidly on his horse to meet the attack. When they came together, each ran his spear through the body of the other, and both were killed.

The death of Brutus maddened the Romans, and they fought fiercely until dark. Then the armies went to their camps, and no one knew which side had won. In the middle of the night a loud voice came from a wood near the camp of the E-trus´cans, as the people of Etruria were called. The voice said, "One man more has fallen on the side of the Etruscans than on the side of the Romans; the Romans will conquer in this war."

The Etruscans were known in ancient times for their religion and interest in magic. They were also known for being very superstitious.

The Etruscans believed that this was the voice of the god Jupiter, and they were so frightened that they broke up their camp and quickly marched back to their own land.

XI - Disciplīna Ūndecim (*Famous Men of Rome* VI)

Publicola

Lars Porsena tries to restore Tarquin and attacks Rome.

The Sublician bridge

Horatius Cocles

The nickname *cocles* means "blind in one eye." Horatius was called by this name because he had lost one eye in a previous battle.

For a time Rome was ruled by Valerius. He was a good man. He caused laws to be passed for the benefit of the people and was therefore called Pub-li'co-la, which means *the people's friend*. He had to fight Tarquin frequently. The banished king was constantly trying to capture Rome and get back his throne. He got help from various nations and fought very hard but was never successful in his efforts. At one time he was aided by Lars Por'se-na, king of Clu'si-um, a city of Etruria, who gathered a large army and set out to attack Rome.

Porsena, however, could not enter the city without crossing the Tiber, and there was only one bridge. This was called the Sub-li'ci-an Bridge. It was so called from the Latin word *sublicae*, which means *wooden beams*. When the Romans saw the great army of Etruscans in the distance, they were much alarmed. They were not prepared to fight so powerful a force. The consul thought for a while, and then he resolved to cut down the bridge as the only means of saving Rome. A number of men were at once set to work with axes and hammers.

It was hard work, for the bridge was very strongly built. Before the beams supporting it were cut away, the army of Porsena was seen approaching the river. What was to be done? It would take a few minutes more to finish the work, and if the farther end of the bridge could be held against the Etruscans for those few minutes, all would be well for Rome. But how was it to be held, and who would hold it? Suddenly from the ranks of the Roman soldiers, the brave Ho-ra'ti-us Co'cles stepped out and cried to the consul, "Give me two good men to help me, and I will hold the bridge and stop the enemy from coming over."

Immediately two brave men, Spu'ri-us Lar'ti-us and Titus Her-min'i-us, ran to his side. Then the three hurried over to the other end of the bridge and stood ready to keep off the enemy.

When the army of Etruscans saw the three men standing to keep them back, a shout of laughter went up among them. Three men to keep back thousands! How ridiculous! There the three brave Romans stood, however, at the entrance of the bridge, with determined faces and fearless eyes.

Very quickly three Etruscans – stout, able fighters – came forth from the army to give battle to the three Romans. After a sharp combat, the Etruscans were killed. Three more came out and continued the fight, but they too were beaten by Horatius and his companions.

Now the bridge began to shake and crack. Horatius felt that it was about to fall, and he cried to Spurius and Titus to run back to the other side. While they did so, he stood alone and defied the whole Etruscan army, which was now rushing upon him. A whole army against one man! Javelins were hurled at him, but he skillfully warded them off with his shield.

Just as the Etruscans reached him, the last beam was cut away, and the bridge fell with a tremendous crash. As it was falling, Horatius plunged into the Tiber, and praying to the gods for help, he swam to the other side in safety. The Romans received him with shouts of joy, and even the Etruscans could not help raising a cheer in admiration of his bravery.

The three Romans were well rewarded. A fine statue of Horatius was built in one of the squares of the city. On the base of the statue was placed a brass tablet, with an account of the heroic deed engraved on it. The Senate also gave Horatius as much land as he could plow around in a day.

XII – Disciplīna Duodecim (no history lesson)

XIII – Disciplīna Tredecim (*Famous Men of Rome* VII)

Porsena still remained with his army on the other side of the river. He thought that by preventing food from being sent into the city he could force the inhabitants to surrender. So he got ships and stationed them on the Tiber to drive away or seize any vessels that should attempt to come to Rome with food.

Porsena besieges Rome.

There was in Rome at this time a very brave young man named Ca´i-us Mu´ci-us, and he thought of a plan to save the city. His plan was to march boldly into the enemy's camp and kill King Porsena, so he concealed a sword under his tunic, went across the river to the Etruscan camp, and made his way to the place where the king was sitting.

Caius Mucius

It happened that it was payday in the army, and the soldiers were getting their money. A secretary, who sat beside the king and was dressed very much like the king, was talking to the men and giving them orders. Mucius mistook the secretary for Porsena. He rushed forward and stabbed him to death. Instantly the daring Roman was seized by the guards. He heard soldiers crying out that the secretary had been killed. Then he knew what a mistake he had made.

Porsena was greatly enraged at seeing his secretary killed. In a loud and angry voice, he commanded Mucius to tell who he was and why he had committed such a deed. Without showing a sign of fear, the bold Mucius answered, "I am a Roman citizen. I came here to kill you, because you are an enemy of my country. I have failed, but there are others to come after me who will not fail. Your life will constantly be in danger, and you will be killed when you least expect it."

On hearing these words, Porsena jumped from his seat in a great fury. He threatened to burn Mucius to death if he did not at once tell all about the others who were coming to kill him. But Mucius was not frightened. To show how little he cared about the king's threat, he thrust his right hand into the flame of a fire which had been lighted close by and held it there without flinching. At the same time, he cried out to the king, "Behold how little we Romans care for pain when it is to defend our country."

Porsena was astonished at this sight. He so much admired the courage and patriotism of the Roman that he ordered the guards to set him free. Then Mucius said to the king, "In return for your kindness, I now tell you of my own free will what I would not tell you when you threatened me with punishment. Know then that 300 Roman youths have bound themselves by oath to kill you, each to make the attempt in his turn. The lot fell first on me. I have failed, but the attempt will be made again and again until someone succeeds."

King Porsena was so terrified when he heard this that he resolved to make peace at once with Rome. He immediately sent messengers to the Senate, and terms of peace were quickly agreed upon.

The Senate rewarded Mucius by giving him a tract of land on the banks of the Tiber. This land was afterwards called the Mucian Meadows. Mucius himself got the name of Scae'vo-la, a Latin word which means *left-handed*. He had lost the use of his right hand by burning it in the fire.

XIV – Disciplīna Quattuordecim (*Famous Men of Rome* VIII.1-2)

One of the great men of Rome who lived soon after the Tarquins were banished was Caius Marcius. He was a member of a noble family, and from his youth he had been noted for his bravery.

Caius Marcius, also known as Coriolanus

In his time there was a war between the Romans and the Vol'sci-ans, a people of a district in Latium. The Romans attacked Co-ri'o-li, the capital city of the Volscians, but they were defeated and driven back. Caius Marcius reproached the Roman soldiers for running from the enemy. His words made them ashamed, and they turned again to the fight. With Caius at their head, they sent the Volscians flying back to the city. Caius followed the enemy to the gates, which were partly open. When he saw this, he shouted to the Romans, "The gates are open for us; let us not be afraid to enter!"

War with the Volscians, an Etruscan people

Caius himself sprang in and kept the gates open for the Romans. After a short fight, the city was taken.

Then everybody said that it was Caius who had taken Corioli and that he should be called after the name of the city he had won. So ever afterwards he was known as Co'ri-o-la'nus.

Alhough Coriolanus was a brave soldier and always ready to fight for Rome, he had some qualities that were not so good. He had great contempt for the common people, and he took part with those who tried to oppress them.

Only a little while before the taking of Corioli, there was serious trouble between the people and the patricians. Many of the people earned their living by farming. But when there was a war, the strong men had to become soldiers. Since Rome was almost constantly at war, the men were nearly always away from their farms. Because the Roman soldiers received no regular pay, they very often had to borrow money to support their families while they were away fighting, because at this time Roman soldiers received no regular pay.

Quarrels between the patricians and plebeians

Now it was the rich patricians who loaned the money, and if it was not paid back at the time agreed upon, they could put the people who owed it in jail, or they could sell their wives and children as slaves.

In this way the plebeians often suffered much hardship. At last a great number of them resolved to leave Rome and make a settlement for themselves somewhere else in Italy. The patricians did not like this very much, for if the common people went away, there would be a scarcity of soldiers for the army. The Senate, after thinking the matter over, proposed that the plebeians should elect officers of their own, to be called trib´unes, who should have power to veto laws they did not like, that is, to prevent them from being passed. The word *veto*, which is Latin for *I forbid*, is used in the same way in our own country. The President of the United States and the governors of some states have, within certain limits, power to prevent the passing of laws they do not approve. This is called the veto power.

The tribunes

The plebeians were pleased with the proposal, so they returned to Rome. For a time there was peace between them and the patricians.

But Coriolanus and other patricians were opposed to the election of tribunes, because they thought it gave the common people too much power. Once, when there was a famine in Rome, and the poor were suffering greatly from lack of food, the Greeks living in Sicily sent several ships laden with corn to Rome to relieve the people in distress. When the corn arrived, the Senate was about to order that it should be divided among the people who needed it, but Coriolanus interfered.

"No, no," he said, "if the people want corn, let them first give up their tribunes. It must be either no corn or no tribunes."

The people were so angry when they heard this that they talked about killing Coriolanus. And they would have done so except for the wise advice of the tribunes.

"No, no," said the tribunes, "you must not kill him; that would be against the law. But you can have him tried for treason against the people, and we will be his accusers."

Coriolanus was then ordered to appear before the assembly of the people to be tried, for the people had power to try persons charged with such offenses in their assemblies. But Coriolanus was afraid the assembly would condemn him, so he secretly fled from the city, leaving his family behind, and he went to the town of the Volscians.

The chief of the Volscians received Coriolanus in a friendly manner. Coriolanus then told him why he had left Rome. The Volscian chief was glad to hear it. He had long wanted to fight the Romans, but he had been afraid to make the attempt. With the aid of such a soldier as Coriolanus, however, he was sure that Rome might be taken. So he raised a large army and put it under the command of the great Roman.

XV – Disciplīna Quīndecim (*Famous Men of Rome* VIII.3)

The Volscian army, led by Coriolanus, captured many cities belonging to the Roman Republic. At last, Coriolanus resolved to attack Rome itself, and he marched his army toward the city. The Romans just then were not very well prepared for a battle, so the Senate decided to send messengers to Coriolanus to beg him to spare his native city and make terms of peace.

Coriolanus becomes an enemy of Rome.

The messengers chosen were five of the leading nobles, and they at once set out for the Volscian camp. Coriolanus received them cordially, for they were old friends; but he said that he would not spare Rome unless the Romans would give up all the lands and cities which they had taken from the Volscians in former wars.

The Senate would not agree to this, and Coriolanus refused to listen to any other terms. The Romans then began to prepare for battle though they feared very much that they would be defeated.

While the men were thus in fear and doubt, the women of Rome saved the city! Va-le´ri-a, a noble Roman lady, remembered that Coriolanus had always dearly loved his mother.

"Perhaps," thought she, "he may listen to her though he will hear no one else."

The Roman women save their city from Coriolanus.

So Valeria, with a large number of noble ladies, went to the house of Ve-tu´ri-a, the mother of Coriolanus, and said to her, "The gods have put it into our hearts to come and ask you to join with us to save our country from ruin. Come then with us to the camp of your son and beg him to show mercy."

Coriolanus's mother at once agreed to go, so she got ready immediately and set out for the camp of the Volscians, accompanied by a great number of ladies and her son's wife and little children. It was a strange sight, this long line of Roman ladies, all dressed in mourning. Even the Volscian soldiers showed them respect as they passed along.

Coriolanus happened to be sitting in front of his tent in the Volscian camp, with a number of officers around him, as the procession came into view. "Who are these women?" he asked. Before an answer could be given, he saw that among them were his mother and wife and children. He stood up and hastened forward to meet them. They fell on their knees and begged him to spare his native city.

Coriolanus seemed deeply distressed. He made no answer, but he bent his head, pressed his hand to his breast, and gazed down upon the dear ones who knelt at his feet. Then his mother said, "If I had no son, Rome would not be in this danger. I am too old to bear your shame and my own misery much longer. Look to your wife and children; if you continue in your present course, you will send them to an early death."

Coriolanus was so grieved that for some minutes he could not speak. At last he cried out, "Oh, Mother, what have you done to me? You have saved Rome, but you have ruined your son."

Then he embraced his mother and looked at her sadly for a moment.

He also embraced and kissed his wife and children and told them to go back to Rome, for they would be safe there. The women then returned to the city, and Coriolanus marched away with the Volscian army. Rome was saved!

Coriolanus lived the rest of his life with the Volscians, but he never again made war against his native city. It is supposed that he died about the middle of the fifth century before Christ.

XVI – Disciplīna Sēdecim (*Famous Men of Rome* IX)

At about the time in which Coriolanus lived, the family of the Fa´bi-i were very powerful in Rome. Among the leaders or chief men of the family at that period were Quin´tus Fabi-us, Marcus Fabius, and Cae´so Fabius.

Quintus and Caeso Fabius

In those times the Roman nobles were very rich and powerful. They held all the high offices of the government and cared very little about the welfare of the plebeians. Often they treated them very harshly.

The Fabii also treated the plebeians harshly. Once when Quintus Fabius defeated the Volscians in a battle, he sold all the valuable things he took from the enemy and put the money into the public treasury. Such things were called spoils. The Roman generals usually divided the spoils among the soldiers. This was the way the soldiers were paid in those days. But Quintus Fabius would not divide the spoils, so the soldiers were very bitter against him.

Some time afterward Marcus Fabius was elected consul, and once, after a great battle with the Vei-en´-ti-ans, a people of Etruria, he took over the entire care of the poor wounded soldiers, and he supplied all their wants at his own expense.

The next year his brother Caeso Fabius was consul, and he tried to convince the Senate to divide the lands that had been taken from the Veientians and other people whom the Romans had defeated in war among the poor citizens. Often afterwards in the Senate, the voice of a Fabius was heard speaking for justice for the plebeians. The common people, therefore, soon loved the whole family of the Fabii instead of hating them as they had before.

The nobles were very angry, because the Fabii took the side of the plebeians, and they threatened to do all they could against them. Now the Fabii saw clearly that it would be useless to attempt to fight the nobles, because the nobles had a great deal of power and could do almost whatever they pleased in Rome. Therefore, the Fabii thought that it would be better for them to move from the city and make a new home for themselves somewhere else. They resolved to do this, and they selected a place on the banks of the River Crem´e-ra, a few miles from Rome.

At this time, the Romans were again at war with the Veientians. These people lived in Vei´i, a city on the Cremera River. One day, when there was a discussion in the Roman Senate about this war, Caeso Fabius said,

War with the Veientians, an Etruscan people

"As you know, we of the house of the Fabii are going to leave Rome and settle on the borders of the country of the Veientians. If you give us permission, we will fight those people and try to defeat them for the honor of Rome and the glory of our house. We will ask neither money nor men from the Senate. We will carry on the war with our own men and at our own cost."

The senators were glad of the chance to get rid of the Fabii. They at once gave the Fabii the permission for which they asked. The Fabii then began to make preparations for their departure. There were over 300 men, in addition to women, children, and servants, and when all were ready, they marched out of the city to their new home with Caeso at their head.

At first the Fabii had only a camp on the Cremera River, but afterward they built a small city with a strong fortress. Many good Roman soldiers came and joined them, and soon they had a fine army of earnest, devoted men.

The Veientians were soon conquered. Fabius and his brave men defeated them in several battles, and at last the Veientians made up their minds that they had had enough of war. They returned to their own city of Veii and remained quiet for a long time. But they declared that they would destroy the Fabii whenever they could get the chance.

Now it was an old custom of the Fabii to have a special worship of the gods on a certain day of every year. Early in the morning of that day, all the men of the family would go in a body to a famous temple on a hill near Rome and have religious services for several hours. The men took no arms with them, as it was thought improper to go armed to religious worship.

The defeat of the Fabii

The Veientians heard of this annual religious service and saw in it a chance for revenge. They resolved to kill the Fabii the next time they went to the temple for their special service. When the day came, the Fabii set out as usual. On their way to the temple, they had to go over a road which had high, steep rocks on each side. A large number of Veientian soldiers had hidden themselves there, and when the unsuspecting Fabii came along, the Veientians attacked them furiously from front and rear. Without arms the Fabii could not fight very well. They made the best defense they could, but it was useless. They were all killed except for one young man who escaped to Rome. Thus the cowardly Veientians had their revenge.

XVII – Disciplīna Septendecim (*Famous Men of Rome* X)

War with the Aequians

In the mountains east of Latium there lived a rather wild people called Ae´qui-ans, who were very often at war with Rome. After some time of peace and good conduct, these people suddenly began to plunder the rich farms of the Romans. This was about 450 years before the birth of Christ and not long after the Veientians had destroyed the Fabian family. As soon as the Roman Senate heard what the Aequians were doing, the

Senate sent messengers to the Aequian king to complain of the wrong. The messengers found the king in his camp, sitting near a huge oak tree. But when they spoke to him, he answered them rudely, saying, "I am too busy now with other matters. Go tell your message to the oak yonder!"

This made the messengers very angry, and one of them said, "We shall tell it to the oak, but we shall tell it also to the gods and call them to witness how you have broken the peace! And they shall be on our side when we come to punish you and your people for the crimes you have committed against us."

It is said that the angry messengers did tell the message to the oak, and to all the other trees around, and boldly shouted that war would come from this insult to Rome.

Then the messengers returned to Rome and told the Senate how they had been insulted by the Aequian king. The Senate at once declared war against the Aequians and ordered the Consul Mi-nu′ci-us to lead an army against them.

The Romans easily won a few battles at first. Then the Aequians began to retreat as if they did not mean to fight anymore. The Romans followed swiftly until they were drawn into a narrow valley on each side of which were high, rocky hills. It was a trap, and the Romans knew it before they had marched very far from the entrance.

The Aequian king then closed up the valley with strong barricades and placed his troops at the entrance of the valley and along the hills, so that the Romans could not get out.

There was very little grass for the horses and no food for the men in the valley, so that if the Romans were not soon relieved, both they and their horses would die of hunger.

Fortunately for the Romans, a few of their horsemen had managed to get out of the valley before the Aequians closed it. These horsemen rode as fast as they could to Rome and told the Senate how Minucius and his soldiers were placed. What was to be done? No one seemed to know at first, but after a good deal of discussion, a senator said, "Let us make Lucius Quinc′ti-us dictator. He is the only man who can save us."

Cincinatus elected dictator

The Senate agreed to this, and so Lucius Quinctius was chosen dictator. A dictator had more power than the Senate or the consuls. All his commands had to be obeyed just as if he were a king. A dictator, however, was appointed only when there was some great danger, and he held office only for six months.

Lucius Quinctius belonged to a noble family. He was a great soldier and had won many battles for his country. He had such beautiful, long curly hair that people called him Cin′cin-na′tus, which means *curly-haired*, and this is the name by which he is known in history.

At the time Cincinnatus was appointed dictator, he lived on a small farm outside of Rome. He worked on the farm himself, and when the messengers from the Senate came to tell him that he had been chosen dictator, they found him plowing in one of his fields. He left his plow where it stood and hastened to Rome, where he was welcomed by all the people.

The first thing Cincinnatus did was to raise a new army. He gave orders that every man of suitable age should buckle on his sword and be ready in a few hours to march to the help of Minucius and his soldiers.

Before evening, Cincinnatus and his army marched out of the city for the Alban hills, where the Romans were shut up. They reached the place in early morning and formed a line all around the hills. The Aequians then found themselves hemmed in on every side between two Roman armies – the army of Minucius and the army of Cincinnatus. They fought as well as they could, but they were quickly overpowered. They could do nothing but cry to the Roman commander to spare their lives.

Cincinnatus spared their lives, but he made them *pass under the yoke*. The yoke was formed of two spears, fixed upright in the ground; a third was fastened across near the top, from one to the other. Cincinnatus made the Aequians lay down their arms and walk, every man of them, under the yoke of spears. They had to bend their heads as they did so, for the spears were not very long, and the one on the top was only a few feet from the ground. The yoke was set up between two lines of Roman soldiers, and as the Aequians passed under it, the Romans jeered at them and taunted them.

Having to *pass under the yoke* was regarded as the greatest disgrace that could happen to soldiers. Many much preferred to suffer death. The practice has given to our language the word *subjugate*, meaning to subdue or conquer, from the Latin words *sub*, meaning *under*, and *iūgum*, meaning a *yoke*.

When the soldiers of Consul Minucius came out of the valley, they shouted for joy and crowded around Cincinnatus, thanking him as their deliverer and protector. "Let us give Cincinnatus a golden crown!" they cried, but the great general only smiled, shook his head, and gave the order for the homeward march.

Great was the rejoicing in Rome when news of the victory was received. The Senate ordered that there should be a general holiday and a grand parade through the city, so the victorious army marched into Rome amid the shouts and cheers of the people.

Cincinnatus rode in a splendid chariot drawn by six handsome black horses. He wore the dress of a dictator of Rome, and on his head was a laurel wreath. Behind his chariot the Aequian king and his chiefs walked, looking very humble and forlorn. Following them were slaves laden with the arms and other valuable things taken from the enemy's camp. With bugles and trumpets gayly sounding, the parade went through the city. The chariot of Cincinnatus was followed by a throng of people cheering and crying, "Hail to the Dictator! Hail to the Conqueror!" Flowers were showered upon him and thrown before his chariot wheels.

A few days afterward Cincinnatus gave up the office of dictator and went back to his little farm.

After he had proved so good a dictator, the people wished to make Cincinnatus king, but he refused. Following his example, George Washington declined to be made a king by the grateful citizens of the new United States of America. Instead, like Cincinnatus, he returned to his home and farm. Because of this, both men were honored by the title *Pater Patriae* (*Father of His Country*).

XVIII – Disciplīna Duodēvīgintī (*Famous Men of Rome* XI.1-3)

About 380 years before the birth of Christ, the Romans had another war with the Veientians. During this war, they tried to take the rich city of Veii, which was about twelve miles from Rome. But there was a great wall of stone all around the city, and the gates, which were of brass, were very high and strong. So the Romans, though they tried as hard as they could for seven years, were not able to take Veii.

To make matters worse for them, it was reported that twelve Etruscan cities were going to send armies to help the Veientians. It was also said that as soon as the twelve armies had driven the Romans away from the walls of Veii, they would march to Rome and destroy the city.

The Romans were very much alarmed by these reports, and they resolved that there should be a dictator. The Senate appointed a dictator, and the man appointed was Marcus Fu′ri-us Ca-mil′lus.

Marcus Furius Camillus appointed dictator

Camillus was one of the greatest men of Rome. He belonged to a very rich and powerful family, and he was a great soldier. When he was made dictator, he raised a large army and marched at once to Veii. He tried to break down the walls or gates for a long time, but he could not do it. Then he thought of the plan of digging a tunnel under the walls.

This seemed a good idea, so Camillus set a great number of his men to work. Soon they had dug a tunnel under the walls and so far under the city that they thought they were as far as the great temple of Juno, which was in the fort or strongest part of Veii. Here they stopped to consider what next to do. Suddenly the sound of voices, as of people talking in the temple above them, reached their ears. They sent for Camillus, and when he came, he listened to the voices.

Deep channels and tunnels may be still seen in the ruins of Veii. These were used to channel and store rainwater, for Veii was built upon a rocky hill and has no natural source of fresh water. Perhaps Camillus entered the city by tunneling into one of these waterways.

Now it happened that at that moment, the king of Veii was in the temple preparing to offer an ox as a sacrifice to Juno and praying to the goddess to save the city from the Romans. The ox was killed, and its carcass was ready to be laid on the altar. After the king had prayed, one of the priests, pretending that he had received an answer from Juno, cried out, "The goddess declares she will give victory to him who offers this as a sacrifice upon the altar."

As soon as Camillus, who was listening all the time, heard these words of the priest, he ordered his men to break an opening in the earth over their heads. This was quickly done, and the Romans sprang through into the midst of the worshipers. They at once seized the carcass of the ox, and Camillus himself offered it upon the altar to Juno. Then he and his companions rushed out of the temple and opened the gates of the city before the astonished and frightened people knew what was being done.

As soon as the gates were opened, the Roman soldiers poured in by the thousands. The Veientians fought bravely, but they were quickly defeated, and their great and rich city was at last in the hands of the Romans.

In those times, as has already been said, it was the custom to divide the valuable things taken from a defeated enemy among the victorious soldiers. The riches of Veii were, therefore, divided among the Roman soldiers, and there were so many precious things – gold and silver and jewelry – that the men were quite rich when each got his share.

Sometime after the taking of Veii, the Romans were at war with the Fa-lis´ci-ans, another people of Etruria, and Camillus went with an army to besiege their chief town, which was called Fa-le´ri-i. He made his camp in front of the walls, stationed soldiers all around, and tried hard to take the town. But the Faliscians were very strong and brave, and they defended their town so well that Camillus began to be afraid he would not be able to take it at all.

The schoolmaster of Falerii

Now there was at that time in Falerii a schoolmaster who taught the sons of the chief citizens of the town. This schoolmaster used to take his boys every day for a walk outside the walls. One day he led them within the lines of the Roman army and brought them into the camp of Camillus.

Camillus was surprised at seeing the boys. He asked the schoolmaster who they were and why he had brought them there. The schoolmaster told him who the boys were and then said, "I bring them here to give them up to you. In doing this, I give you the city, for their fathers will surrender the city to you in order to get back their children."

Camillus stood for a moment in silence, gazing at the traitor with a look of disgust. Then in an angry voice he cried out, "Villain, we Romans are not so bad as you are. We do not make war upon children but upon men who do us wrong."

Then he ordered some of his soldiers to tie the schoolmaster's hands behind his back and to give each of the boys a rod, telling them to drive the traitor before them back into the city. This the boys did with a hearty good will. They whipped the unworthy schoolmaster into Falerii, and when the people saw the sight and heard of the noble conduct of Camillus, they resolved not to fight any more against so good a man. They sent ambassadors to Rome to make peace, and the Romans and Faliscians became good friends.

Not long after this time, one of the tribunes brought a charge against Camillus that he had kept for his own use more than his fair share of the spoils of Veii. Some valuable things were noticed in his house, and it was said that he had not gotten them as part of his share. It was believed, therefore, that Camillus had taken them secretly from Veii.

The Romans were very particular upon this point. They had strict laws for the division of spoils obtained in war, and no one was permitted to take more than he was entitled to, according to his rank in the army.

Camillus leaves Rome and goes into exile.

Camillus was summoned to appear in the people's court to answer the charge made against him. But he would not humble himself to go before the plebeians to be tried. He preferred rather to leave Rome forever. So the great Camillus departed from his native city, intending never to return. As he passed out of the gates, he prayed to the gods that some dreadful thing might happen to the Romans so they would be forced to call him back again to Rome to save the city.

And very soon something did happen which compelled the Romans to ask for the help of Camillus. For a long time a people called Gauls had been doing a great deal of mischief in some parts of Italy. These people came from the country now known as France, which in ancient times was called Gaul. Thousands of them made their way across the high mountains called the Alps and settled on the plains of northern Italy. For many years they lived in this region, but when they heard that farther south the country was very beautiful and was rich in corn and cattle, they started out in great numbers to conquer it.

The Gauls

They were a strange, savage people, very different from the Romans or the Etruscans. They were very tall and strong and had long shaggy black hair and dark, fierce faces, so that they appeared very terrible to the Italians. In battle they showed all their savage nature. They rushed furiously at their enemies, yelling at the top of their voices, flourishing enormous swords, and blowing trumpets.

The chief or king of the Gauls at this time was called Bren´nus. He was a man of great strength and size. He wore a golden collar called a torques around his neck, and on his arms, which were bare, he sometimes wore bracelets of gold.

The Gauls found the southern lands very much to their liking. They robbed farms, attacked some of the Etruscan cities, and then, after a short time, they marched for Rome. A great Roman army went out to fight them, and the two armies met on the banks of a river called the Al´li-a.

The Roman soldiers had never before seen the dreadful Gauls. They were therefore greatly terrified when the tall, fierce-looking savages came running over the plains in vast numbers, shouting furiously and blowing their trumpets. Though the Roman general, Marcus Man´li-us, tried to make his men go forward bravely to meet the Gauls, it was useless. They fought badly and were killed by the thousands. At last they ran from the field and fled toward Rome.

XIX – Disciplīna Ūndēvīgintī (*Famous Men of Rome* XI.4-7)

When the defeated soldiers reached Rome and told what had happened, there was great terror in the city. Most of the people bundled up their household goods and fled to hiding places in the mountains close by, where they thought they would be safe from the Gauls.

The Gauls invaded and plundered the city of Rome in 390 BC. The Romans never forgot this terrible disaster, for it was the first time Rome had ever been occupied by an enemy. Rome would not be invaded again for another 800 years!

But many of the senators and other brave nobles and plebeians, instead of running away from the city, went up to the Capitol, fastened the gates, and made ready for a siege. The Capitol was the most sacred part of the city. It contained splendid statues of Jupiter, Juno, and Minerva, and, as you know, the famous Sibylline Books.

Some old men who had been consuls resolved to remain in the city and wait for the Gauls to come. They thought that if the Gauls should kill them, they would then be satisfied and would spare the city. So the patriotic old men dressed themselves in their finest robes and sat in chairs in the Forum, each with an ivory staff in his right hand.

When the Gauls reached the city, there was no one to oppose them. They marched on to the Forum and found the old men, with long white beards, sitting in their chairs, so still that they looked like statues. A Gaul went up to one of them and pulled his beard to see if he were a living person. Instantly the old man raised his staff and struck the barbarian in the face. The Gauls then fell upon the patriots and killed them. Then they began to plunder.

After they destroyed the greater part of the city, the Gauls turned their attention to the Capitol. The rock on which it was built was high and steep.

Brennus led his soldiers up the hill, but the Romans in the Capitol rushed down the narrow road and after a few minutes of brave fighting, drove them back. The Gauls made another attempt, but it was no more successful than the first.

Brennus saw that the Romans could not be driven from the Capitol. He therefore decided to starve them out. He put a strong guard at the entrance so that the Romans could not come out to get food. For weeks the Capitol was thus besieged, but its faithful defenders held out manfully.

Meanwhile, the people who had fled from Rome took courage again. They gathered at the city of Veii and organized a strong army to fight the Gauls, but they had no commander – and then they thought of Camillus. All agreed that he would be the right man to be their general.

They resolved to send for him, but first they thought they must have the approval of the Senate. Here was a difficulty. How could a messenger get to the Senate while the Gauls were around the Capitol? This puzzled them for a good while, but at last a young man named Pon´ti-us Com-in´i-us volunteered to carry a message to the Capitol.

Pontius left Veii on a very dark night and swam down the Tiber until he reached the Capitoline Hill. Then he went on shore and crept up the hill as far as the great rock. The Gauls had put no guard there, for they thought no one could climb the rock because it was so steep.

By great efforts Pontius managed to climb up. Several times he was near falling, but by clinging to the vines and bushes that grew on the rock, he came to the top at last. His countrymen in the Capitol were delighted to see him. They were also very glad when they heard about the army at Veii, and the Senate at once approved of the proposal about Camillus. It was agreed not only to make him general but to make him dictator. Then Cominius went down the rock and the hill by the way he had come up and hastened off to Veii.

The next day some of the Gauls, while walking along this side of the hill, noticed footmarks in the soil. They also noticed that bushes, growing high up on the rock, were crushed and torn. Then they knew that someone had gone up or come down the cliff, and they resolved to try to go up themselves that night.

Veii had been and captured by Camillus and the Romans in their earlier war and was now a Roman possession. it was strongly fortified and only a few miles from Rome. That is why the Romans fled there for safety.

Camillus elected dictator a second time

Shortly after midnight, when they thought that the Romans would be fast asleep, a party of Gauls began cautiously and silently to clamber up the steep rock. Some placed their shields across their shoulders for others to stand upon, and in this way they supported one another, until at last some of them made their way very near to the top; one of them got just to the edge of a balcony of the Capitol. No one within the building heard them, not even the watchdogs.

But at that moment there was a loud cackling of geese. These birds were thought to be the favorite birds of the goddess Juno. Many were kept in the Capitol, and some of them happened just then to be at the side the Gauls were climbing up. The movements of the climbers, quiet though they were, disturbed the geese, and they began to cackle and flap their wings.

The noise aroused Marcus Manlius from his sleep. He sprang from his bed, seized his sword and shield, and ran to the balcony. There he saw a Gaul climbing on to the parapet and others scrambling up behind. Marcus rushed upon him, struck him in the face with his shield, and the Gaul tumbled headlong down the rock.

As the Gaul fell, he knocked down some of his companions who were climbing behind him. The geese still kept up their loud cackling, and soon all the Romans were awakened and came quickly to the assistance of Marcus. The Gauls were hurled back as they mounted the rock, and in a few minutes, all who had come up were dashed down the steep cliff and killed. Thus the Capitol was saved by the cackling of geese. For his brave action on this occasion, Marcus Manlius was honored by being called Marcus Cap´i-to-li´nus.

Marcus Manlius called "Capitolinus"

Brennus now saw that he could not take the Capitol, so he thought it would be useless to remain in Rome any longer. He therefore offered to go away if the Senate would give him a thousand pounds of gold. The Senate thought it better to do this. Food was very scarce in the Capitol, and in a few days the brave men there would have nothing left to eat. They had heard nothing from the army at Veii, and they were not sure help would come in time to save them.

The Senate resolved to give the thousand pounds of gold to the Gauls. An officer named Quintus Sul-pi´ti-us was sent with some lictors to deliver it to Brennus, but first the gold had to be weighed, and the Gauls attempted to cheat the Romans by using false weights. When Sulpitius complained of this, Brennus took off his sword and threw it, belt and all, into one of the scales. When Sulpitius asked what that meant, Brennus answered, "What should it mean but woe to the conquered?"

At that moment Camillus appeared at the gates with his army. He soon learned what was going on. Quickly he marched to the spot and ordered the lictors to take the gold out of the scale and carry it back to the Roman treasury. Then he turned to Brennus and, addressing him in a stern voice, said, "We Romans defend our country, not with gold, but with steel."

Immediately there was a battle, and the Gauls were driven out of the

Camillus honored
with the title *Pater
Patriae* for his service.

city. The next day there was another battle a few miles from Rome, and the Gauls were again defeated and thousands of them slain.

Camillus then returned to Rome at the head of his victorious army. The people received him with shouts of joy and for several days held celebrations in his honor. They called him the second Romulus, meaning that he was the second founder of the city. They also called him the Father of his Country.

It was in the time of Camillus that a great hole or chasm, caused perhaps by an earthquake, suddenly appeared in the ground in the middle of the Forum. Workmen were sent to fill it up, but no matter how much earth they threw into it, the hole seemed to be as large and as deep as before. The Senate then consulted augurs, and they said the hole could not be filled up until what was most valuable in Rome was cast into it. Then the people began to throw in gold and silver and jewelry, but still the hole was as deep as ever. At last a young man named Cur´ti-us said that the most valuable things the Romans had were their arms and their courage. Then he put on his armor and his sword and, mounting his horse, rode into the Forum and leaped into the great hole. Immediately it closed up behind him, and neither he nor his horse was ever seen again.

In the old Roman stories, Curtius is much praised as a patriot and hero. The people thought he had saved his country from some great evil, which they believed would have happened if the hole in the Forum had not been closed up.

XX – Disciplīna Vīgintī (*Famous Men of Rome* XII)

Marcus Manlius, who commanded the Roman army at the battle of Allia and who defended the Capitol against the Gauls so well, belonged to a family known as the Man´li-i. This family gave many brave generals to the Republic. One of them was named Titus Manlius.

Some years after the siege of the Capitol, Titus had a remarkable fight with a huge Gaul. The Gauls had come back to make war again upon Rome. Their army camped near a bridge on the A´ni-o, a small river a few miles from the city, and the Roman army was waiting on the other side of the river for a good opportunity for battle.

Every day a Gaul of gigantic size, who wore round his neck a collar or chain of twisted gold threads, used to come to the bridge to insult the Romans. He would call them cowards who were afraid to fight. One day he dared them to send someone out to fight with him. Manlius at once accepted the challenge, and the two immediately took their places in an open space within sight of both armies.

The Gaul was so tall and strong that the Roman appeared like a boy beside him. Everybody thought the big warrior would have an easy victory, but Titus was very quick in his movements. For a few moments after the fight began, he skillfully dodged the furious blows of his opponent. Then he suddenly ran up close to him, sprang under his great shield, and plunged his sword deep into the Gaul's body.

The Gaul fell to the ground dead. Then Titus took the golden collar from the dead man's neck and put it on his own. Afterward he was called Manlius Tor-qua´tus, from the word *torques*, which is Latin for *a twisted collar*.

Manlius Torquatus became consul, but he was not liked much by the people, for he was a very stern and severe ruler. During a war the Romans fought against the Latins and some tribes of southern Italy, Manlius was in command of the Roman army. He marched to meet the enemy, who were assembled in force at the foot of Mount Ve-su´vi-us.

While the two armies were encamped opposite each other, Manlius ordered that none of his men should fight with any of the Latins until the word for battle was given. Soon after, a Latin officer met young Manlius, the consul's son, riding in front of the lines with a troop of his comrades. They entered into conversation about the coming battle, and each boasted of the valor of the soldiers on his own side. At last the Latin officer challenged the young Roman to single combat.

"Wilt thou," he cried, "measure thy strength with mine? It will then be seen how much the Latin horseman excels the Roman."

Manlius accepted the challenge, and in the fight which immediately took place, he was the victor. He killed the Latin, and according to the custom of those times, stripped him of his armor and carried it to the Roman camp. Then he went to tell his father what he had done.

"Father," said he, "I present you this armor, which I have taken from the enemy. I hope you will accept it as proof that I am ready and able to do my duty as a Roman soldier."

Torquatus looked at his son sadly and then said, "My son, you say you are willing to do your duty as a soldier, but the first duty of a soldier is obedience. This duty you have not performed, for you have just now disobeyed me, your commander. You have fought with the enemy without receiving orders to do so. But you shall not escape the punishment because you are my son."

Then, turning to his lictors, he said, "Go, bind him to a stake and cut off his head."

At this cruel order, loud cries of horror came from the soldiers. Young Manlius threw himself at his father's feet and begged for mercy. But the stern consul turned away from him and ordered the lictors to perform their duty. So the brave young Manlius was led to a stake and bound, and with one stroke of the lictor's ax, his head was cut from his body.

Soon afterward there was a battle between the two armies, and the Romans gained a great victory. The war continued for some time longer and ended in the defeat of the Latins. Manlius took possession of one of their towns – the town of An´ti-um, on the Mediterranean coast – and compelled the inhabitants to give up their warships.

War vessels and galleys in those times had sharp prows made for the purpose of running into and breaking through the sides of other vessels.

The Romans honored Titus Manlius as a patriotic hero because he placed the well-being of his country above his own.

The prow was a beam with pointed irons fastened to it and a metal figure resembling the beak or head of a bird or other animal mounted on it. This beak was called a *rostrum*.

When the Romans captured the warships of Antium, they broke off the beaks and carried them to Rome. There they fastened them as ornaments to the platform in the Forum, from which orators addressed the people. Hence, the word *rostrum* came to mean a platform or pulpit for public speaking. It is now used in our own language in this sense.

XXI - Disciplīna Vīgintī Ūna (*Famous Men of Rome* XIII.1)

Soon after the defeat of the Gauls, a great man named Ap´pi-us Clau´di-us lived in Rome. He belonged to one of the highest families of the city. He was consul for two years, and for several years he held the office of censor (312-308 BC).

The censor was a very high and important officer. He was not only head of the department for taking the census, but he had charge of collecting the taxes, of erecting public buildings, and of making roads and streets.

Appius Claudius was a great soldier. Every Roman citizen had to be a soldier, and every man who was consul had to be able to lead armies to fight and win battles. But Appius Claudius was chiefly famous for the great public works he planned and directed in Rome, which at that time was a city with a population of about 300,000. One of these works was an aqueduct which brought water to the city from a lake eight miles distant. The Roman aqueducts were the best in the world. Some of them that were built over two thousand years ago are still in use.

However, the greatest work of Appius Claudius was the making of a road from Rome to Cap´u-a, a distance of 120 miles. This road was called the Appian Way in honor of Appius. It was also called the "queen of roads," because it was so well built. Parts of it are still in existence. The Romans had good roads as well as good aqueducts. They were the best road builders in the world.

While he was censor Appius Claudius made many improvements in Rome. He was called "the greatest of his countrymen in the works of peace." Even after he retired from office, he had great influence in public affairs. Both plebeians and nobles asked for his advice.

Once during the first war between the Romans and the Greeks, the advice of Appius was of great benefit to Rome. At that time there were many Greek settlements in the south of Italy. One of the Greek towns was called Ta-ren´tum. It was built close to the sea and had a very good harbor.

Many of the people of this town were well-educated. In those days the Greeks were mostly an educated people. They were fond of learning and of art. They called the Romans barbarians and were not friendly to them.

Once when a Roman fleet entered the bay of Tarentum, the people of

The rostrum

Appius Claudius the Censor

The Aqua Claudia, or aqueduct built by Appius Claudius

The Via Appia, or Appian Way, built by Appius Claudius. Many years later, St. Paul travelled this road on his way to Rome.

Long before Rome was a town of any importance, most of southern Italy and the island of Sicily had been colonized by Greeks. The entire region was even called *Magna Gracia*, or Great Greece.

the town attacked it, and after taking five of the ships, they put the crews to death. When the news of this outrage reached Rome, the Senate sent ambassadors to demand satisfaction. One of the ambassadors was a man named Lucius Pos-thu′mi-us. When they arrived at Tarentum, they were met by a noisy crowd of people of the town, who made fun of their dress.

The Romans wore an outer dress called a toga. It was a large white woolen cloth in the shape of a half circle, four or five yards long and of nearly the same length. In putting on this garment, they doubled it lengthwise, then passed one end over the left shoulder and under the opposite arm and again over the left shoulder, the other end reaching nearly to the ground in front. The Tarentines laughed at the toga of the Roman ambassadors. They said it was a dress fit only for savages.

In a short time, the ambassadors were taken to the public theater where the people had assembled to hear the message from Rome. Posthumius spoke to them in Greek, but as this was not his own language, he pronounced many of the words in a peculiar way, and the Tarentines laughed. The Roman went on, however, in a dignified manner and finished his speech as if he had not noticed the insult.

Just then a Tarentine moved forward to the place where Posthumius stood and threw some dirt on his white toga. The ambassador held up the soiled garment with his hand and said that Tarentum would be made to suffer for the outrage. Then the theater rang with laughter and offensive cries.

"Laugh on," said Posthumius, "You may laugh now, but you shall weep hereafter. The stain on this toga shall be washed out in your blood!"

Then the ambassadors left the theater and at once set out for Rome. When they appeared before the Senate, Posthumius showed the stain on his toga as proof of the insult offered to Rome by the Tarentines. The Senate at once declared war on Tarentum and sent a powerful army to attack it.

XXII – Disciplīna Vīgintī Duo (*Famous Men of Rome* XIII.2)

At this time the Tarentines had no general who they thought would be able to fight the Romans, so they sent across the sea to E-pi′rus, in Greece, for the king of that country to come and help them. The name of the king was Pyr′rhus. He was a great soldier and commander and was nearly always engaged in war. He consented to help the Tarentines and crossed over to Italy with a great army in which there was a number of fighting elephants.

Pyrrhus

When Pyrrhus entered Tarentum, he made himself master of the city. The Tarentines were very fond of plays and amusements of all kinds. Pyrrhus closed the theaters, stopped all the amusements, and made the people drill as soldiers all day long.

As soon as he was ready to fight, Pyrrhus marched out with his army of Greeks and Tarentines against the Romans, and there was a great battle near the city of Her´a-cle´a. Both sides fought well for hours, but the Greeks at last began to fall back. They could not stand against the steady, fierce attacks made by the Romans.

Then Pyrrhus brought his elephants upon the field. He had 70 of them, and they were thoroughly trained to fight. The elephants would run into the ranks of the enemy, knock the soldiers down and trample them to death, or lay hold of them with their trunks and throw them high into the air.

As the elephants stood in line waiting for the order to charge, the Romans looked at them with wonder and fear. They knew nothing about elephants, for they had never seen any before. When the huge beasts came charging furiously across the field making strange noises, many of the Roman soldiers were terribly frightened, and in a few minutes the Roman army was put to flight.

Only one thing saved the Romans: a Roman soldier was brave enough to rush at an elephant while it was charging and cut off a part of its trunk with his sword. The animal, wild with pain, turned and ran back to the Greek lines, trampling down the soldiers and causing a great deal of confusion. In the excitement, the Romans managed to escape across a river to a friendly city where they were safe.

Pyrrhus won the victory, but he lost thousands of men. When he saw the great number of his soldiers who lay dead on the field, he exclaimed, "A few more such victories and I must return to Epirus alone!"

XXIII - Disciplīna Vīgintī Trēs (*Famous Men of Rome* XIII.3)

Shortly after the battle, Pyrrhus sent his friend and favorite minister, Cin´e-as, to Rome to offer terms of peace to the Senate. Cineas was a very eloquent man. Often when Pyrrhus could not conquer people in battle, Cineas, by his clever speeches, induced them to submit to the king and be his friends. This was why the Greeks used to say, "The tongue of Cineas wins more cities than the sword of Pyrrhus."

The Greeks propose peace.

Cineas proposed to the Roman Senate that the Romans should not make war any longer on the Tarentines nor on any of the Italian tribes that had helped them. He further proposed that all the lands Rome had taken from these tribes in past years should be given back. If the Romans would agree to these terms, then Pyrrhus would be their true friend.

The terms were not good for Rome, but Cineas was so smooth-spoken and pleasant in proposing them that many of the senators were inclined to accept them. One day while they were discussing the matter in the Senate, a thrilling scene occurred.

Appius Claudius was still living in Rome. He was very old and had become blind. For this reason, he got the name Cae´cus, a word which is Latin for *blind*. But his mind was remarkably clear, and he had not lost interest in public affairs. When he heard that the Senate was going to accept the terms offered by Pyrrhus, he rose from his bed, declaring that he would go and speak against the proposal.

So he was carried by his slaves to the Senate house, and his sons led the aged man to his seat. He began his speech amidst the deepest silence. His youth seemed to come back to him. Once more he was a bold censor of 30 years before. In fiery words he spoke against the plan for peace, saying it would be base and cowardly to yield to the Greek king.

"Let us fight on," he said, "as long as we have soldiers. Shall we submit to this Greek invader merely because we lost one battle? Never! Never! I say. Better to lose all that we have than to disgrace ourselves by submitting!"

The patriotic old man went on speaking in this way until his strength failed him and he sank exhausted into his seat. His speech had so much effect on the senators that they immediately voted against the proposal of Pyrrhus and ordered Cineas to depart from Rome.

The terms of peace rejected

Then the war proceeded vigorously. A great battle was fought at As´cu-lum, and again the Romans were defeated by the Greeks. But they were not discouraged. The consul Cu´ri-us Den-ta´tus fought another battle against Pyrrhus at Ben´e-ven´tum and won. The Greeks were utterly defeated, and Pyrrhus soon afterward left Italy and returned to his own country.

Then the Romans speedily took possession of Tarentum and made its people pay well for their insult to the Roman ambassadors.

www.ingramcontent.com/pod-product-compliance
Lightning Source LLC
Chambersburg PA
CBHW081424090426
42740CB00017B/3176